ON MODERN WOMEN AND THEIR RIGHTS

By
CARMEN DE BURGOS

PROFESSOR AT THE CENTRAL NORMAL SCHOOL
OF MADRID, AND GENERAL PRESIDENT OF THE INTERNATIONAL
LEAGUE OF IBERIAN AND HISPANIC AMERICAN WOMEN

TRANSLATED AND EDITED BY
GABRIELA POZZI AND KEITH WATTS

Title: *On Modern Women and Their Rights*
Original title: *La mujer moderna y sus derechos*
ISBN-10: 1-940075-62-9
ISBN-13: 978-1-940075-62-4

Design: © Ana Paola González
Cover Design: © Jhon Aguasaco
Author's photo: ☻ Carmen de Burgos (Colombine), 1901.
E-mail: carlos@artepoetica.com / aguasaco@gmail.com
Mail: 38-38 215 Place, Bayside, NY 11361, USA.

© *On Modern Women and Their Rights*, by Carmen de Burgos, Translated and edited by Gabriela Pozzi and Keith Watts.
© *On Modern Women and Their Rights*, 2018 for this edition Escribana Books an Imprint of Artepoética Press Inc.

ON MODERN WOMEN AND THEIR RIGHTS

By
CARMEN DE BURGOS

TRANSLATED AND EDITED BY
GABRIELA POZZI AND KEITH WATTS

escribana
books

NEW YORK, 2018

Contents

Introduction

Carmen De Burgos and Feminism at the Turn of the 20th Century

Shortly after Francisco Franco's death, in an interview with Linda Gould Levine, Spanish feminist Charo Ema explained, "There have been women here who were feminists and no one knows about it. It's as if feminism were suddenly a new fashion that just arrived here [...] what we really should do is look for the parallels between past and present, examine the feminism that existed here before, and see what its importance and relevance is to us now" (291). The "before" Ema refers to is, of course, the pre-Franco era, the first third of the 20th Century, a time when, if we are to believe literary manuals and histories, there were no women involved in literature, politics or the "regenerationist" movement. If some of the writings of the members of the generations of 1898, 1914 and 1927 were subjected to serious scrutiny and censorship during the Franco years, even the names of feminists, like Margarita Nelken, María Zambrano, Federica Montseny and Carmen de Burgos were erased from the historical record. Only relatively recently, years after the death of Franco, have scholars like María del Carmen Simón Palmer, Maryellen Bieder, Roberta Johnson, Susan Kirkpatrick and Janet Pérez, among others, begun to shed light on the very real and strong presence of a literature written by women, and especially of a feminist movement in Spain. In fact, Neus Samblancat Miranda argues that Spanish modernity is created and informed by women in all areas of culture and society, from literature and the arts, to medicine, to philosophy, to music. The objective of the present translation is to introduce English speaking readers to one of the most important and active Spanish feminist writers of the beginning of the last century, Carmen de Burgos (1867-1932), a.k.a. "Colombine."

Born in 1867, Carmen de Burgos straddles two eras: the end of the nineteenth Century and the start of Modernity. In many ways, her thinking follows a similar path to that of Spanish society, albeit in the liberal strain. Her attitudes towards women's rights change as she matures, and she becomes progressively more militant. Towards the beginning of her writing career, she is mainly concerned with women's education and does not question the ideology of domesticity, whereas by the end of her life, as the present translation evinces, she has a fully developed set of demands including political, civil and reproductive rights.

Burgos grew up in the province of Almería and was married young to a man 14 years her senior, of whom her parents did not approve.[1] Her husband turned out to be a womanizer and an alcoholic, who often mistreated her. To make ends meet, she worked as a typesetter at her husband's journal, and frequently was forced to write his articles for him. Due to her economic insecurity, and her dependence on an unreliable man, Burgos studied to become a school teacher – one of the few careers open to women at the time – and obtained her degree in 1898 followed by her certificate a year later. At this same time, she separated from her husband – divorce was not an option within Spanish law. In 1900 she published her first book, *Literary Essays*, at her own expense, which contains a variety of genres: legends, stories, poems and essays. Most importantly, it includes an article on the education of women that evinces a timid feminism tempered by religious dogma. The following year Burgos obtained a teaching position and left Almería for Madrid, taking her daughter with her. In 1903 she became the first Spanish woman columnist when the new *Diario Universal* gave her a daily column ("Readings for Women"), and its editor dubbed her *Colombine*, the name by which she became known to the readers of her novels and novellas. It was from the pages of the *Diario Universal* that in 1904 she launched the survey designed to gauge public opinion on divorce which made her famous,[2] and in 1906 she did the same for women's suffrage. From this point on she would continue working as a journalist for a variety of newspapers, the *Diario Universal*, *El Heraldo de Madrid* and, the newly founded *ABC*, among others.

Burgos took full advantage of the new mass publishing industry so disparaged by male high Modernist writers, and the majority of her novellas were published in pulp weeklies. Yet among her many projects she also began the publication of *Revista Crítica*,[3] a journal whose motto was "Libertad, Arte, Amor" [Liberty, Art, Love], and which had on its editorial board some of the most well-known Modernists and Vanguardists of the day: Juan Ramón Jiménez, Antonio de Hoyos y Vinent, Andrés González Blanco, Rafael Cansinos Assens, Francisco Villaespesa, and Ramón Gómez de la Serna, among

---

1 All the biographical information comes from Concepción Núñez Rey's new biography, the most extensive, and certainly the most authoritative biography of Burgos to date.

2 Her detractors called her "La divorciadora" for this survey.

3 Through this journal, Burgos promoted the Alianza Hispano Israelita which called attention to the plight of Sephardic Jews all over the World, and attempted to atone for

others. The journal was short lived, lasting only about six months, but through it Burgos met Gómez de la Serna, twenty years her junior, not yet known as one of the most important Spanish Vanguard writers, and with whom she would have a romantic relationship lasting two decades. Today his name is more recognized than hers, but at the time, she was the more famous of the two. She was an author in her own right who published something in the vicinity of 111 novellas, 12 or 13 long novels, five travel books, four biographies; six manuals for women on health, cooking and domestic economy; and myriad translations (of Bracco, Keller, Nordau, Salgari, Ruskin, Montegazza, Renan and Tolstoi, to name a few) (Núñez Rey). [4] And in 1909 she became the first woman war correspondent when *El Heraldo* sent her to cover the war in Morocco. Most importantly, she wrote a number of monographs on the status of women in Spanish society: *Women in Spain*, *On Women's Social Mission* and, of course, *On Modern Women and Their Rights*. These provided powerful arguments for change and a specific program. She was invited to give lectures throughout Spain, as well as in Rome (1906), Buenos Aires (1913), Lisbon (1920), Paris (1922), Mexico City (1925), and Havana (1925), among other cities. She also traveled extensively throughout Europe, writing her experiences as she went. In August of 1914, she found herself in Germany at the start of World War I, and her chronicle constitutes an important first-hand account of the dangers and fears experienced by a woman traveler at the time.

The Great War had a profound impact on Burgos, as her writing attests; as a result, she became an uncompromising pacifist and also began to be involved in direct political activity. As the founder of the Crusade of Spanish Women (1920) she demanded: the establishment of divorce; the investigation of paternity; equal rights for illegitimate children; equal rights for women in the Civil Code (Núñez Rey, 489). Later, the Crusade organized the first street demonstration on behalf of women's rights which presented a nine-point manifesto adding to the prior demands: the right to vote and to be elected; equality in the Penal Code; the establishment of centers of moral and civic education for women; the abolition of prostitution. (Núñez Rey 507). She also formed part of the National Council

---

the wrongs the Jewish people had suffered in Spain.

4   Given the status of "throw away" literature of the weeklies in which Burgos published, they are often difficult to find today, except for the small number that have been published in the last few years. It is also difficult to know with any certainty how many novellas she wrote.

of Women, and became president of the International League of Iberian and Latin American Women. And in 1927 she published her most extensive and important feminist treatise: *On Modern Women and Their Rights*. When the Second Republic was proclaimed, the Radical Socialist Republican Party included in its platform many of the demands she had detailed in the treatise and chose her as one of their candidates for representative in the 1933 elections. She was not to fulfill this last act, however. On October 8, 1932, while speaking at the Radical Socialist Circle on sex education, she felt ill, and as the doctors carried her out of the hall, according to the newspapers of the time, she proclaimed, "I die happy, because I die a Republican. Long live the Republic! I beg you to say it with me: Long live the Republic!" (Núñez Rey 617). She died of a heart attack at 2:00 a.m. the following morning. With the advent of the Republic, Burgos sensed a new Spain coming into being, and the fulfillment of many of the changes she had fought for; according to Núñez Rey, she stated, "I believe the future belongs to us" (593). With the Civil War (1936-1939) and the dictatorship of Franco, of course, these hopes would be frustrated, but she was not to see it.

One of the main concerns of Spanish intellectuals at the start of the century was progress. Yet for many of Burgos' male contemporaries, this did not include an improvement in the status of women. These writers' lack of interest in the "woman question" can be gleaned from Miguel de Unamuno's reply to Burgos' survey on divorce: "What happens to me with the issue of divorce is the same that happens with novels of adultery; rarely do they manage to interest me. I have always seen everything that refers to the relations between the genders as subordinate to other kinds of problems. This is why feminism appeals little to me; I consider that some of the issues it poses have to do with the organization and regulation of work, and others with education in general. A majority of the wrongs about which women complain are wrongs that we men also suffer" (*On Modern Women and Their Rights*) So Unamuno waves away feminism as being too tied to details, to the everyday world, the apparent, perhaps even for him it is too "personal." But this curt dismissal fails to see the more profound ways in which gender is inscribed into cultural, as well as political, economic and social discourses. These discourses act on women at various different levels —intellectual, emotional, physical, spiritual— in order to keep them in their position of permanent minors solely due to their biological sex. Because of this women are, by definition, affected differently from men —the evils that they suffer under patriarchy are not and cannot be the same as those suffered by men. Burgos specifically ties a society's progress to women's status: "the progress of humanity lies in direct relation to the privileges and social influence that the female gender can develop" (*On Modern Women and Their Rights*). The entire purpose of the treatise, *On Modern Women and Their Rights*, is to show the specific ways in which women are oppressed in Spain and large parts of the world, and the ways in which women in a few other countries have escaped that oppression. In this sense, the book is a veritable history of women throughout the ages and all over the world.

As an organized movement, feminism arrives belatedly on the peninsula when compared with the rest of Europe and part of the Americas. Whereas the second half of the 19th Century saw numerous organized attempts to improve conditions for women and children in many places, in Spain these were mainly limited to isolated voices who restricted their discussion to issues of inequality in education during Pedagogical Congresses. Aside from a few exceptions such as Emilia Pardo Bazán, Rosalía de Castro, Concepción Arenal, Rosario de Acuña and a handful of others, women writers rarely ventured beyond the "domestic novel" which upheld the image of the Angel of the House (Deutsch). And yet, as Anja Louis has stated, Burgos can be seen as an "important precursor of Beauvoir's Deuxième Sexe / The Second Sex" from 1949 (128).

At the turn of the century, in response to an untenable economic situation for the majority of the Spanish populace, a series of political and regionalist associations came into being, many of which included feminist branches. The Galician nationalist party, Irmandades de Fala (1916) for example, had its Irmandade Feminina; the Basque party its Organización de Nacionalistas Vascas; the Socialist Workers' Party, the Agrupación Femenina Socialista de Madrid (1906-1927); the anarchists, Mujeres Libres. Alongside these, there appeared some workers associations for women such as the Feminist Association for Assistance and Mutual Aid (1900), which drew its membership from shoe factories. And the Association of Spanish women, one of the most important feminist organizations in Spain, came into being towards 1919. There was also the International League of Iberian and Spanish American Women, presided over by Carmen de Burgos, modeled after U.S. suffragist organizations, and originally founded by Mexican Elena Arizmendi. As the name of the Liga indicates, it took up the causes of women in Latin America as well as Spain and Portugal. Its main goal was to challenge laws that, under the guise of protecting women, only kept them in a subordinate, subservient position within the society, the legalized patriarchy.

In *On Modern Women and Their Rights*, Carmen de Burgos elaborates extensive and erudite arguments to counter the anti-feminist assertions that female difference leads of necessity to inferiority. She challenges the phrenological definition of women as intellectually inferior to men by bringing to bear recent findings which point to the fallacy of a direct relationship between the size of the brain and an individual's intelligence. She refutes the notion that women are by nature, due to their nervous system, more volatile and passionate than men by highlighting the numbers of crimes of passion committed by men as opposed to women, and noting that it is men who start wars and abuse their mates. Burgos also provides a historical overview of women's participation in important historical and cultural movements. And she presents the demands her organization and allied groups proposed to the Spanish government on several occasions, as a well-thought out, coherent program to improve the lot of women and attain political and civil equality. Specifically, the League sought for women the following rights: to vote; to form part of the military and receive military training; to pursue professions and trades hitherto closed for them (women could not be notaries, judges, or pharmacists for example); the right to form part of a jury and to act as witness in a trial; the right to equality before the law and especially the repeal of article 438, which effectively legalized the murder of an adulterous woman who was caught in the act; the right to equal pay for equal work; and the right to work and dispose of her salary without authorization from her husband; the right to enter into contracts, buy and sell property, make donations and accept inheritances; the right to choose her place of residence and to maintain her citizenship regardless of her husband's nationality; the right to equal education; the right to sue for paternity and broken contract when a marriage offer is not honored; the same say as the father with respect to their children's care, education, and life commitments; equal rights for illegitimate children; the right to divorce and remarry; and, finally, the right to birth control.

This fairly long list of demands clearly suggests the desperate situation of women in Spain at the beginning of the 20th Century; a situation which, even in the early years of the second Republic, had seen little change for centuries. Along with other women, Carmen de Burgos sought to abolish this legalized slavery through multiple means. Her petitions to Congress and her essays on women in Spanish society (such as *On Modern Women and Their Rights*) constitute the most explicit enunciation of this attempt, but they are far from the only means she employed. Neither are they the most effective in that they appeal to a reader who holds a fair level of education and sophistication, and one who is willing to follow her arguments. Her other writings evince a feminist agenda in varying degrees of overtness. In her newspaper columns, of course, she openly polemicized in favor of divorce in 1904, and for women's suffrage in 1909. She also placed before public scrutiny many of the issues mentioned above, advocating women and children's rights, in addition to hygiene in the home and schools, the fight against alcoholism, the abolition of prostitution, the reform of the penal code, and the repeal of the death sentence. Her domestic manuals teach women rudimentary principles of physics, chemistry and accounting and suggest possible occupations and small business ventures which would give her readers more independence.

In many ways, what makes Burgos unique among first wave feminists, however, is her concern with the working classes. She develops strong and cogent arguments for the benefits feminism could bring to working class women on many fronts, even, as Roberta Johnson notes, arguing for "class equality via fashion" ("Carmen de Burgos's Place" 46). And, she "inextricably links happiness to equal rights and social justice" (Louis 128). In fact, Burgos specifically addresses the pay and legal status of women factory laborers, and she rejects the rationales for prohibiting women from taking on certain jobs. She also calls on women to unionize to demand the same rights as their male co-workers: pensions, insurance, freedom to choose their work, as well as an equal workday and equal wages.

While Spain entered Modernity somewhat later and more unevenly than did most other European nations, in the first third of the 20th Century there are clear signs of the same rapid changes that characterize this epoch in other countries. In her book *Las modernas de Madrid [Modern Women of Madrid]*, Shirley Mangini describes a Madrid fully in the process of modernization at the start of the century; she notes medical and scientific advances, the incorporation into daily life of the phonograph, electric lighting, film, the streetcar, the telephone, the automobile, the airplane, the telegraph and the microphone (30). We also see a shift from a predominantly agricultural to a more industrial and service economy, and there is a concomitant demographic movement from the rural countryside to the urban centers.[5] As a result of the liberal campaign for education, the literacy level also rises dramatically during the first third of the century.[6] Additionally, Spain benefits from continuous economic expansion, growth in population, and greater use of industrial technologies (Kirkpatrick 8-9). And, of course, along with these changes, there is also an expansion of cultural production and consumption. In fact, *El Cuento Semanal*, the first pulp weekly to be published in Spain (and in which several of Burgos' novellas appeared), began publication in 1907 and issued between 50,000 and 60,000 copies of some novellas (Mangien 28 n.22).[7]

The above numbers indicate a general tendency towards Modernity, but they do not necessarily reflect the material situation of women at the time. Women lagged behind men in education: in 1930 47.5% of women were illiterate, as opposed to 36.9% of men (Morcillo, True Catholic Womanhood 17); and, although women entered the university in 1900, thirty years later, there were only 1,681 female students versus 38,114 males (Garrido González 467). Between 1900 and 1930 there is a progressively larger percentage of women working in industry, particularly in the food, chemical, textile and garment industries (ibid 480); still, a sizeable number of women garment workers labored at home (Nash, Mujer, familia, trabajo 51). Female shop clerks, office workers or telephone operators were still relatively rare (Nash, Mujer... 59). The entrance of women into business, government work or liberal professions was slow and riddled with obstacles (Nash, Mujer... 59), and even in 1927, as Burgos testifies, there were still professions that were closed to them. While, as Susan Kirkpatrick observes, Modernity eventually brought positive changes for many women, especially in the urban centers (13), these changes did not come easily, as Burgos' writings show, and were often in conflict with the influence that the Church still held over Spanish society, as well as with the more modern gender models constructed by science. These latter tended to reinforce the

---

5   In 1900, 65% of the population worked in agriculture, whereas by 1930 this had decreased to 46% (Álvarez Junco, 82). 67% of the population lived in rural municipalities or small centers with fewer than 10,000 inhabitants at the start of the century, in comparison to 57% in 1930 (Álvarez Junco, note 1, 89).

6   From 41% in 1900 to 68% thirty years later (ibid. 82).

7   This growth in the publishing industry can be more clearly apprehended by contrasting it with the editions of Benito Perez Galdos' novels in the late 19th Century which reached only an average of 4,000 or 5,000 copies per edition (Botrel 124).

public-private divide by making motherhood the sole, defining role for women. By the 1920's, however, the New Woman, working in an office, wearing makeup, a short bob and less restrictive clothing makes her appearance in the cities and in Burgos' fiction as well.[8]

Within the history of early 20th Century Spain, *On Modern Women and Their Rights* can be seen as what Michel Foucault termed "subjugated knowledge," a kind of knowledge that has been repressed, whose "historical contents have been buried and disguised" ("Two Lectures" 81), a kind of "popular knowledge" that has not attained the status of "science" or "discipline" and has been disqualified. In this kind of knowledge resides "the memory of hostile encounters", and resurrecting it is essential for the reconstruction of a history of resistance and struggle (Sawicki 57). Certainly, this is the case with "throw away" literature, such as the pulp weeklies, and it is particularly applicable to the work of a writer, such as Burgos, who was erased from the pages of literary history during the Franco regime.

To fully understand the history of feminism in Spain, then, we must take into account the work of women like Carmen de Burgos. Her project is manifold. To begin with, her speaking out through the mass media can be seen as an exercise of power, and an attempt to create knowledge, or counter-discourses that refute and de-naturalize many of the masculinist premises in legal, scientific and religious discourses. She denounces numerous small social practices that constrain and discipline women, as well as the punishments suffered by those who cannot or will not subject to them. She also highlights the complicity of women in their own oppression. And, though less so, she sketches possibilities for different feminine subjectivities.

The following translation is based on the first edition of Burgos's *La mujer moderna y sus derechos*. Valencia: Sampere, 1927.

---

8 Ana María Díaz-Marcos traces the relationship between Modernity, the new woman and *On Modern Women and Their Rights*, as well as *The Art of Being a Woman*.

WORKS CITED

Álvarez Junco, José. Rural and Urban Popular Cultures. *Spanish Cultural Studies: An Introduction*. Edited by Helen Graham and Jo Labanyi. Oxford: Oxford UP, 1995. 82-90.

Bieder, Maryellen. "Carmen de Burgos: Modern Spanish Woman." *Recovering Spain's Feminist Tradition*. Ed. Lisa Vollendorf. New York: The Modern Language Association of America, 2001. 241-59.

---. "Contesting the Body: Gender, Language, and Sexuality. The Modern Woman at the Turn of the Century." *Women's Narrative and Film in Twentieth Century Spain*. Ed. Ofelia Ferrán & Kathleen Glenn. New York, London: Routledge, 2002. 3-18. Includes discussion of "El veneno del arte"

---. "Self-Reflexive Fiction and the Discourses of Gender in Carmen de Burgos." *Self-Conscious Art: A Tribute to John W. Kronik*. Ed. Susan L. Fischer. Lewisburg: Bucknell U. P., 1996. 73-89.

Botrel, Jean-François. "Le succès d'édition des oeuvres de Benito Pérez Galdós I: essai de bibliométrie." *Anales de Literatura Española* 3 (1984): 119-157.

Deutsch, Lou. *Narratives of Desire. Nineteenth-Century Spanish Fiction by Women*. University Park: Penn State P, 1994.

Díaz-Marcos, Ana María. "La 'mujer moderna' de Carmen de Burgos: feminismo, moda y cultura femenina." *Letras Femeninas* XXXV. 2 (2012): 113-132.

Foucault, Michel. "Two lectures." *Power/Knowledge: Selected Interviews and Other Writings 1972-1977*. New York: Pantheon Books, 1972.

Gould Levine, Linda. "The Censored Sex: Woman as Author and Character in Franco's Spain," *Women in Hispanic Literature: Icons and Fallen Idols*, ed. Beth Miller (Berkeley, CA: U. of California P, 1983) 291.

Garrido González, Elisa, et al. *Historia de las mujeres en España*. Madrid: Síntesis, 1997.

Graham, Helen and Jo Labani, eds. *Spanish Cultural Studies: An Introduction*. Oxford: Oxford UP, 1995.

Johnson, Roberta. *Gender and Nation in the Spanish Modernist Novel*. Nashville: Vanderbilt UP, 2003.

---. "Carmen de Burgos's Place in a Genealogy of Spanish Feminist Thought." *Multiple Modernities: Carmen de Burgos, Author and Activist*. London: Routledge, 2017: 43-58.

Kirkpatrick, Susan. *Mujer, modernismo y vanguardia en España (1898-*

1931). Madrid: Cátedra, 2003.

Louis, Anja. "In Search of Feminist Happiness: Burgos's *La entrometida.*" *Multiple Modernities: Carmen de Burgos, Author and Activist.* London: Routledge, 2017: 127-145.

Mangien, Brigitte, et al. *Ideología y texto en El Cuento Semanal 1907-1912.* Madrid: Ediciones de la Torre, 1986.

Mangini, Shirley. *Las modernas de Madrid. Las grandes intelectuales españolas de la vanguardia.* Barcelona: Península, 2001.

Morcillo, Aurora. *True Catholic Womanhood. Gender Ideology in Franco's Spain.* Dekalb: Northern Illinois P, 2000.

Nash, Mary. *Mujer, familia y trabajo en España, 1875-1936.* Barcelona: Antropos, 1983.

Núñez Rey, Concepción. *Colombine en la Edad de Plata de la literatura española.* Seville: Fundación José Manuel Lara, 2005.

Pérez, Janet. *Contemporary Women Writers of Spain.* Boston: Twayne, 1988.

Samblancat Miranda, Neus. "Los derechos de la mujer moderna." *Cuadernos Hispanoamericanos* 671 (mayo 2006): 7-19.

Sawicki, Jana. *Disciplining Foucault. Feminism, Power and the Body.* New York: Routledghe, 1991.

Simón Palmer, María del Carmen. "Escritoras españolas del siglo XX." *Arbor* CLXXXII. 721 (septiembre-octubre 2006): 661-703.

Works by Carmen de Burgos

Al balcón. Valencia: Sempere, 19??

Alucinación. Madrid: Viuda de Rodríguez Serra, 1905.

Los amores de Faustino. Madrid: La Novela Corta, 1920.

El anhelo. Madrid: La Novela Semanal, 1923.

Los anticuarios. Madrid: Biblioteca Nueva, 1989.

Arte de saber vivir. Valencia: Sempere, 19??

El arte de saber vivir. Valencia: Prometeo, 19??

El arte de ser amada. Valencia: Sempere, 19??

Las artes de la mujer. Valencia: Prometeo, 19??

Una bomba. Valencia: La Novela con Regalo, 1917. Pedido a la BNM, año 2, no. 4

El brote. Madrid: La Novela Corta, 1925.

Cartas sin destinatario. Bélgica. Holanda. Luxemburgo (Impresiones de viaje). Valencia: Sempere y Compañía, 19??

La ciudad encantada. Madrid: La Novela Corta, 1921.

Confidencias. Madrid: Los Contemporáneos, 1920.

La confidente. Madrid: La novela de noche, 1926.

Cuando la ley lo manda. Madrid: Atlántida [La Novela de Hoy], 1932.

Cuentos de Colombine. Valencia: Sempere, 19?? Includes: "Un momento (por Pierrot)," "La muerte del recuerdo," "Por las ánimas," "Madre por hija," "Alma de artista," "El viejo ídolo," "¡Ay del solo!" "La incomprensible," "¡Triunfante!" "Historia de Carnaval," "El último deseo," "Los que no vivieron,""Como flor de almendro" "Aroma de pecado," "En pos del ensueño," "El tesoro," "En la sima."

El desconocido. Madrid: Los Contemporáneos, 1917.

El divorcio en España. Madrid: Viuda de Rodríguez Serra, 1904.

Don Manolito. Madrid: Los Conmporáneos, 1916.

El dorado trópico. Madrid: La Novela de Hoy, 1930.

Dos amores. Madrid: La Novela Corta, 1919.

Ella y ellos o ellos y ellas. Madrid: Los Contemporáneos, 1916.

La emperatriz Eugenia. Su vida. Madrid: La Novela Corta, 1925.

Las ensaladillas. Madrid: La Novela Corta, 1924.

Ensayos literarios. Almería: n.e., 1900. Includes: "Zahara," "La mariposa", "Dos madres," "Salud de los enfermos," "Locura," "El repatriado," "Una venganza," "El pajarillo," "Cantares," "Las almas hermanas," "La flor del valle," "Cantares," "Desesperación," "La educación de la mujer."

El extranjero. Madrid: La Novela Semanal, 1923.

El fin de la guerra. Madrid: Los Contemporáneos, 1919.

La flor de la playa y otras novelas cortas. Ed. Concepción Núñez Rey. Madrid: Castalia, 1989. Includes: "En la guerra," "La flor de la playa," "El permisionario," "El perseguidor," "El último contrabandista," "El veneno del arte," "Vida y milagros del pícaro Andresillo Pérez."

Frasca la tonta. Madrid: El Libro Popular, 1914.

Guiones del destino. Madrid: Atlántida [La Novela de Hoy], 1932.

Hasta renacer. Madrid: La Novela Corta, 1924.

El hastío del amor. Madrid: La Novela Corta, 1923.

La herencia de la bruja. Madrid: Ed. Gráfica [La Novela Gráfica], 1923.

El hombre negro. Madrid: Emiliano Escolar, 1980.

El honor de la familia. Madrid: El Cuento Semanal, 1911.

La hora del amor. Madrid: V.H. de Sanz Calleja, 19??.

Los inadaptados. Granada: Biblioteca General del Sur, 1990.

La indecisa. Madrid: El Libro Popular, 1912.

Lo inesperado. Valencia: Novela con Regalo, 1916.

Influencias recíprocas entre la mujer y la literatura. Logroño: Imp. "La Rioja," 19??

La ironía de la vida. Madrid: Atlántida [La Novela de Hoy], 1931.

La justicia del mar. Madrid: El Libro Popular, 1912.

Luna de miel. Madrid: La Novela Corta, 1921.

La malcasada. Valencia: Editoria Sempere, 1923.

Malos amores. Madrid: El Libro Popular, 1914.

La mejor film. Madrid: La Novela Corta, 1918.

La melena de la discordia. Madrid: La Novela Semanal, 1925.

La miniatura. Madrid: La Novela Corta, 1924.

Mis mejores cuentos. Ed. Ana Martínez Marín. Sevilla: Editoriales Andaluzas Unidas, 1984. Includes: "Autobiografía," "El artículo 438," "El abogado," "El novenario," "Los huesos del abuelo," "La mujer fría."

Mis viajes por Europa. Madrid: V. H. de Sanz Calleja, Editores, 19??

La misionera de Teotihuacán. Madrid: La Novela Mundial, 1926.

Misión social de la mujer. Bilbao: José Roja Núñez, 1911? Conferencia Pronunciada en la Sociedad "El Sitio", la noche del 18 de febrero de 1911.

El "misericordia." Madrid: La Novela Mundial, 1927.

Los míseros. Madrid: La Novela para Todos, 1916.

La mujer en el hogar. Valencia: Sempere, 19??.

La mujer en España. Valencia: Sempere, 1906.

La mujer fantástica. Madrid: La Novela Corta, 1923.

La mujer fría. Madrid: La Novela Corta, 1922.

La mujer moderna y sus derechos. Valencia: Sempere, 1927.

La mujer moderna y sus derechos. Intro. Pilar Ballarín. Madrid: Biblioteca Nueva, 2007.

Los negociantes de la Puerta del Sol. Madrid: La Novela Corta, 1919.

La nostálgica. Madrid: La Novela Semanal, 1925.

Pasiones. Madrid: La Novela Corta, 1917.

La pensión ideal. Madrid: La Novela Corta, 1923.

Perdónanos nuestras deudas. Madrid: La Novela de Hoy, 1931.

El perseguidor. Madrid: La Novela Corta, 1917.

¡La piscina! ¡La piscina! Madrid: La Novela de Hoy, 1930.

Por Europa (Impresiones). Francia. Italia. Barcelona, Madrid, Buenos Aires: Casa Editorial Maucci, 19??.

La princesa rusa. Madrid: La Novela Corta, 1922.

"Prólogo." *Panorama errante. El caso del periodista español*. Madrid: Imprenta de "La Mañana," 1917. 11-15.

La prueba. Madrid: Los Contemporáneos, 1922.

Puñal de claveles. Ed. Miguel Naveros. Almería: Editorial Cajal, 1991.

La que quiso ser maja. La Novela Pasional. Sevilla: Renacimiento, 2000.

La que se casó muy niña. Madrid: La Novela Corta, 1923.

Quiero vivir mi vida. Madrid: Biblioteca Nueva, 1932.

La rampa. Madrid: Renacimiento, 19??
La rampa. Madrid: Los Contemporáneos, 1921.
La rampa. Ed. Susan Larson. Buenos Aires: Stockcero, 2006.
"Recuerdos.". *Homenaje a Manuel del Palacio*. Madrid: [n.e.], 1932. 19-21.
El retorno. Novela espiritista (basada en hechos reales). Lisboa: Lusitania Editora, 19??
Salud y belleza. Valencia: Sempere, 19??
Se quedó sin ella. Madrid: Atlántida [La Novela de Hoy], 1929.
Senderos de vida. Madrid: El Cuento Semanal, 1908.
Siempre en tierra. Madrid: Los Contemporáneos, 1912.
El silencio del hijo. Barcelona: Publicaciones Mundial [La Novela Femenina], 19??
Sorpresas. Madrid: La Novela de Bolsillo, [1914].
El suicida asesinado. Madrid: La Novela Corta, 1922.
El tesoro del castillo. Madrid: El Cuento Semanal, 1907.
El tío de todos. Barcelona: Ribas y Ferrer, 1925.
El tocador práctico. Valencia: Sempere, 19??
Todos menos ése. Madrid: La Novela Corta, 191?
La tornadiza. Madrid: Los Contemporáneos, 1923.
Las tricanas. Madrid: Alfa (La novela romántica), 19??
Los usureros. Madrid: Los Contemporáneos, 1916.
Vademécum femenino. Valencia: Prometeo, 19??
Venganza. Madrid: La Novela Corta, 1918.
Villa María. Madrid: La Novela Corta, 1916.

SCHOLARSHIP ON CARMEN DE BURGOS

Adam Muñoz, María Dolores. "El cuento de Carmen de Burgos "El srtículo 438" de código penal y su posible vigencia." *Romper el espejo. La mujer y la transgresión de códigos en la literaturaEspañola: Escritura. Lectura. Textos*. Ed. María José Porro Herrera. Córdoba: Universidad de Córdoba, 2001. 235-54.

Arranz, Carmen. "El discurso de raza como pretexto feminista: Carmen de Burgos desde Melilla." *Ciberletras* 25 (julio 2011).

---. "Más allá del género: Carmen de Burgos, modernidad y clases sociales." *Hispanófila* 167 (Jan 2013): 39-49.

Bell, Amy. "Rewriting Symbolic Psychoneuroses: Carmen de Burgos's *Quiero vivir mi vida*." *Letras Peninsulares* 17.2-3 (Fall/ Winter 2004-2005): 271-284.

---. "Deconstructing the "Sleep-Death Equation" and the Misogynistic Marquis: Carmen de Burgos's *Ellas y ellos ó ellos y ellas*." *South Atlantic Review* 71.2 (Spring, 2006): 31-47.

Bieder, Maryellen. "Carmen de Burgos: Modern Spanish Woman." *Recovering Spain's Feminist Tradition*. Ed. Lisa Vollendorf. New York: The Modern Language Association of America, 2001. 241-59.

---. "Contesting the Body: Gender, Language, and Sexuality. The Modern Woman at the Turn of the Century." *Women's Narrative and Film in Twentieth Century Spain*. Ed. Ofelia Ferrán & Kathleen Glenn. New York, London: Routledge, 2002. 3-18.

---. "Self-Reflexive Fiction and the Discourses of Gender in Carmen de Burgos." *Self-Conscious Art: A Tribute to John W. Kronik*. Ed. Susan L.Fischer. Lewisburg: Bucknell U. P., 1996. 73-89.

Bravo Cela, Blanca. *Carmen de Burgos (Colombine). Contra el silencio*. Madrid: Espasa-Calpe, 2003.

Cabañas Alamán, Rafael. In *Género y géneros: Escritura y escritoras iberoamericanas: V. I*, edited by Encinar, Angeles, Löfquist, Eva, Valcárcel, Carmen. Madrid, Spain: Universidad Autónoma de Madrid, 2006: 189-201.

Casas, María Lourdes. "Escritura femenina, mujer moderna y ciudad en La Novela Mundial (1926-1928)." *Ciberletras* 27 (April, 2011)

Naveros, Miguel and Ramón Navarrete-Galiano, eds. *Carmen de Burgos: Aproximación a la obra de una escritora comprometida*. Almería: Instituto de Estudios Almerienses, 1996.

Castañeda, Paloma. *Carmen de Burgos. "Colombine."* Madrid: Dirección General de la Mujer, horas y HORAS la editorial feminista, 1994.

Caulfield, Carlota. "Tórtola Valencia bajo la mirada de Carmen de Burgos y Antonio de Hoyos: moda y tipismo español." *Monographic Review/Revista Monográfica* 25 (2009): 120-44.

Charpentier Saitz, Herlinda. "Carmen de Burgos-Seguí (Colombine), Escritora Española Digna de Ser Recordada." *La escritora hispánica. Actas de la decimotercera conferencia anual de literatura hispánica en Indiana University of Pennsylvania*. Ed. Nora y Juan cruz Mendizábal Erro-Orthmann. Miami, Florida: Ediciones Universal, 1990. 169-77.

Clémessy, Nelly. "Une Page d'histoire sociale de l'Espagne: Carmen de Burgos et la polémique sur le divorce." *Histoire et Civilixations Ibériques*. Nice: Annales de la Faculté des Lettres et Sciences Humaines, 1978. 155-67.

Davies, Catherine. "The 'Red Lady': Carmen de Burgos (1867-1932)." *Spanish Women's Writing 1849-1996*. Ed. The Athlone Press. London and Atlantic Highlands, N.J., 1998. 117-36.

Doyle, Kathleen. "Body of Evidence: The Legislation of Female Desire in *El artículo 438* by Carmen de Burgos." *Letras Femeninas* XXX.1 (verano 2004): 155-64.

Epps, Brad. "Modernity, Gender and the Spectre of Coloniality in the 'Moroccan Texts' by Carmen de Burgos and Aurora Bertrana." *Anales de la Literatura Española Contemporánea* 41.4 (2016): 105-129.

Establier-Pérez, Helena. *Mujer y feminismo en la obra de Carmen de Burgos "Colombine."* Almería: Instituto de Estudios Almerienses, 2000.

Estrada-López, Lourdes. "Marginalización secundaria en *Quiero vivir mi vida*' (1931) de Carmen de Burgos." *Letras Femeninas* 40.2 (2014): 217-32.

Imboden, Rita Catrina. *Carmen de Burgos "Colombine" y la novela corta.* Benn, Berlin, Bruxelles, Frankfurt am Main, New York, Oxford, Wien: Peter Lang, 2001.

Johnson, Roberta. "Carmen de Burgos and Spanish Modernism." *South Central Review* 18.1-2 (Spring-Summer 2001): 66-77.

---. "Carmen de Burgos: Marriage and Nationalism." *La generación del 98 frente al nuevo Fin de siglo.* Ed. Jesús Torrecilla. Amsterdam: Rodopi, 2000. 140-51.

Kirkpatrick, Judith. "Skeletons in the Closet: Carmen de Burgos Confronts the Literary Patriarchy." *Letras Peninsulares* 8.3 (Winter 1995-1996): 389-400.

Krauel, Ricardo. "Hacia una redefinición de la sensualidad femenina en la modernidad: 'La mujer fría' de Carmen de Burgos." *Bulletin of Hispanic Studies* 80 (October 2003): 525-36.

Larson, Susan. *Constructing and Resisting Modernity*: Madrid 1900-1936. Madrid: Iberoamericana, 2011.

Louis, Anja. "Carmen de Burgos and the Question of Divorce." *Tesserae: Journal of Iberian and Latin American Studies* 5.1 (June 1999): 49-63.

---. "Inferior, Superior or Just Different? A Woman's Sense of Justice in Carmen de Buergos's *El abogado*." *Hispanic Research Journal* 6.1 (February 2005): 13-27.

---. "Melodramatic Feminism: The Popular Fiction of Carmen de Burgos." *Constructing Identity in Contemporary Spain.* Ed. Jo Labanyi. Oxford: Clarendon Press, 2002. 94-112.

---. *Women and the Law: Carmen de Burgos, an Early Feminist.* Suffolk, Great Britain: Tamesis, 2005.

Mangini, Shirley. "The Female as Battleground: Carmen de Burgos's *Quiero vivir mi vida.*" *Visions and Revisions. Women's Narrative in Twentieth-Century Spain.* Ed. Kathleen M. Glenn and Kathleen McNerney. Amsterdam, New York: Rodopi, 2008. 19-35.

Martínez Garrido, Elisa. "Amor y feminidad en las escritoras de principios de siglo."

---, ed. *Carmen de Burgos: Aproximación a la Obra de una Escritora*

Comprometida. Almería: Instituto de Estudios Almerienses, 1996.

---. "El mito de la "virgen perseguida" en una novela femenina y feminista." *Actas del IX simposio de la Sociedad Española de Literatura General y Comparada*. Ed. María Teresa Cacho Túa Blesa, et al. Zaragoza: U. de Zaragoza, 1994. 253-61.

Minesso, Bárbara. "Malcasadas, vencidas y liberadas: Anhelos de cambio en la narrativa de Carmen de Burgos, Colombine." *Cuadernos de Aleph. Revista de Literatura Hispánica* 9 (2011): 173-183.

Núñez Rey, Concepción. *Carmen de Burgos, Colombine en la Edad de Plata de la literatura española*. Seville: Fundación José Manuel Lara, 2005.

Pérez, Janet. "The Turn-of-the-Century Generation." *Contemporary Women Writers of Spain*. Boston: Twayne, 1988. 15-36.

Paredes Méndez, Francisca. "Elisa se ha comprado zapatos de tacón: moda, género y clase social en *La flor de la playa* de Carmen de Burgos." *Anales de la Literatura Española Contemporánea* 34.1 (2009): 203-28.

Pozzi, Gabriela. "Carmen de Burgos and the War in Morocco." *MLN* 115.2 (March 2000): 188-204.

---. "Viajando por Europa con Carmen de Burgos (Colombine). A través de la Gran Guerra hacia la autoridad femenina." *Literatura de viajes. El Nuevo y el Viejo Mundo*. Ed. Salvador García Castañeda. Madrid: Castalia, 1999. 299-307.

Ragan, Robin. "Carmen de Burgos' *La Mujer Fría*: A Response to Necrophilic Aesthetics in Decadentist Spain." *Disciplines on the Line: Feminist Research on Spanish, Latin American, and U.S. Latina Women*. Ed. et al Anne J. Cruz. Newark, DE: Juan de la Cuesta, 2003. 235-55.

Rodriguez, Maria Pilar. "Modernidad y feminismo: Tres relatos de Carmen de Burgos." *Anales de la Literatura Española Contemporánea* 23.1-2 (1998): 379-403.

---. "Desviación y perversión en *El veneno del arte* de Carmen de Burgos." *Symposium* 51 (Fall 1997): 172-85.

Sharp, Michelle and Anja Louis, eds. *Multiple Modernities: Carmen de Burgos, Author and Activist*. London: Routledge, 2017.

Sharp, Michelle. "Carmen de Burgos: TEaching Women of the Modern Age." Kiosk Literature of Silver Age Spain. Modernity and Mass Culture. Chicago: U of Chicago P, 2017. 313-328.

Starcevic, Elizabeth. *Carmen de Burgos. Defensora de la Mujer*. Almería: Librería-Editoria Cajal, 1976.

Suárez-Galbán Guerra, Eugenio. "Sobre Dos Novelas Cortas Recuperadas de Carmen de Burgos." *Ínsula* 37.430 (Sept 1982): 7.

Torres Pou, Juan. "El viaje a Oriente en la literatura femenina

española: Carmen de Burgos, Aurora Bertrana y Rosa Regàs."
Neophilologus 90.1 (Jan. 2006): 39-51.

Truxa, Sylvia. "Corrientes y prácticas literarias en la obra de Carmen de Burgos." *Literatura y Pensamiento en España: Estudios en Honor de Ciriaco Morón Arroyo.* Newark, Delaware: Juan de la Cuesta, 2003.

Trautenberg, Ezekiel. "The Yoke of the Hat. Consumption, Middle-Class Values, and Social Mobility in Carmen de Burgos's La Flor de la Playa." *Hispanic Review* 84.1 (winter 2016): 25-46.

Ugarte, Michael. "Carmen de Burgos ('Colombine'): Feminist Avant la Lettre." *Spanish Women Writers and the Essay: Gender, Politics, and the Self.* Ed. Kathleen M. Glenn and Mercedes Mazquiaran de Rodriguez. Columbia, MO: U. of Missouri P, 1998. 55-74.

---. "Feminist Madrid: Carmen de Burgos." *Madrid 1900. The Capital as Cradle of Literature and Culture.* University Park, Pennsylvania: The Pennsylvania State U. P., 1996. 79-104.

---. "The Generational Fallacy and Spanish Women Writing." *Siglo XX/20th Century* 12.1-2 (1994): 261-76.

Urioste Azcorra, Carmen. *Narrativa andaluza (1900-1936). Erotismo, feminismo, regionalismo.* Sevilla: Universidad de Sevilla, 1997. Cap. III, "Canon y literatura de mujeres. Carmen de Burgos", 65-95.

Urioste, Carmen de. "Canonicidad y feminismo: Los textos de Carmen de Burgos." *Romance Languages Annual* 5 (1993): 527-32.

Wood, Jennifer. "A Woman Writing War in 1909: Colombine in Melilla." *Letras Peninsulares* 12.2-3 (Fall-Winter 1999-2000): 373-85.

Zapata-Calle, Ana. *"En la guerra* de Carmen de Burgos: crítica del proceso de nacionalización e imperialismo español en Marruecos." *Decimonónica: Journal of Nineteenth Century Hispanic Cultural Production* 8.2 (2011): 91-112.

Zaplana, Ester. "Feminist Parallels: Carmen de Burgos and Virginia Woolf on the Themes of Militarism and Pacifism." *Donaire* 15 (Noviembre 2000): 52-58.

---. "Rewriting the Patria: War, Militarism and the Feminine Habitus in the Writings of Rosario de Acuña, Carmen de Burgos and Emilia Pardo Bazán." *Bulletin of Spanish Studies* LXXXII.1 (2005): 37-58.

CHAPTER 1
FEMINISMS

Social transformation. —Origins of Feminism. —Feminism's various tendencies. —What modern Feminism means. —Unfairness of a Proclamation for Human Rights that disregards gender.

One of those profound evolutions that transform society is unfolding before our very eyes, of the type barely perceived by those who suffer from the clash of new ideas, the type of evolution that sweeps along everything that had served as a foundation of society in order to transform ideas and emotions. If the beginning of Christianity marks a New Era, and the French Revolution is the beginning of an Age, there can be no doubt that the Great War, which erupted in 1914, heralded the beginning of a new period in history and profoundly transformed principles and customs.

We are at a time when more is being torn down than is being constructed, in which old materials are being collected in order to build with them, and they are being torn apart by hand; this is the precise moment for one to prepare oneself for a future that is trying to break with the past, in a flood, all the more daring the greater the obstacles that oppose it. In the midst of uncertainty and vagueness, in which everything is stirred up by anxiety for the insatiable renewal that has accompanied humanity during its entire pilgrimage on earth, women seem confused, most intensely because their transformation is more abrupt. Women are somewhat like the patient who gets a cataract operation and whose bandages are removed in full sunlight, exposing her to dazzling light and blindness.

Although the vast majority of women are prepared for the social mission that they must undertake in the post-war world, there needs to be a period of adaptation, we could say of transplantation. Much like during the season when trees lose their leaves and keep the buds that will become new shoots, women must lose the false foliage of their preconceived notions, false ideas and arbitrary customs, while keeping the noble and fundamental aspects of nature that constitute a true orientation. The foundation (for this) is found in the law, in the proclamation of "Equal Rights." Customs have evolved significantly in favor of women. What is needed is for the civil codes to march in step with customs, and for them not to attempt to dictate life within rigid guidelines.

One could say that we are passing through a period analogous to Roman times, when women gained a degree of freedom in their customs, and equality with and even prevalence over men, which even the most feminist states of North America have not yet surpassed. These women did not worry about their status in the legal Code, they did not argue; it was all action and feminism, which we could call a pragmatic approach. But all this disappeared along with the Roman Empire without leaving a trace. The influence of customs vanished, leaving only the written law, which has served as a stamp to mark women as slaves for so many centuries.

Freedoms gained through customs must be guaranteed by law. The true concept of feminism must be established definitively. Few doctrines have been so strongly resisted and so poorly understood. Disrepute fell over all of feminism, but was only deserved by some women whose conduct indicated that they misunderstood its significance. The campaigns of men and women who ridiculed those who fought for the liberation of a large portion of humanity contributed to this image. Feminism's first significant victory was to ensure that it was taken seriously, putting an end to the facile jokes and quips in poor taste, prompting eminent men to take women's liberation seriously, and clearly defining the *meaning of feminism to be*: A SOCIAL PARTY THAT WORKS TO ACHIEVE A JUSTICE THAT DOES NOT ENSLAVE HALF OF THE HUMAN RACE, IN DETRIMENT TO ALL. The concepts of imbalance and ridiculousness, and the ideas of feminine hegemony and danger to society, were banished from the word feminism.

Rarely is it possible to limit an idea to the narrow confines of a single definition, much less in the case of feminism, which has such broad interpretations. Feminism involves more action than doctrine in its pursuit of liberating women and improving their condition so that their individual rights are guaranteed in the name of the principle of human rights and in the interests of the entire community. Feminism will complete its mission more easily by counting upon the collaboration of the two halves of which it is made up. And so, as a doctrine, feminism includes the purest principles of freedom and justice, and as an endeavor, has great social usefulness.

Feminism, the name of this movement and doctrine, is of French origin and is attributed to Fourier,[9] that great defender of women, who in his *System*, expressed the conviction that the progress of humanity lies in direct relation to the privileges and

---

9 French socialist philosopher Charles Fourier (1772-1837) was an influential intellectual and utopianist.

social influence that the female gender can develop. In no way did he mean that there should be a reversal of the genders or their roles, much less an aspiration for equality, which would go against the laws of nature. Once the word "feminism" was accepted as meaning the cause of women's liberation, in accordance with the laws of nature, untrustworthy people discredited it and at times came to present feminism as a terrible thing capable of dissolving society. At other times, it was presented as a ridiculous, laughable thing that did not deserve to be taken seriously.

With the desire to find a new, less polemical word to label women's just aspirations, some used the word "Humanism," which never gained universal acceptance. Actually, the point is trivial at bottom. The word "Feminism" is destined to stop being used soon, with no need to find a substitute for it, as is happening with the word "Masculinism." Once both halves of the human genus gain the right to govern each other, there will be no need to make that distinction, which has required a word to represent women's vindication. The word is nothing more than a sign that represents the problem that churns in society's soul, not a problem that we could deem secondary because it only affects a limited number of individuals or because it was born of conventionalism. Feminism exists, independent from free will, and comprises the whole of society. It was born of the injustice and malaise that a portion of humanity suffers. It can only be resolved by reestablishing the integrity of justice so that all may have their rights guaranteed.

Thus, we see that feminism is not a mere theory, but a fact. It represents the oppressed, mistreated woman's desire for freedom. Although its roots are ancient, there have been periods when the struggle and mistreatment have intensified, above all since greater cultural involvement as well as the spread of a more critical nature prompted a great number of women to throw off the paralysis, indifference and deception of gallantry. The modern winds that stoked the flames came from American soil, not just because America is a young country, freer from the prejudices that history engenders, overflowing with a rich productive vitality and abundant restiveness, but rather because the American struggle was violent, heated, and required the development of every resource. The seed came from Europe; the mature fruit would come from America.

With this impetus, the personality of the modern woman developed rapidly, growing in freedom as well as dignity and authority. Although some detractors would pretend something different, and include within the movement, with respectably independent protests, a scant number of women who are mentally imbalanced and who, as Marie Martin[10] states: "hide under the mantle of feminism a most erroneous conduct or immoral eccentricities. Under the false pretext of emancipation, they give free reign to their strange habits and capricious fantasies." It is neither a matter of censuring them nor of arguing whether they are doing good or evil. We can only affirm that their behavior has nothing to do with feminism and that they are knowingly putting forth an insincere, disloyal argument. In light of this, there are those who shout: "You see what kind of example the feminists are setting?"

But feminism is something more serious. Its bonfire was lit in the world driven by the economic necessities that fanned its flames, stoked by the pain and suffering of female servitude. Almost without being noticed, an evolution in the family and in the economic conditions of nations was taking place, certainly not because of women's influence. A type of family organization, within which women felt morally supported even though they had no rights, disappeared almost completely. Those homes that once sheltered a loving family in the glow of faint lamplight, whose head of the family protected all the women related to him by birth, no matter how distant the relationship, have almost ceased to exist. Women always found refuge in homes where the strictest rectitude was the norm. Their economic needs were met; worries and ambitions had not yet penetrated into their spirits and they resigned themselves to monotonous lives. But now that only a minority of homes of this type remains, and women no longer find themselves to be respected and their lifestyle guaranteed, not even in their own home, at times they have to feel a deep sense of unease and irradiate it over the entire society, victims of their own egotism. As Novicow[11] rightly said, "the happiness of nations stands in direct relation to the sum of justice that each nation distributes among the individuals that form them."

The family's transformation accompanied economic transformation. Life became more difficult. Along with the great factories and industrial enterprises came a scarcity of daily wages and jobs. To earn her keep, since she could not count on a man to support her, a woman had to leave the home and go out to labor in

---

10 Martin (1839-1910) was a French suffragette who launched the publication *Le Journal des femmes*.

11 Yakov Aleksandrovich Novicov (1849-1912) was an important Russian sociologist opposed to war and social Darwinism.

the workshop or the factory. She could not live by "counting stars," as in the English legend. She had to choose between working and enduring an abject existence, since women are normally not granted a means of subsistence because of their touching weakness, but rather in exchange for their dignity. This was the root of the feminist movement. Women availed themselves of the doctrine that advocated for their social equality with men, full of the same fervor that had thrown the slaves into confusion when they heard Christian theories of equality centuries before.

And in the face of feminism an ancient anti-feminism also intensified. This involved unjust men protective of their hegemony and selfish women who feared losing their privileged positions. They proclaimed with moving tones that nature determines the mission of both sexes: men should work, and women should be nothing but mothers, angels of the home, a commingling of grace and beauty. All of this, translated into common language, means that women should be no more than servants and playthings for men. But if a law had been passed that coincided with this lyrical song, that obliged all men to support this "angel of the home," whose wings they were asked to clip, without her needing to work and without detriment to her dignity as a woman, the protest would have been widespread. Invoking maternity in order to maintain servitude implies a high degree of cynicism which inexplicably ignores the existence of women who have not been mothers and of widows and wives who, after raising and educating their children, thus fulfilling their maternal mission, have energies that demand to be used. But that song, with which men played the role of SIRENS, deceived many unfortunate women who accepted as dogma the notion of their inferiority.

One of the greatest difficulties that feminism faced was opposition from women themselves. Accustomed to servitude, they were afraid of liberation, which included responsibility. Others did not realize, in the midst of their ignorance and irresponsibility, the importance of freeing themselves from the ills that afflicted them; some wished to please their husbands by being submissive. The phenomenon that played out when slaves and servants were freed repeated itself; women opposed their own emancipation, motivated by the fear of freedom that their heritage and the experience of a long period of servitude had imprinted on them. Some had an envious fear of a refined class of women: doctors, lawyers, artists, in the midst of whom they would go unnoticed. They did not want to make any effort to emulate these women in order to lift their spirits. For some their value was dependent on their pots and pans, for others upon their social graces, and they despotically imposed their authority on the family, shielded by the role of "Housewife." There was the case of women who unwittingly imitated the subjects of Ferdinand VII[12], cheering for their own chains. There were some who congratulated Moebius[13] for his attacks against the entire gender in such an overblown way that he, ever the enemy of women, was forced to defend them, assuring us that "luckily, there are women who have wholesome souls." And Mrs. Fanny Sewelpf concluded that Moebius' book disabused her of the notion that women could have the same faculties as men. It is certainly true that any comedian could make use of these words.

In England Humphry Ward,[14] a talented woman, opposed feminism. In France, where one could pay tribute to many noble, sensible feminists, a mediocre writer, Mrs. Barbat de Chosel, widow of Dardanne de la Granjerie, donated several thousand francs to the French Academy to fund a prize under the pseudonym "Philippe Cerfant." She established the condition that women who applied for it be excluded "because of their spirit of intrigue." The Academy rejected the bequest by mutual agreement.

Feminism finds itself obligated to free these women in spite of themselves. They are like suicidal patients who must be placed in straightjackets and made to take their medication, because healthy individuals have the right to defend their health and avoid contagion. In the face of struggles, mockery, and accusations, even men of good will distrusted feminism, much like the colonists who were suspicious of the emancipation of the slaves. Subconsciously they experienced the displeasure of seeing their absolute control escape them, a control which, in Napoleon's words, led them to believe that women belonged to them much as fruit trees belong to the gardener. They were led to believe that feminism was man's enemy, that it broke up homes and represented the denial of love. They could not convince themselves that feminism is neither a battle of the sexes, nor hostility toward men, but rather women's desire to collaborate with them and work side by side.

---

12   The king of Spain during the French invasion under Napoleon, at the start of the 19th Century.

13   Paul Julius Moebius (1853-1907) was a German neurologist who in 1900 published the pamphlet "On the Physiological Idiocy of Women," which numerous feminists roundly criticized. Burgos reacted by translating it into Spanish, giving it the title "*La inferioridad mental de la mujer*/The Mental Inferiority of Women".

14   Mary Augusta Ward, wife of Thomas Humphrey Ward, was an English novelist.

Both love and home life are strengthened because a free woman gives her love through conscious self-denial, filled with a dignity that a slave does not have. Her husband finds her not to be a frivolous, idle, inferior, irresponsible person, but rather an equal in whom he can confide all of his ideas, feelings and aspirations. No one benefits more from the triumph of feminism than men themselves, since they cannot aspire to greatness while continuing to sacrifice the dignity of their companions to their own selfishness. All of society has to be suffering the effects of this situation for women. José de Maistre[15] has said that "the most effective way to perfect society is by ennobling women." In his article "The New Woman," Jules Bois[16] adds that "the real wonders will be reserved for future centuries [when] the splendor of a woman's soul will be completely understood."

Fortunately, the strength of the facts swept away all the unfounded ideas, and feminism manifested itself in ways that responded to specific needs. These clearly defined movements can be recognized as:

- ○ Workers' Feminism.
- ○ Bourgeois Feminism.
- ○ Worldly Feminism, and
- ○ Professional Feminism.

Philosophical ideas and political parties were quick to support these movements, and they established the feminist doctrines of:

- ○ Christian Feminism.
- ○ Revolutionary Feminism, and
- ○ Independent Feminism.

The feminist movement originated among the lower-class women who suffered the effects of economic hardship more profoundly. Workers' feminism developed first, and gained more followers in the city than in the country. Their husband's debauchery and absolutism forced women, wives and mothers to rebel. It could not have had a more honorable, just origin. Today, thanks to the triumph of feminism, many homes shelter children whom only the women support, while their husbands spend their wages at the tavern. Nevertheless, among us, the law still makes a man the head of the household, and tradition sanctions this.

---

15 Giuseppe de Maistre (1753-1821), a Sardinian politician, writer and philosopher whose primary concern was social unity.

16 Henri Antoine Jules-Bois (1869-1943), a French playwright, poet and scholar whose topics included experimental psychology, occultism, and metaphysics.

The middle class took longer to raise the feminist flag, which it now waves with great enthusiasm. Implicit in feminism is the obligation to work, and the middle class—intelligent, educated, and instilled with great respect for traditions—was nevertheless undermined by vanity and lack of foresight. The lower-class origin of feminism distanced the middle class from it. In the desire to erase the border that separates members of this class from the aristocracy, poverty was hidden as if it were a crime and all types of deprivations were imposed to keep up appearances and to honor last names. People lived a life more idle than pure. A lack of foresight accompanied this vanity. A family that could live well on the father's salary raised its daughters in an atmosphere of luxury, pampering and ostentation. Such a natural occurrence as the death of the head of household always caught them unawares. And so, poverty with all its horrors came upon them. If any funds remained, thanks to the women's ignorance they were soon used up. Misery and degradation were tolerated, but no one resorted to working. At times, some supported themselves with handouts from wealthy families, preferring that to seeing any of their relatives' work. It was less disgraceful to have a nephew jailed for fraud than to have a niece who was a worker or an actress. On that basis, women shut themselves up within the walls of their homes as if they were the palaces of the nobility. They were horrified by any custom that was not merely ornamental. Their ideal consisted of being considered loving mothers, submissive wives, early risers, housewives, and skillful in the completion of their tasks. Such charming virtues these were, but for the fact that they were engendered by ignorance, which bears such sad fruit!

In the end, life's pressures and struggles, which became more and more difficult, broke the ranks of the poor bourgeoisie and bourgeois feminism was born. But it was characterized by women's desire to free themselves from manual labor and by all of them taking refuge in professional and artistic careers. Bourgeois women were the ones who fought valiantly to defend their right to practice law and medicine, hold down jobs, educate themselves as men did, and to enjoy the legal right to have the same type of positions as men.

The aristocracy developed worldly feminism. Women of this class took advantage of feminist doctrines, not to participate in arduous struggles and accept their share of work and responsibility, but rather to free themselves from the seclusion into which they were forced. Under the protection of feminism, they displayed their wealth, and won the right to go out unaccompanied, to travel, to introduce themselves to society and take part in sports, all of which were considered to be the exclusive rights of men. They freed themselves from false modesty and began wearing makeup, dressing and styling their hair as they pleased. *They liberated their bodies.* And although it may seem childish, this trend, familiar to women everywhere, has had a very positive influence on feminism. This worldly feminism should not be confused with pseudo-aristocratic feminism that is no more than fundraising for charity and the creation of social clubs, which has nothing to do with feminist work.

Professional feminism is notably propagandistic. Its supporters are not only women motivated by strong feelings of pity toward the suffering of their sisters, but also men of noble heart and superior intelligence who recognize the justice implicit in women's vindication. Both women and men selflessly carry out their ministry of spreading feminist doctrines in universities, through the press and in print, at the same time as they fight to obtain equality under the law.

Unfortunately, there are profound schisms in the feminist world. Some groups fight with others, more or less obviously, in the belief they have opposing interests, when in fact, there is only one women's cause. In practice, these diverging tendencies usually seem mixed up and confused because in all of them there is a desire for liberation and independence. Political elements that get mixed up in feminism are the cause of this division.

Revolutionary feminism is a logical response to the oppression women suffer. As Lucien Descaves[17] says: "Woman is the victim of the masculine law that demands obedience and of a society that keeps her in servitude." She is the perpetual victim of exploitation. There are those who take advantage of this situation by making women instruments to serve their own interests in exchange for the liberation they offer them. The Russian conspirator Pierre Lawroff[18] stated: "If we revolutionize wives and mothers we will have revolutionized the world." Directing his comments to women he remarked: "You will only be made free through revolution." In this way, a revolutionary feminist party is forming, the majority of whose members adhere to socialism. The majority of the party's membership is made up of working women and women from small towns. It seems that the fate of feminism must be tied up with socialism, because just as in America the liberation of women and black men made common

---

17   Lucien Descaves (1861-1949) was a French journalist, novelist and playwright.
18   Piotr Lavrovitch Lavrov (1823-1900), Russian writer, mathematician and philosopher, was forced into exile in France from 1870 on for his affiliation with the Revolutionary Socialist Party.

cause, in Europe feminism is united with the cause of the "white black men:" the workers.

Bebel[19] defended the economic rights of women at the Zurich Conference in 1897, faithful to the statements he had made in 1883: "Women will have social and economic independence; they will not be subjected to excessive authority and exploitation, but rather placed before men on an equal footing of freedom and absolute equality. They will be masters of their own destiny." But independent feminists do not believe in pretty theories. They remember the ingratitude with which women were treated during the French Revolution, in spite of their enthusiastic support of it. They want evolution, peaceful reforms, the triumph of conviction, and they form a homogeneous block with the same spirit in each of the feminist groupings.

The phrase "Christian feminism" appears to be contradictory, since in Christianity women always are subservient to men. Nevertheless, both Protestant and Catholic feminism, in rivalry with each other, seek women's influence. Not long ago the Catholic Archbishop of Paris presided over a feminist conference, and the head of the Anglican Church, the Archbishop of Canterbury collaborated with another.[20] Catholic feminists wish for women to remain subordinate to men, since that is their place in the home, according to St. Peter. But at the same time, they attempt to improve their future and free themselves from the abuses of excessive authority. They seek to combine liberation with obedience, much as the earth revolves around the sun with no detriment to Joseph's miracle.[21]

There are also those who take pains to recognize a racial feminism, making distinctions between Latin feminism, Saxon feminism, etc. This is a new mistake. Differences will result from the laws and customs in each country that its citizens must submit to, but their principles are the same. The different characteristics of the temperaments of women of different races, which at bottom are presented with more theatricality than truth, cannot influence

---

19 Ferdinand August Bebel (1840-1913) published *Woman and Socialism* in 1879, which was considered an important theoretical work that also helped spark interest in Marxist ideas in Germany. Here he argued that the social emancipation of women is an integral part of transforming social relations and overthrowing capitalism.

20 Cardinal Richard, archbishop of Paris, presided over the International Women's Conference, held in Paris in 1900.

21 This is a reference to the so-called "Miracle of the Longest Day," a story from the Old Testament. Joseph asked God to halt the sun's progress over Gibeon so that the Israelites could defeat the Amorite kings who had besieged the city.

the general principles of human rights. The sad thing is that such digressions undermine action—the feminist task is still not completed. At present, women are suffering in many nations, as they do in ours, from:

- ○ Educational inferiority.
- ○ Economic inferiority.
- ○ Civic inferiority.
- ○ Political inferiority.
- ○ Conjugal inferiority.
- ○ Maternal inferiority.

Women are not men's equals even according to penal law, in which the woman gets the worst end of the deal, as in the case of adultery. But if women do not have equal rights they are equal in their obligation to pay taxes to the State. The author[22] of *The Marriage of Figaro* summarized this dearth of logic in a few words: "They [women] are treated like adolescents with respect to their freedoms and punished like adults for their shortcomings." The goal of modern feminism is to find a way to eradicate the injustice of inequality.

In *The Social Power of Women*, Georges Deherme[23] fiercely combats Jules Bois, although he does not equal him in intelligence. Speaking of the sinking of the Titanic, he says: "If feminism had been in practice [on the ship], no one would have been saved." In this way, he shows that he does not understand the matter he addresses and cannot conceive that women do not want a privileged status, just equal status. Who cares whether more women or men were saved? People of both genders would have been saved, surely the elderly, the invalid, children—the same number of human beings, which is all that matters.

Georg Simmel[24] confirms the lack of neutrality involved in discussions of the feminist problem when he states: "Women cannot be judged impartially. For that reason, the attitude of mocking criticism of them is so common and banal. From the male point of view, it is not possible to recognize the independence of the feminist premise. Women remain subjugated to two different measures at the same time, both of masculine origin: one is the absolute measure formed by the

---

22 Pierre-Augustin Caron de Beaumarchais (1732-1799) was the French playwright who wrote the original play, which was later transcribed for the opera by Mozart.

23 Georges Deherme (1867-1937) was a French anarchist who collaborated in the foundation of "L'université populaire". He published *Le pouvoir social des femmes* [Social Power of Women] in 1914.

24 Georg Simmel (1858-1918) was a major German sociologist, philosopher, and critic.

criteria of men and applied to women's activities, to their convictions and to the theoretical and practical components of life. The other is a relative measure, which also derives from men's prerogatives. Men demand not only that women seem desirable in general, but also that they seem desirable to them as men. They demand femininity in the traditional sense of the word, which implies a special nature oriented toward males in order to please and serve them."

This should raise an alarm for women who talk about what they term a "sensible feminism" and speak of "femininity," contrasting that with "feminism." Generally, they are women of little breeding who want to elicit cheap applause from an ignorant, unadventurous crowd. Feminism is not at odds with femininity and a woman will be more feminine the more she is a woman in the broadest sense of the term. To be "feminine," in the way that those gullible women desire, only means being subjugated to sexual duties, aspiring to be no more than nursemaids and governesses. Being a "feminist" means being a conscious, respected woman with a personality, responsibilities and rights; this is not opposed to love, home and motherhood. Feminism, with its diverse branches growing from a single trunk, *is nothing more than the vindication of women's rights*. There cannot be anyone who would support the absurd notion that because a legal subject has those rights recognized, she will vary in her nature and intrinsic qualities.

But the majority of the numerous books that I have consulted for this work, some of which I merely read, others which I studied thoroughly, are written by men. While some books whose authors, because they are highly educated, write tomes free of jealousies, selfishness and vulgarity, others have authors who are more or less underhandedly the enemies of liberated women. Unfortunately, even many books written by women suffer from the fact that their authors do not realize what feminism is. But there is a force in life that rises above all unfounded notions. Our time has arrived.

In the end, everything leads us to believe that Victor Hugo's prophecy at the grave of the great feminist Luisa Jullien is going to come to pass, though a century late. Since it didn't happen in the 19th Century, the 20th Century will be the time when women's rights are declared, although in reality, up to now not even men's rights have been established in a fair and comprehensive way. There are many obstacles, but the social current that forms feminism is advancing. There can be no doubt that this current must triumph because of its inner strength. Since the Great War, it has offered us more deeds than words.

We should note that women have managed to create this great liberation movement—initially unaided by anyone—under male dominance in every domain of activity, weighed down by the cruel load of work and worry. Women are gaining power and freedom; they want to have their rightful place, at the side of their men, with complete dignity, supported by the strength of reason and the law—which must purge from society all vestiges of servitude. It is undeniable that women will achieve this. The march of civilization through time collaborates with feminism: "The chains have grown brittle and fall like fruit from the tree."

Chapter 2
The Uses of Biology to Subjugate Women

Morphological differences determined by sex. –Bisexuality. –Weight and size of the brain. –Various opinions. –Different functions. –Ineffectiveness of experiments to prove the inferiority of a gender.

A brief look at the study of the female gender, however fleeting it may be, shows us that the subordination of women is not the work of nature. For that reason, the triumph of feminism can be considered the reestablishment of justice and the jurisdiction of natural law, which have long been violated by injustice. There is nothing in nature that justifies the servitude of women. One can clearly see that in the germination of existence, both sexes have a clear, extraordinarily important, admirably determined, well defined role that is suitable for the functions that they must carry out.

Women are more than just females, much as men are more than just males, from the moment in which intelligence permits them not to be reduced to mere reproducers of the species. A large number of naturalists who have studied the physiology of both sexes have concluded that women are imperfect, incomplete beings, *men with arrested development.* Many have established that because of their physical makeup, women are closer to being children than men. But this cannot be considered inferiority, unless one wishes to value such arbitrary opinions as those of Moebius,[25] who finds that children are *deficient* in comparison to adults.

It is absurd to suppose that a human being whose evolution has stopped is incapable of progress. Undoubtedly, neither men nor women have achieved perfection, but both fully enjoy the maximum development that they have reached. The female of the human species was formed from the beginning with different physical characteristics than the male, and since then customs have accentuated the differences, since many of them are acquired and transmitted through heredity. Women are not just failed men, and men are not merely degenerate women. Physiologically, there are males and females. Psychologically, there are men and women. Socially, there are fathers

---

25   See chapter 1, note 13.

and mothers. They are like certain instruments that play the same notes but with different tones, whose variety is necessary to an orchestra's harmony.

We could say that organisms in which feminine elements predominate are more active than masculine ones. This can be observed even in the plant world. Observe the male palm tree as its long, pointy branches sway in the wind, crossing back and forth as if in a fencing competition. It will seem like some lazybones to you in comparison to the female tree, which will seem like it is about to break under the weight of bunches of golden dates that it nourishes with its own sap. Observe the fig tree and you will get the same impression. See the male water lily lying in the sun on the surface of the water and the female water lily hidden at the bottom of the pond, painfully gestating its flowers.

And if we move on from plants to the animal kingdom, the effort to conserve the species is always greater among females. The hen burns with the desire to give life to her chicks, an admirable instinct, while the rooster loafs around carefree, like a parody of that braggart Don Juan. Mammals set the example for us that the female is the true head of the family. The female gathers the children, who do not know their fathers, around her. Female cats, dogs, and lions all nurse their young and defend them, while the male is hardly concerned with them. Nevertheless, we do not want to deduce from these observations that the male is inferior, as men have maliciously done. How can one half of the whole be superior or inferior to its other half? Without the pollen that the wind blows off a tree that to us seems barren, without the drones that suffer the injustice of superior numbers in the hive that the swarm owes to them, and without the roosters and male lions that do not deign to seek sustenance for their offspring, the species would not exist. Complementary sexes, both have different shapes, they are entrusted with carrying out different roles in the same mission and are inevitably necessary in fulfilling that role. Neither one nor the other can boast of being superior. The inferiority of one of them equally diminishes both. It would seem that this has been elucidated so well that it would not be necessary to insist upon the point, but still, as Paulina Yhys has stated, "man is the only animal who thinks his companion is inferior."

Aristophanes and Plato wrote the fable of males who were engendered by the Sun and females by the Earth. Hermaphrodites of the Moon resulted from their union, whom Jupiter split in half with a thread, like an egg. They assured that from then on, anxiety ruled among human beings—whole beings seek out whole beings, while half-beings seek their other halves. But the latter carry within themselves a piece of the other. Today this has become a scientific theory. Wise men speak of human beings' early bisexuality, which is not overcome until puberty but which becomes dominant again in old age. Such an authority as Dr. Marañón[26] admits the coexistence of genders, which does not limit their influence to the reproductive organs. He says, "There is hardly a portion of the body that is not assigned the same sex that the entire body has." Among many others, Marañón quotes the opinions of the Viennese doctor Weininger,[27] who affirms, "If at times women are worthy of esteem, it is only because of their masculine traits and, on the other hand, men are kept from succeeding by the female traits that are hidden inside them." Weininger deduced from this that the progress of humanity would come about by eliminating these feminine kernels, which would lead to a generation of sexually pure males without a trace of woman and who would be free from the preoccupation with gender. But since Weininger does not provide proof of the superiority of the masculine principle, one could argue with the same arbitrariness that "women cannot succeed because of the male traits that are in them, and if at times men are worthy of esteem, it is due to the female traits that they possess." And even arguing deceptively one could cite examples of men whose feminine traits undeniably predominate, but who have excelled thanks to their superiority, from Socrates to Oscar Wilde.

With his great sense of justice, Marañón does not speak of the superiority of one sex over another, but rather of the necessity of differentiation, which is more accentuated in animals the higher up they are on the zoological scale. But generally, all men try to proclaim the supremacy of the masculine principle, and consider the gifts they cannot deny women to be masculine traits that stand out. Marañón himself states, "There is a category of women, much larger than is usually acknowledged, who aspire to act (like men) because they are capable of doing so with equal physiological strength. They are women whose femininity is diminished, mixed with obvious masculine traits. This initial bisexuality is often confined to the realm of feelings, and sometimes it can be noted in their anatomy." He adds, "In the eyes of physiologists, great women are the ones who are distanced from their femininity."

---

26 Gregorio Marañón y Posadill (1887-1960) was a Spanish endocrinologist and essayist whose scientific work had national and international renown. Human sexuality was one of his primary research subjects.

27 Otto Weininger (1880-1903), an Austrian philosopher who wrote *Geschlect und Charakter/Sex and Character* in 1903, before committing suicide that same year.

For Moebius, talented women are degenerate beings, although he admits that "double-flowered plants"[28] are also the result of degeneration, and in spite of this are all the more valued." He assures us that the predominance of female traits is so tragic that "human beings would remain stationary if only women existed." One must confess that this state of affairs would not last long if there were only one sex. Inexorably linked together, even within the same organism that they are diffused throughout, both necessary for reproduction, it cannot be argued that one is superior to the other, although there may exist individually determined physiological differences.

The females of almost all species are smaller than the males. Where this rule does not hold as fast is in the human species, since it is frequent to find men of such small stature that they are able to avoid military service. The Venus of Medici, a model of feminine beauty, is a bit more than eight heads tall and the Apollo of Belvedere, a model of masculine beauty, perhaps for its feminine traits, is eight heads tall. Neither is it possible to argue that one man is superior to another based on height. Napoleon and Goethe were very short; Mariano José de Larra was small and Ribera owed his nickname, Spagnoletto (Little Spaniard), to his shortness.

It is not unusual for women to have less pulmonary capacity, smaller heads, hearts, feet and hands, since they are smaller in stature. From the point of view of superiority, it means nothing that women have physical differences. They have longer waists and shorter lower extremities. Their cheekbones are smaller, as are their mastoid and styloid processes.[29] They have less pronounced hairlines and thinner eyebrows. The outer half of women's eye sockets are thinner and sharper, their mouths are smaller and their noses rarely aquiline. Their eyelashes are more abundant, the whites of their eyes clearer, their skin smoother and their figures rounder. However, there is no general rule that determines all of this. A large number of these differences may be attributed to a sedentary lifestyle, and at times these characteristics predominate in men.

If women were to argue arbitrarily, as men have done, they could recognize signs of superiority in their differences, such as having shorter arms, smaller, better formed and wider jawbones. In many instances women lack *wisdom teeth* and their facial features are more open, which means that their craniums are higher. Women

---

28 These are plants with an abundance of petals that lack the means to reproduce themselves by seed, such as the camellia and most types of rose.

29 Two points at the base of the temporal bone of the skull where muscle tissue is connected.

have smaller larynxes, and their *Adam's apples* are barely visible. Their smaller, narrower glottis makes their voices higher pitched, higher when they sing, more emotional when they shout and more persuasive and penetrating when they speak.

It has been stated that the hair could be sufficient to characterize both sexes, but it is a proven fact that women's hair is much longer just because of how they style it. A man's hair can be just as long and voluminous as a woman's. In general, women's follicle systems are not as extensive, but there are light bearded men in the world and women with beards and mustaches. Carib men are beardless.

Nature has given women more well-developed hips, and a pelvis that is more than fourteen millimeters wider so that they can fulfill their maternal mission. After dedicating fifteen years to patient study of anatomy and psychology, a wise French doctor, one L. Manouvrier, [30] states "that women are the equals of men when it comes to their reproductive roles. Women's eggs are every bit as worthy in dignity and importance as men's semen. Both must come together to create an embryo. The embryo develops at the expense of its mother, and also at her expense, lives inside her like a parasite until birth, and for ten to twenty months afterwards. So, it is that all in all, women's reproductive role is more highly developed." Manouvrier avows that women's digestive systems are more highly developed, destined as they are to nourish the baby. Women must breathe, eat and digest for the both of them. The doctor also concedes that the muscle mass needed for strength and movement are less developed in women, but he adds, "It would be just as absurd for a man to be proud of his biceps as it would for a woman to be conceited because of her womb." He concludes the following:

ROLES	SUPERIORITY
Reproduction..............	Women.
Nutrition....................	Women.
Movement..................	Men.
Intelligence.................	Both.

But detractors of the female sex put more emphasis on this last point. Since the days of Geist, Ribra and Peach, anthropologists have never stopped weighing, measuring and observing the feminine brain,

---

30 Léonce Pierre Manouvrier (1850-1927) was an important French anthropologist who studied the ratio of the weight of the brain to parts of the human body, and to the comparison of male and female brains.

with the desire of proving their intellectual inferiority. Manouvrier finds that it is difficult to connect the shape of the skull to intelligence. He says, "Variations are insignificant from the physiological perspective. In the case of people with brachycephally,[31] what the cranium gains in width it loses in length. For anthropologists, the ideal cranium is dolichocephalic,[32] and nevertheless, this type of cranium is found among savages and primitive peoples. Cranial shape is modified according to physical makeup and the effects of nutrition, with men as well as with animals." Women's craniums are shorter and longer, they have smaller heads and occipital bones,[33] wider facial features and foreheads that bulge at the top and are narrow at the bottom.

Hoffman assures us that men's brains weigh two ounces more and Lauret, who measured the brains of two thousand people, maintains that the diameter of the encephalic circumference[34] is less for women. The craniums of women of the superior races are a bit more evolved than those of savage women, with respect to size. This proves nothing. Broca[35] considers the pretense of saying that one's level of intelligence is dependent upon the dimensions and shape of the head to be ridiculous. He maintains that intellectual stimulation increases the weight and volume of the brain as well as the development of intelligence. Pancharpe, Lacassagne, Chiquet, Ferri, Vitalis, Galton, Van Finot, and many others share this opinion. Women have been deprived of the pursuit of intellectual endeavors for a long time, and have even been denied the chance to learn to read and write. It is no surprise that men have lager craniums. The great anatomist Sappey has compared the weights of the brains of thirty-two individuals, sixteen men and sixteen women, and found that the men's brains with cerebella weigh 1,550 grams, while the women's brains with cerebella weighed 1,250 grams. The men's brains alone averaged 1,187 grams while the women's averaged 1,093 grams. The men's cerebella weighed 143 grams, while the women's weighed 137 grams. So, the difference that favors the men was as follows: brains and cerebella, 300 grams, brain alone, 94 grams, and cerebella alone, six grams.

---

31 A condition frequently associated with Down Syndrome.
32 Oval shaped.
33 A saucer shaped bone situated at the back and lower part of the cranium.
34 The circumference of the brain.
35 Pierre Paul Broca (1824-1880) was an important French neurologist, surgeon and anthropologist.

The difference is minimal, but even so, we are not talking about an absolute difference. Height is NOT taken into account. If the comparison is made in proportion to height, as fairness would require, the women's brains are larger than the men's. Finot[36] has established the proportion between the brains of cats and of lions. According to his deductions, cats should be three times smarter than the other felines that are larger than they are. The proportion of the brain to the body of the smaller animal is more advantageous to it. So, it can be observed that the smaller animals are relatively more intelligent than the larger ones. Long ago Aristotle concluded that humans are more intelligent than the other animals because their heads have relatively small dimensions. The brains of small men are proportionately larger, and the same goes for women. Broca discovered an intelligent woman whose head had the same dimensions as the head of an idiot. For him intelligence is never in direct proportion to the volume of the head.

Using similar measurements, Pancharpe discovered men of normal intelligence whose heads were smaller in dimension than the heads of idiots. Based on this research he concludes that intelligence is never proportional to the volume of the head. Bischoff has also refuted the relationship between intelligence and the size and weight of the brain that others have tried to establish. One must take into consideration the thickness and height of the cranial cavity. One brain can be bigger than another that it is compared to, even though it has a smaller circumference.

A voluminous brain is not needed for one to have mental ability, but rather, it must be well formed, since an ingenious idea can be conceived in a billionth of a micron, in other words, in a trillionth of a millimeter. Bischoff himself had a small brain. Gambetta, Voltaire, Lamennais and Liebig had brains that weighed less than normal. The brain of the great Anatole France weighed little more than a kilo, 1,017 grams. But on the other hand, all of their brains were deeply ridged and furrowed by convolutions. Rudinger asserts that mental ability depends on the number of these convolutions. He says that the male insular cortex is larger than the female insular cortex, but the latter is more convex, and has deeper convolutions. Adult women have smaller lower frontal lobes, especially the sections that are directly connected to the central lobe. The numbers of convolutions located around the lateral fissure are simpler and less sinuous in newborn

---

36   Jean Finot (1859-1922), was a French author who criticized the racial science that emerged in the late 19th and early 20th Centuries.

females than in newborn males. And from all these studies, which prove nothing but that men and women are different morphologically, some have wanted to deduce that women are inferior. They rest on these studies to keep women in servitude.

Some physiologists, like Bonnet, Wolf and Lamarck, point out differences that are related to what we could call animal life, which is noticed less in women than in men. They say that women's temperaments are more lymphatic than sanguine, and rarely irritable, and that their nervous systems are more impressionable, in order to leap arbitrarily to this conclusion: "The precise nature of women— their weakness, dependence on their makeup, emotional temperament, impressionability, emotional character, vocation, social mission, and natural destiny—are resistant to all changes and create an irrational incompatibility between the duties of a mother and the functions of a citizen. Women's existence can be entirely summed up in their maternal nature."

Although human life may be influenced by sex, although a *sexual accent* may exist, as Marañón says, it is absurd to forge out of this a new link in the feminine chain. It is monstrous to give sex the importance that Freud gives it to such a degree that it infiltrates and subordinates all else. In realms of thought, in the ability to act freely, within the egalitarian sphere of justice and the law, an individual's gender should not be an issue.

CHAPTER 3
THE RIGHT TO A SINGLE MORAL STANDARD

*Psychological differences. –Consequences that derive from these differences. –
The right to one moral standard. –Prejudices sanctioned by law. –Infanticide.
–Paternity testing. –Limiting births. –State sponsored immorality. –Ways
of abolishing such immorality.*

The theory of the existence of *two different moral codes* is born of a false
analysis of female nature. Antifeminists have deduced that women
are inferior or too sentimental because their nervous systems reach
a heightened state of sensitivity. They maintain, as Diderot did, that
women do not understand absolute principles, that they are not
interested in ideal abstractions, and that they only become moved
and share the treasure that is the generosity of their souls when one
speaks to them of pity, love, and forgiveness. They appeal to women's
saintly goodness and to the maternal instinct that fills their hearts.
Antifeminists also maintain that women's greater sensitivity makes
them get exited or exasperated more easily, and that they are prone
to explosive passions.

The spuriousness of this line of argument is even more
notorious because it is disproved by all that women actually do.
Just look at history to see who have allowed themselves to get more
worked up with violent emotions. Men, who are more prone to attack,
have more overbearing emotions which, due to their intensity, are
generally short-lived. Men more frequently suffer emotional dramas
of jealousy, revenge, and selfishness. Statistics show that men have
a higher rate of suicide and more impassioned emotions, which are
not always amorous but rather, prideful. Men are greedy, money-
hungry glory seekers. Spanish prison statistics from 1926 show that
there are 13,294 male inmates and only 871 female inmates. Talk
about explosive feminine emotions!

Generally speaking, typical well-balanced women are not
passionate in the sense that this term implies. Their upbringing has
accustomed them *to knowing how to wait,* by their nature they need
only a hint to be able to respond to that upbringing. Malicious people
claim that because of the predominance of women's nervous systems,
they are rash and impulsive, instead of recognizing that women's
temperaments make them more suited to the arts. Claiming that

women are selfish and false is a popular saying, a set phrase. But these are defects that men and women tend to share equally. If these vices could ever be forgiven it would be in the case of slaves, in whom they might be instilled by fear and the instinct of self-preservation.

According to Moebius,[37] "Women's shrewdness is not a sign of mental acuity. They are compelled to hide their sensual needs, and they do so instinctively, because deception, or rather, lying, is women's natural, indispensable weapon. It can be no other way. Women's lies can be judged more leniently than men's lies." It can be noted that even in the middle of his diatribe, Moebius' recognition of the truth comes out. In his evaluation of the morality and social value of women he attacks them ruthlessly. He slanders them, humankind's basest weapon. Moebius says that both physically and morally, women are "highly dangerous" creatures. He claims that "women are conservative and accept all sorts of absurdities as good things," that "morality born of reason is inaccessible to them." "Anything that does not pertain to the family does not interest them." "They have no sense of justice." "Their discontented or wounded vanity awakens storms in them that do not allow for any reflection." Moebius believes that progress is made only thanks to men. He even denies women their role as the inspiration and stimulus that contribute to artistic creativity. He claims, "Women are a heavy burden to men that prohibits them from using their full energies." His viciousness toward *his rival gender* is so great that he himself distorts his own attacks with exaggerations when he exclaims, "As a consequence of the critical period, when women grow old, we can do no more than observe a weakening of their mental faculties." Or when he says. "Men grow old; in addition to growing old, women become disgusting and ridiculous."

Schopenhauer, who does not forgive Christianity for having modified "the fortunate state of inferiority that women had in antiquity, with the gallantry and stupid veneration of Germanic-Christian foolishness," states that "European ladies are monsters, the products of human bestiality, a money-spending machine. Nature has denied them strength but has given them meanness and deceit to make up for their weakness." In saying this he is doing nothing more than parodying Anacreon,[38] who wrote, "God has given women beauty in exchange for the judgment he endowed men with." But

---

37 See chapter 1, note 8.
38 A Greek poet (570-488 B.C.E.) whose verses spoke of love, and who feared nothing but the coming of old age.

Schopenhauer also denies their beauty, which his abnormal nature could not comprehend. He exclaims, "Instead of being called beautiful, the sex of the wide hips, long hair and limited ideas could more properly be called anti-esthetic." Being incapable of knowing love, he is surprised by feminine mystique and charm, and by the fact that there are people of generous spirit who love women and hold on to their pictures and locks of hair as if they were treasures. As with all misogynists, his hate stems from the feelings of the indeterminate gender toward those he envies for their complete triumph in life. His is the fury of a *frustrated woman* who suffers from the torment of jealousy.

Lebon[39] writes, "Women only have feelings, and they lack ideas. They exhibit the inferior characteristics of human evolution, and in terms of mental capacity, they hardly surpass black people. They do not reason, nor do they let themselves be convinced by rational arguments. But it is easy to put thoughts into their heads, which makes them politically dangerous." Proudhon[40] claimed that women *invented* love in order to tyrannize men with their emotions and miserable feelings. He considers them to be a species half way between a man and an animal. He asserts that women have false spirits, are anti-metaphysical, are incapable of generalizing and synthesizing, lack a sense of justice, and are shameless children of privilege. They even believe women's virtues to be defects. Marital fidelity in women is considered to be a sign of their animalistic nature, since it distinguishes the human female from the other mammals. Maternal love is considered to be animalistic as well. Women are compared with female Rhesus monkeys that die of grief when they lose an offspring.

Although in legends, extreme pain has always been embodied in the figure of a woman, Lombroso[41] denies that painful sensations and feelings reach as high a level of intensity for women as they do for men—he believes that women are less sensitive. The meekness and compassion that women have managed to cultivate, since they are more removed from social struggles, are perceived by some as being signs of inferiority. They say that if women are less criminal,

---

39 Gustave Le Bon (1841-1931) was a French social psychologist known for his study of the psychological characteristics of crowds.

40 Pierre-Joseph Proudhon (1809-1865) was a well-known French social theorist, anarchist and politician.

41 Cesare Lombroso (1835-1909) was an Italian physician and criminologist who stated that criminals were born that way and could be identified by certain physical defects.

it is because they are not as strong. And so, they also consider women's pacifist tendencies to be a weakness. In light of this unfair characterization, one must remember the famous phrase that if killing is a virtue, the tiger is superior to man.

Ughetti, a professor at the University of Catania, studies the manifestation of humor evident in both genders. He claims that not only are women incapable of humor, but they cannot even understand it. He assures us that comedy and humor do not give women the least bit of pleasure. Unfortunately, by making this assertion he is confusing two different concepts. Even if at times comedy is not lacking in artistry, it does not please those with more refined sensibilities, who are disgusted by the grotesque and the slapstick. Conceiving comedy is easy for people of a vulgar nature, and it generally disgusts superior people who long for more delicate esthetic displays. But comedy cannot be confused with humor, just as humor should not be confused with satire or irony.

Humor is similar to a sadness that gives rise to clarity in superior people. But this sadness is not accompanied by the morbid bitterness that leads to pessimism, but rather, it is accompanied by greater understanding that accepts the type of misfortune that the longed-for perfection does not deny. Humor encourages a great goodness in order to show beauty mixed with defects in a soft chiaroscuro that has neither bitterness nor preachy or moralizing airs. Humor does not laugh at things, it smiles benevolently. Women are capable of humor because they are able to give it the most delicate shades of meaning. They also include all the tenderness that is necessary to diminish its flaws. The fact that there have been few female humorists in literature is because women have been denied what is required—maximum development and intelligence, as well as refinement. Nevertheless, when women experience in their lives the clash between ideal aspirations and the materiality of things, they know how to smile with resigned kindness. That smile is humor.

Humorists can be found among the ranks of superior female writers, although they have not dedicated themselves exclusively to that literary genre. In this regard, they have surpassed men, who insist on creating humorous literature without having a true vocation for it, which proves to be ridiculous when it is not sincere and spirited. Women retain a sense of the ridiculous because in public life they still have not confronted all the failures that weaken it. They still need some time to learn to smile at what used to make them cry. Women love humor as they love a perfume or a soft, fragrant balm for the spirit, but satire and the grotesque disgust them. With respect to the exceptional mental faculties that humor requires as an artistic manifestation, there are few men and women who have them. But they are not exclusive to either of the two genders.

Feminine condescension is taken as a lack of will, a notion found in the satires of Aristophanes, Xenophon, Aristotle, Simonides as well as Cato and Juvenal. Mistreating women was in style. Seneca, who was married twice, said that "women are immodest animals" and Hippocrates[42] defined them this way: "women are an illness". Spencer,[43] who does not denigrate women, asserts that they suffer from intellectual myopia because of their excessive kindness, and they reject all that has nothing to do with their own worlds. He believes that in the face of an imminent problem, women do not prevent the consequences and damages that they could have avoided had they acted differently. But the great naturalist forgets that you cannot predict outcomes based on actions that have not happened. If women had thrust forward a different way than humanity has, we do not know how history would have played out, since every action has a value that connects it to its origin, at times in remote or hidden ways.

This double standard makes women out to be of less worth. Weininger[44] says that women are neither evil nor moral, but rather, simply amoral, indifferent to moral concerns. On the other hand, Goethe has said that due to their nature, women aspire to have good habits, "which many times are hampered by men." He adds, "Women's morality is akin to the casing of feminine substance." Georg Simmel[45] does not believe that women are amoral, and even maintains that characteristically they are much more faithful than men. He states, "With regard to the soul, clearly it cannot be claimed that women are all *beautiful souls*, but nevertheless, their psychic makeup includes a certain inclination toward that harmonious, non-conflictive state. Women have a constitution that spontaneously resolves the contradictions of masculine life, and a way of being that includes the world of ideas in its reality."

Since Simmel is not able to deny, as Moebius does, women's role as an inspiration to men, and thus a primary promoter of civilization, he resorts to subterfuge and says, "The type of person who gives to another that which that person does not have is executed

---

42 These men were all famous Greek or Roman poets, playwrights, philosophers or statesmen.

43 Herbert Spencer (1820-1903) was a British biologist and philosopher.

44 See chapter 2, note 28.

45 See chapter 1, note 24.

perfectly in the relation that women have with men. The lives and spirituality of countless men would certainly be different and much poorer if they had not been influenced by women. But I must warn that what benefit men gain from women is not a previously existing condition within them. On the other hand, what men contribute to women's spiritual lives really tends to be substantial. Although it may seem paradoxical, women give something immediate, an essence that dwells permanently in them, an essence that, when it comes in contact with males, sprouts within them something that does not have the least phenomenological resemblance to women. In men, this becomes 'culture'. This is the only sense in which it is possible to affirm that women 'stimulate' males' cultured creations—but not in the immediate sense, that would include the content itself. Because in all honesty, it makes no sense to say that Rachel is the driving force behind Jacob's work, nor that Don Quixote's heroic deeds were prompted by Dulcinea, nor that Ulrike von Levetzow inspired the Marienbad Elegy."[46]

In his essay on the psychology of the two genders, Simmel only manages to present a less-than-satisfactory solution—the absurd idea of people being able to pass on to others that which they do not possess. He claims, "In typically feminine women, we feel that there is a vital preeminence in their very course of life, over the particular content of their lives, such as science, economics, etc. A submersion of themselves, so to speak, in the profundities of life as such. This is the reason why for women, normative, abstract ideas (ideally, distinct from life itself), truth, moral standards and artistic beauty never reach the same level of independence and fullness as they do for men." According to him, women bring together *ideas* and *reality*, that is, for women life and reality are unified concepts, and the value of women's internal world is established upon this unity. For men, the only possibility is to distinguish between or separate these concepts. Simmel assures us that if women are offended more easily than men, under the same circumstances, it is because their entire organism feels an attack that was only directed at a single point. Simmel says: "Women have more unitary, closed natures than men. For women, in a manner of speaking, the whole is not separated from the individual

---

46 Jacob and Rachel were biblical characters who fell in love, and Dulcinea was the fictitious "true love" of Cervantes' famous character Don Quijote de la Mancha. Ulrike von Levetzow was a 17-year-old with whom the then 72-year-old Goethe (the German writer and politician) fell in love and proposed to. With the elegy, Goethe lamented the loss of her love (she declined to wed him).

parts so that the parts can lead an independent life."

Simmel believes that women have "something conclusive, enclosed within itself, something that slips without falling, a balance of peace and harmony that specific feminine grace is made up of. This can be explained by their lives that persevere in spaces where there is nothing to conquer, so to speak, spaces that have become a bodily extension of their very personalities." "Immersed in universal reality, women's instincts speak to objects as if from a fundamental entity: no intermediary is necessary." "The more deeply immersed women are in their own being, the more they abandon themselves to their own essential nature, then the more they approach reality, cosmic unity, and the more perfectly they reveal and express that universe." Without the author intending to do so, all of this is a declaration in favor of women.

The illustrious philosopher José Ortega y Gasset, a man of such great intellect, expresses the same sentiments when he says, "Women's entire psychic lives are more closely connected to their bodies than men's psychic lives; that is, women's souls are more corporal." "In comparison, men's souls are kept separate from the corporal; their bodies and their souls know little of one another." "Women can withstand greater pain and physical suffering than men and, on the other hand, women are more restrained when it comes to giving in to excessive pleasures, the reason for the surprising graceful movements and courteousness of feminine bearing—women are in complete control of their gestures, and their bodies have a je ne sais quoi in terms of tidiness and complexity." He concludes that men fluctuate between carnal and mystic love, sentimentalism and platonic love; women attain a perfect unity of all their feelings. As can easily be observed, this is the recognition of qualities that I would consider to be neither superior nor inferior to men's qualities.

At the core of the books that treat women poorly, a crudely comedic tone is almost never lacking; there are plenty of buffoons among the ranks of the enemies of the female sex.

William Vogt slanders women in *The Weaker Sex*, a book filled with vulgarities in which he insults all brilliant women by way of degrading biographies. A literary movement has even started up that has attempted to eliminate women from its entire works. But on the other hand, since the turn of the century, the number of meritorious writers who are feminists and who give women credit for their morality has been on the rise.

In reference to women's loyalty, Paul Margueritte says, "When men accuse women of being insincere, cagey and disloyal, they could respond that the men who laid down the law of the survival of the strongest made them that way." In his character Nicolasa, from *Morganatic*,[47] Max Nordau creates a female type who is balanced, gentle and strong. He states, "So women are cunning… underhanded… capable of heroism when prompted by emotion, but in their habitual relationships they have only a vague notion of sincerity, and they do not consider sacrificing honesty to convenience to be a fault…? The portrait may not be flattering but it is fair. But whose portrait have you painted? A portrait of women? How misogynous! You have painted a portrait of our species. All of this can be said about men much more correctly than about women."

Marcel Prevost is of the opinion that "the fact that historically, women have been condemned to being the weaker sex has made them develop shrewd instincts, something that will disappear when women have the same social rights and status as men, because at that moment, shrewdness will not be 'necessary.'" Alfred Rouillée assures us that "the progress made by the great moralists Buddha, Confucius and Socrates only consisted of insinuating that some of women's fundamental virtues—tenderness, mercy, self-denial—are in men's hearts." Daniel Lesueur adds that even if one concedes that women's status has developed some defects, their morals being stricter than men's, this has made women more scrupulous in many ways. Thus, women are moralists and instill moral principles in their daughters to a greater degree than men do. Peggy Wood declares, "As a general rule, I do not believe in the superiority of one gender over the other." But of all the diverse conflicting opinions that exist, the ones that are averse to women tend to prevail. This has given rise to the existence of *two different moral standards*, one for each gender, as if *Morality*, *Justice* and *Truth* could be multiplied or divided.

Nevertheless, women are bound by moral principles that enslave them and abusive sanctions that men can escape. The absurd notion of believing that there are two weights and measures for the same object is fulfilled. Professor Bridel has stated, "It is patently unfair to speak of a lack of dishonor for women if the same is not said of men. What dishonors one dishonors the other. Where there is no dishonor for males there can be none for females." But the *morality of a society* is not an inherent thing within which women behave naturally and with a clean conscience. Rather, it is a system of conventional rules that women believe will assure their stability. For

---

47 A morganatic marriage is between a noble man or woman and someone of lower social status. Neither the lower-class spouse nor the offspring may inherit.

that reason, the prejudice of two different moral standards is allowed, the disappearance of which is necessary for social development and for the fundamental morality of all of humanity. The fact that in sexual relations different moral standards are applied to the two genders is an absurdity that day by day makes men more incorrigible and women more hopeless.

One of the great ills of the different moral standards that are applied to sexual relations is the concept of disgrace that stigmatizes unwed mothers and young women who have been seduced, although they may have been driven by love. On the other hand, most of the time, men are not disgraced if they seduce without love but rather, as a whim or a vice. These tales of scorn for the single mother do not fit in with the hymns to maternity, the protection with which mothers are surrounded, nor do they fit in with the praise that is lavished upon mothers. Many cases of abortion and infanticide committed by women derive from the fear that young women experience when they must publicly confess what is considered a disgrace.

Society censures women, at the same time giving males complete freedom to ignore all the duties that have been established with respect to sexuality. It is as if an exclusively female sin existed. Men, who are considered to be stronger, to be more aggressive and to take greater initiative, can sing their own praises while still being considered decent people. And so, men demand purity of their wives as a fundamental basis of the new home, which seems to be founded on the purity of women. No one thinks about how monstrous it is to turn over a pure, decent young woman to one of those tired, worn-out, sick old men who are mired in all sorts of vices. Some even believe that this is a guarantee of happiness for the poor woman, the flowers of whose ideals she sees being stomped on and withered. The justification given for men's vices is reflected in the vulgar phrase that even women unwittingly utter: "Any bachelor who isn't a skirt chaser will be one when he's married."

In "A Lady," Jacinto Benavente has portrayed this type of woman, the one with no concept of the nature of her servitude who is left abandoned in a house that does not deserve to be called a home—berated by her husband, all her dreams dashed—and yet she still enjoys the status of *lady of the house*, which encompasses the notion that she is a *legitimate* spouse, and feels proud of the idea that her husband cheats on her with other women who are envious of her situation. Benavente's character is an irresponsible type of woman who has lost her dignity and forgotten her responsibilities to her gender. She has been led astray by the applause of the bourgeoisie, who believe that this type of resignation is the height of virtue, because it protects the selfishness of the majority. Benavente understood the spirit of the public well. It is necessary to write highly successful plays and novels by making fun of the public and following its tastes. A few years ago, when Björnson broached the subject that Justice, like Morality, should be the same for all of humanity, and advocated for men's chastity and for the necessity that both spouses be virgins when they marry, thus creating a happy, honorable home, the scandal in Norway was tremendous. When *The Glove* (a play in which the great writer develops this theme) was enacted, women received it passionately. Many young women wanted their fiancés to swear an oath of purity, and thousands of weddings that were about to happen were broken off.

The influence of the theory has been moralizing. Just as the majority of men in Latin countries are embarrassed if they are not considered to be seducers and womanizers, afraid to be virtuous as if abstinence were ridiculous—thus giving a sad testimony of their moral value—Scandinavians pride themselves for maintaining their purity. A sense of modesty, innate in human beings and not exclusive to one gender, will develop when a corrupt upbringing does not destroy it. Men and women feel the shame of intimacy equally if love does not mask the harsh realities of sexual relationships. Public customs have been cleaned up with the absence of vices and how much young people of pure habits gain in health has been proven.

One of the causes of infanticide, almost the only one for a long time, has been the sense of disgrace that results when children are born out of wedlock. The Penal Code, in title VIII on crimes against people, defines parricide this way: "Whoever kills his father, mother or child, be they legitimate or illegitimate, or any other progenitor, ancestor or spouse, shall be sentenced as a parricide to life in prison." But then there is a mitigating factor that should not exist, because it should not be considered disgraceful to have children if the right to maternity derives from the right that an individual has over his/her physical and moral self.

In *Love and Marriage* Ellen Key[48] says, "A single mother who has given her body out of love is more respectable than the wife who finds her husband to be repulsive. Love is not just for the propagation of the species, it should give pure joy, although puritanical people may think otherwise." For this reason, the mitigating factors that the

---

48 Ellen Key (1849-1926) was a Swedish feminist and writer whose ideas on love, sexuality, marriage, education and morality had broad influence.

Penal Code establishes for parricide should not exist. For example, "The mother who kills her baby under three days of age in order to hide her disgrace shall be sent to a correctional facility for a sentence of medium or maximum degree. For maternal grandparents who commit this same crime in order to hide the mother's disgrace, a prison sentence of maximum degree. Beyond these cases, whoever kills a newborn, according to the circumstances, shall receive the same sentence as a parricide or murderer."[49]

It is clear that in countries where tests to establish paternity are conducted infanticide is reduced. Our Civil Code establishes (except in cases in which paternity is proven by way of an unquestionable document) that "No suit shall be allowed at trial that directly or indirectly has the objective of testing the paternity of illegitimate children who do not at the same time have legal status as natural children."[50] On the other hand, maternity is tested. Provided that the birth has been proven, the mother is obligated to feed the child.[51] The opponents of paternity testing is base their argument on the idea that "we must put an end to the perversity of women." The idea of women's amorality, which in no way is worse than the amorality of men, should neither deny children rights that belong to them nor of the support that their father would give them. Because of their innocence, children's rights are always much worthier of respect than the rights of their parents.

Countries where paternity testing is allowed affirm that the interests of the State demand it. Statistics reflect a much lower number of infanticides and abortions and therefore a higher birthrate. In France the Convention, whose Civil Code is a little-known marvel, established paternity testing, but quite soon after it was abolished. Tranchet says, "Young women who wanted to give their children a father would chase after the richest of the men who had spent time with them, and men of high standing were exposed to this type of defamatory persecution. In particular, priests were the object of true persecution." But the prohibition of testing favored licentiousness, and so after a century of struggle, French law reauthorized it in 1912 for cases in which there had been rape, seduction, physical abuse or abuse of authority, a promise of marriage or written proof. Testing is also authorized if it is well known that the mother and the presumed

---

49 Author's note: Section 2, chapter IV, title V.

50 The Spanish legal code of 1904 defines "natural" children as those conceived by unmarried parents who had the ability to marry each other.

51 Author's note: Article 143 of the same title.

father have had a public relationship during the time of conception. The ostensible act of protecting a child allows for a paternity test. It is obvious that paternity testing, for fear of the law and abuses, puts a halt to masculine immorality.[52]

Abortion can be considered infanticide, although the law distinguishes between the crimes of taking the life of a human being who is older or younger than three days of age, as if life did not have the same value from the moment of inception. The law punishes women who induce abortions, or who allow another to do so, with the same sentence as for those who commit the infanticide of a baby younger than three days of age. But it allows the mitigating factor that only a single mother with a good reputation may invoke. Article 427 says, "Any woman who induces abortion or gives consent for another person to do so shall receive a prison sentence of medium and maximum degree. If she does it to hide her dishonor, she will receive a prison sentence of minimum and medium degree." It follows that married women, and women who will not tarnish their reputation, will not be able to avail themselves of these mitigating circumstances either for abortion or infanticide.

The Code also establishes penalties for anyone who induces an abortion on purpose or out of recklessness, for those who induce it without the consent of the mother and even for those who induce it with her consent. Any doctor who abuses his craft by inducing an abortion or taking part in one is also punished, as is any pharmacist who sells abortion-inducing drugs without a doctor's prescription. But in many countries women have wanted to avoid giving birth for economic or health reasons.

During the war, the physical abuses that the invaded countries suffered prompted the rise of the theory of the right to abortion, in cases where conception occurred against the will of the mother, since, as George Sand says: "The womb does not reason." But no Code has given legal recognition to this principle.

In Russia, the Commissariat of Hygiene strictly controls the number of births, in accordance with the economic conditions of the country. Workers and peasants are subjected to a constant advertising campaign so that they will restrict the size of their families to reasonable limits. The advertisements encourage them to prefer three or four healthy children rather than many offspring. Abortion is permitted in state hospitals, provided that women give a satisfactory

---

52 Author's note: In 1921, the Crusade of Spanish Women, presided over by the author, presented to the Courts a petition to establish paternity testing.

reason, but it is severely punished when practiced in secret.

The right not to have children has always been recognized for women who wish to remain chaste, and all have been granted the freedom to avoid conception. But it has not managed to gain acceptance as a general theory because it is such an affront to the rights of the State, as are Malthusian theories.[53]

In some nations women have wanted to get the scientific training needed to limit birthrates from the State, alleging that having many children goes against the purpose of the family, since children cannot be raised and fed properly in poor homes. Nothing can give us a better idea of the nature of this difficult issue like the words of the English writer Dora Russell when she talks about the Conference held in Margate by the English labor party. "English working women have requested that the Ministry of Health not prohibit State maternity clinics from giving scientific instructions to regulate the number of births." According to them, the prohibition is an issue of class privilege, because they believe that "rich women can get such instructions from specialists, while poor women do not have that benefit within their reach."

In one of her interesting works, Dora Russell[54] makes the reference that in the prior Labor Party conference, held in Liverpool, women were cautioned that they would not be allowed to even discuss the matter as an issue that would form part of the program. She says, "This year the women repeated the attack and found strong opposition on the part of the Executive Committee of the party. The argument that this opposition was founded upon was that certain members had powerful reasons of a religious nature against everything that tends to prevent conception. And they even find themselves disposed to oppose for the State to give the requested instructions, even to people who might not have the same reasons. So, it was demonstrated to the women who made the request (some of whom have fifteen children and who suffer from the consequent nightmares and anxieties) that the only remedy that they and their offspring have is to continue suffering and enduring the situation, so that the delicate sensibilities of other charmingly tolerant people could remain pure and calm." One must confess that for those women who already had fifteen children, seeking solutions to limit the birthrate comes a bit late.

Dora Russell states that English women are not trying to

---

53   The Rev. Thomas Malthus (1766-1834) was an English proponent of population control.
54   Russell (1894-1986) was a British feminist, author and socialist campaigner.

compel anyone to use procedures that prevent conception, but they do not want to be forced not to use them by ignorance or intolerance. They believe they have the right to have the State give them the necessary instructions, with complete scientific rigor, and they declare that the Labor Party has to support their demand, just as it supported miners in their fight for a seven-hour workday. Dora Russell who, together with Dorothy Jewson, spoke in support of this feminine demand, asserts that "for mothers, the regulation of births is like the seven-hour workday for miners, a matter that affects their health and happiness."

The Trade Unions voted with the women, since they judged that the discussion of such an important issue should not be impeded. Also, the International Congress of Women for Peace and Freedom recommended that all of its national sections examine this problem from the point of view of each one of them having access to this right themselves. They asked that obstacles not be put in the way of giving out the most complete scientific instructions regarding methods for limiting births. An excessive birthrate favors neither the State nor the family. In one of his admirable books, Doctor Marañón[55] speaks of women who are mothers of numerous children who, still young, arrive at his clinic sick and exhausted due to their excessive fertility. He says that he has determined that the majority of the children of such fertile families die in infancy.

One must not confuse the tendency to limit the birthrate with Malthusian theories. The former is about knowing how to channel human instinct from infancy, and training feelings so that indulgence and vice are not placed above love and modesty. In this way, the waywardness of youth and abuse within sexual relationships would largely be avoided. There is no doctrine in existence that has enough power to totally triumph over instinct.

It has been seen that the influence of Christianity did not manage to eliminate vice. During the Crusades, when faith prompted thousands to conquer the Holy Places, thousands of miserable women followed the army, supported by the male vice. It is well known how the number of these women is always in direct proportion to the troops bivouacked there.

In spite of the fact that marriage has been raised to the level of a sacrament, monogamy has very rarely been a reality among men, who are less faithful to their marriage vows than women, thanks

---

55 See chapter 2, note 27.

in large part to how easy things are made for them. It is a fact that prostitution increased along with the institution of matrimony and the suppression of concubinage and of secret affairs. Those who have involved themselves in these matters, such as Martínez Marina,[56] observe that as legal concubinage in Spain was coming to an end, the prostitution that the Partidas[57] meant to repress was on the rise. In the "Novísima Recopilación"[58] there are laws, among them one from the time of Phillip II, that prohibit prostitutes from wearing scapulars, having pages or servants younger than forty years old, and taking a pillow, cushion or rug into a church. Phillip IV strictly prohibited brothels in every city, village and place in Spain. From the same monarch came a law established in 1661 that required that women who walk the streets and plazas be removed and taken to the Women's Prison. Although it seemed ethical, this established the bad precedent of separating a number of women from social interaction, creating a class apart, without taking care that they not lose all notion of dignity and leaving them un-absolved.

And each time that we go further down the moral path that would lead us to the establishment of a profession or trade that is permitted and regulated—which would be equivalent to promoting it—people make false displays of morality, as we can see in the laughable laws included in the third book of the "Novísima Recopilación." One could say that these laws are meant to protect the greater immorality, just as import taxes protect domestic production. While houses of ill repute were tolerated, like some sort of barracks for vice, holding dances at night in the streets or in the country was prohibited. People of the opposite sex were banned from being present at the same time at the homes of dance teachers as well as from putting on plays in private homes and other things of that nature. The laws of *hygiene*, as they are paradoxically called, date from 1815 and 1818, and their regulation, as it has lasted with minor modifications until now, dates from July 4, 1877.[59]

---

56 Franciscom Martínez Marina (1754-1833) was a Spanish lawyer, legal historian and priest.

57 The Partidas were a set of legal codes first set forth by King Alphonse the Wise in the 13th Century. Their purpose was to establish a unified body of normative rules for the kingdom.

58 The "Novísima Recopilación de las leyes de España," edited in 1806, systematized Spain's entire legal code.

59 Prostitution was legal and regulated before the Second Republic in Spain (1931-1936). Each city had its own regulations, but most required a prostitute to carry a card certifying

I do not wish to dwell on the analysis of the ups and downs that have brought about this shameful state of affairs, not only for women but also for all of humanity. It is repugnant to go into detail about the organization in which unfortunate women *are enrolled*, the disgraceful *tax* that the State charges, the degradation and filth of the Madams, Go-Betweens, Pimps and Scoundrels, all who are parasites that prey on misfortune and torturers of wretched women who must endure all kinds of humiliation and torment. All of this is repulsive to the one who writes about it and for those who read about it. Nevertheless, we cannot silently pass over immorality. In order for the wounds to heal they must be touched, although without probing deeply into them.

Fortunately, since the International Conference of London took place in 1899, many institutions have been founded to redeem these unfortunate women and combat the absurd notion that vice can be regulated. In Spain, the Council for the Suppression of Human Trafficking was created by Royal Decree in 1902. Later the Spanish Abolitionist Society appeared, now joined with the International Federation. But these institutions are not progressing as far as one would hope. They have limited somewhat this national and international immoral traffic, above all in connection to the corruption of minors. They work to create a public atmosphere with conferences and publications, but the regulations still exist and women are all humiliated by them. With the complicity of the State there is a class of women who are truly slaves, while men safely and irresponsibly enjoy vice. Only the woman is made to bear the brunt of the consequences of an act committed by two people. Exceptions cannot be made for women without violating the female quest for justice. Responsibility, the foundation of all morality, should be the same for women and men. The State cannot fail to recognize this principle without abusing its authority and inciting anarchy.

Among the noble women who are fighting for the dignification of their sex, Josephine Butler and Mme. Avril de Sainte-Croix cannot be left out. In one of the latest Congresses, the latter requested, to general applause, that the regulation of prostitution by the State[60]

---

she did not have a disease. She was to undergo a vaginal exam on a regular basis, and could not be seen in the street at certain times of day. The Royal Orders of March 1 and 16, 1908, established a Prostitution Hygiene Service in the entire country that was charged with making sure prostitutes did not carry venereal diseases and were registered with the state.

60   Author's note: This petition is included in the request presented to Congress by the

be abolished. Her arguments are irrefutable. She bravely studied all aspects of the problem and one by one dismantled the false arguments that regulation provides a measure of public order and is a safeguard for the very same society that it ridicules. With admirable inspiration she says, "We are combatting this regulation not only because it has been demonstrated that it is absolutely useless with respect to anything that has to do with improving public health and making honorable women safer, but also because it is a declaration based on the false, highly demoralizing principle of the *necessary evil*." Actually, it has been demonstrated how absurd it is to try to prove that husbands, wives and children are all happily living together, thanks to the daily sacrifice of thousands of women who are looked down upon. The role that is attributed to these unfortunate women, that they are the *guardians of virtue,* is paradoxical, as is the idea implied about them that they are degraded and ignoble. It is a sad virtue that needs to be propped up in this way!

The unfortunate women who are caught up in this horror are generally the poorest, the ones who were abandoned and had no one to raise and protect them. And the State, which in this case should have been their guardian and refuge, agrees to take them away from common law. It leaves them subjected to special regulations that permit them to be treated like veritable slaves, without taking into account the fact that systematic corruption destroys morals. This is like the stain left when oil is spilled on a folded cloth. It does not stay on the surface, it penetrates the other layers.

In a recent report, the Physicians Society of Berlin has done away with the argument of those given to vice who wish to keep the regulation—along with its retinue of despicable consequences— without stopping to consider, when offending women, the sacred nature of every human being, and that each woman is an image of one's own mother. The German physicians have declared that:

1. Prostitution is neither recommended nor necessary for either hygiene or morality.
2. It is a matter of individual morality that does not concern the State.
3. Instead of promoting the vice and corruption that underage females are victims of, both sexes should be educated, and women given the means to live independently.

Spanish Women's Crusade in 1921.

Mrs. Stanfeld says, "The inscription of *profession* is an attack on freedom and common law, just as the obligatory visit is an affront to women, a monstrous inequality." Doctor Forel of Zurich adds, "The State does not have the right to place unfortunate women at the disposal of the police, subject them to an immoral regulation—which leaves them unabsolved—nor jail them in the name of Hygiene."

This is all the more deplorable when one observes that, aside from the sad exceptions, women accept this way of life neither willingly nor with pleasure. There is nothing sadder and more immoral than seeing one of these unfortunate women appear in court, when the judge asks for her *name and occupation*. There are women who hesitate, who doubt themselves, or who blush when they utter the horrible word that names their *profession*. This shows that modesty has not been extinguished in their hearts, they still have memories of pure days, they still harbor noble feelings which are stomped upon daily, and they still aspire to having love, a home, children and independence.

The great poet Alfred de Musset synthesized what causes the ruin of so many unfortunate women when he exclaimed:

"Poverty! Poverty!
You are the courtesan!"

There are those who go so far as to try not to understand how a State could survive without this scourge. All we need do is take a look around.

In England and Switzerland prostitution is banned, and those who buy and sell women, lead them to prostitution or do any trade by dishonoring them in these ways are punished. In the United States women are too well-respected for that system of regulation to ever be put into place. Three states tried to legalize prostitution, but had to give up in the midst of broad disapproval. Today women have so much social influence there that it is impossible for this sordidness to exist.

The three known systems related to this scourge are: repression, whereby moral transgressions are punished; regulation, which supports the absurd notion of a *necessary evil;* and abstention, in which case prostitution is considered to be a private matter with the belief that the State should not intervene. This last case has the drawback of requiring the State to regard an immorality that is a danger to the community with arms folded, in the name of individual freedom.

There are nations that use mixed systems, such as Austria and some Swiss cantons. There, whatever happens in private is not investigated, but public displays are punished. The Code in Neuchâtel punishes public gestures, words and displays and holds the men who solicit or pay for immoral acts accountable. The methods established in Switzerland to eliminate prostitution are:

1. Not allowing brothels.
2. Improving the economic conditions for women so they can avoid the hardships that lead to a life of prostitution.
3. Regulating the protection of minors and strictly penalizing anyone who seduces them or leads them into lives of crime.
4. Giving instruction in public schools in order to eliminate ignorance regarding sexual matters, since ignorance is not innocence. Truly valuing all the natural phenomena related to puberty and reproduction so that they will neither draw children's attention to them nor seem to them to be wrapped in a veil of provocative mystery.
5. Demanding that men be punished as strictly as women, considering that prostitution is a crime that women cannot commit by themselves.
6. Promoting paternity tests.
7. Respecting moral law, which should be in everyone's conscience.

Marañón[61] says, "The huge mistake about morality that we have grown up with is to warn men about women and women about men, when in the battle of the sexes, the enemy is within us. We believe that a progressive differentiation of the sexes is necessary, *not only in men*, but also in women." An artist as well as a thinker, Marañón exclaims: "All men, or at least the vast majority of them, carry within themselves the specter of a woman, and not an imaginary specter—that would make it too easy to drive it out—but rather, circulating in the blood. And all women have a more or less concrete specter of a man within them. These outlines of women and men, not the ones on the outside, are what lead to pain and sin."

The notion that the other sex is inside us is what disturbs purity. The salvation of ethics lies in differentiation. Marañón adds,

---

61   As an endocrinologist, Marañón had a propensity to explain matters in terms of hormones.

"Be men and be women to the utmost, that is what the sexual progress—this is in part like saying 'moral progress'—of humanity must fundamentally rest upon." It is worth meditating upon his formula for achieving a superior morality, a single and true morality: "Kill the specter of the other sex that everyone carries inside of them. Be men, be women, and then the women and the men who walk the earth will only appear to you to be fountains of virtue."

CHAPTER 4
THE RIGHT TO EDUCATION

The right to learn. —Women in the Arts and Sciences. —Teachers, doctors, lawyers. —Business women. —Access to all professions. —The situation of women in Spain. —The Laws of the Partidas.[62] —The Constitution. — Women's struggle for cultural inclusion. —Friends and detractors. — Feminine education.

Women have had to put up a veritable battle to claim their cultural rights. Departing from an arbitrary psychological analysis in order to show their inferiority, everything surrounding women has been distorted. Even legends wove their nets around women to imprison them further. All of these legends are pernicious: Eve, Maya the Indian, Isis, Tanit, Milita, Minerva, Diane (the fierce virgin who punishes unfortunate Calisto mercilessly for having loved), Brunhilde (who loses her standing as a Valkyrie when she marries), Psyche, Proserpina and Pandora.

Some legends praise the chastity to which virgins from all religions are sacrificed, and develop customs in which the virginity of women is the foundation of the whole society. Others portray women as being the source of all evils and the ruination of the human race. Humanity creates images of women that parallel religious ideals. When humanity worships the God of Mount Sinai with his crown of lightning bolts and omnipotent arm, the God of armies, its legends construct strong women: Judith, Deborah, Jezebel, or Herodias. When the God is merciful, legends of pious women arise: Veronica who, being a pagan, wipes the sweat from Jesus' brow, Mary Magdalene, who anoints him, and Martha, who serves him. Pain is embodied in the figures of women such as the Virgin Mary and the beautiful Niobe. Supreme love is embodied in women in the same way. Psyche, who lost her husband because of her curiosity, works to recover him; Ishtar descends into hell in search the *Only Son;* Sita is a martyr of her faithfulness to Rama; Olympus, Parnassus, and heaven are filled with women lovers and sufferers, which gives the idea and creates the habit of regarding the female gender as being destined only to love and to suffer.

---

62   See chapter 3, note 57.

Greek literature embodies hate, crime, vengeance and furious passions in its women, including the horrible characters of the Furies and Cassandra. In his theory of Metempsychosis, Plato maintains that a guilty soul will transmigrate to the body of a beast and that during its rehabilitative lives, will pass through female stages before becoming incarnate as a man. Nevertheless, in his magnum opus *The Republic* he confesses that men and women are just as equally suited for ideal communism and that "there are women who are gifted in Music and Medicine, just as there are women capable of governing the State."

The artistic professions were the first that women were able to break into. A few years ago, statistics showed that women were only in the majority among the ranks of nuns and theater performers. Initially, even the latter field was denied to women. The only actors were men, who would dress in women's costume when necessary. Until just a short time ago the profession of actress was considered dishonorable, as was being an actor. Actors were prohibited from being buried in sacred ground, and even in the 19th Century male actors were denied the possibility of being addressed as Sir/*Don*.[63] They were still considered inferiors, in spite of the great, talented artists whom they counted among their numbers. At present, the real successes that women have attained in the dramatic arts, singing, music and dance have prompted these professions to be honored and respected. In his rather antifeminist book (although not as much as one would think—its title, *Intellectual Differences Between Men and Women*, was changed in subsequent editions, and comes down to us as *The Intellectual Inferiority of Women*), Moebius[64] confesses, "In my opinion, of all women, the only ones who are indispensable are actresses and singers. No sensible person can maintain that female painters, sculptors, doctors, etc., etc., are necessary. Only poetry remains, or better yet, only female novelists, since female poets are such rare creatures. I have heard it said repeatedly that the ideas and feelings of female writers are singularly inspired."

Simmel[65] adds, "It is interesting to point out that in the world of popular music there are many towns where women write songs with the same productivity and originality as men. This means that in an undeveloped culture, when there is no objectification of the

---

63   Author's note: See my book *Figaro, His Life and Works*, which extensively describes the Spain of Ferdinand VII.

64   See chapter 1, note 13.

65   See chapter 1, note 24.

spirit, there are no opportunities for there to be differences." This is the broadest confession that only the lack of learning to which the female gender is subjected is the cause of such apparent inferiority. It is not strange that in the fourth record of the Council of Macon,[66] not only having solemnly debated whether women had souls but also whether or not they were human beings, they also tried to deny their ability, genius, and even talent for art. But faced with the facts, Simmel confesses, "It is admirable that while there are very few brilliant women, it has frequently been observed that brilliance has something feminine about it."

Women have excelled at writing literature since ancient times. China offers the example of women having excelled at first more than men. Pan-Hoes-Pan, a poet and preceptor to the Empress, who was well versed in history, poetry, eloquence and astronomy, slyly proclaimed the right to teach herself and to have economic independence when, with melancholy and apparent resignation, she said, "We have to suffer because we have to live." There are also famous Indian poetesses like Radi Padmini, Queen of Chittor, who was surrounded by noteworthy women who excelled at astronomy and philosophy, as well as the rest of the sciences and the fine arts.

Greece produced Sappho, a much-discussed and admirable poet. History still cannot specify whether she was a courtesan or the strict mother of a family. As a beautiful, brilliant woman she was slandered during her lifetime, but her work reveals to us that she was erudite, passionate and artistic. Neither Myrtis, Corinna, nor Pindar managed to exceed her. Aspasia of Miletus ruled Athens, sharing the throne with Pericles. Socrates, who taught her rhetoric, at the same time as he was teaching Alcibiades to dance, said that she [Aspasia] was the author of some of the most eloquent speeches that Pericles delivered. She was also the first woman to hold regular political meetings, and sought equal rights for both genders. She could be called the patron saint of feminism, who scandalized Aristophanes to such a degree that she inspired his famous comedy *The Assemblywomen*, which was abused so much by antifeminists in a later age.

As for Roman women, they became men's equals in every way. Although they were considered to be inferior by the law, in practice they were dominant. When one hears that common phrase, uttered

---

66   A council of bishops celebrated in 585 C.E.

in a school house tone of voice, that "among Romans, women were treated like objects," it is hard not to smile at the ignorance implied by this assertion. It is only in the United States where women now have similar freedoms to those enjoyed by noble Roman women at the time of the Empire. The emperors had broken with tradition to place their wives and mothers in high positions. Octavia and Livia, the sister and wife of Augustus Caesar, respectively, achieved the highest tribunal offices. The Senate conferred upon Livia the title of *Augusta*, and the right to join the imperial ranks. Agrippina attended sessions of the Senate covered by a veil, and Julia Domna, the wife of Septimus Severus and the mother of Marcus Aurelius, had great beauty — perpetuated in goddess-like statues of her — to go with her philosophical erudition. She developed a personal politics, created a Ladies' Senate, and was greeted by soldiers with the title "Mother of the Battlefield."

Vitoria, the mother of Marcus Piavonius Victorinus, was conferred political power. The legionnaires adored her and coins were minted with her name on them. After the empresses, the wives of the proconsuls participated in all political affairs. Women founded an academy and a type of charity organization, they created libraries, instituted a coeducational system with the same teachers, programs and disciplines: Rhetoric, History, Philosophy, Law, Metaphysics, etc. Funerary paintings show that women performed in all roles. So, in the Roman golden age, these women gained a reputation as poetesses: Cornificia; Praxilla, Ovid's wife; Polla Argentaria, Lucan's wife; and the satirical Sulpicia. It is frightening how in such a flourishing age it became possible to enslave the female gender again by the authority of Saint Paul. Nevertheless, in the first centuries of Christianity women did not repudiate learning. The wisdom of some women did not prevent them from being canonized. There is news of Saints Melania, Caesaria and Relindis, who taught Greek and Latin in the monasteries of Arles and Maaseyk (Belgium). Saint Lioba wrote Latin verse. Saint Hersintha composed plays of the Terencian school. Saint Adelaide gave literature lessons. Hilda, who was so learned that kings and prelates went to her for counsel, was Saint John of Beverley's teacher. The monastery at which she was the abbess was converted into a seminary for priests and bishops. Many young women were employed as scribes in the cathedrals.

These examples should suffice for those who have said that "women should be ignorant in order to be virtuous" and that "women fulfill their duties better the dumber they are." Precisely all the examples of illustrious women show us that the most erudite and responsible among them were also the most virtuous. Beastliness and ignorance are no guarantees of virtue.

Knight-Errantry, which made a type of sacrament of the investiture of knighthood and exalted the ideals of love of and respect for women, came about later. A woman became a precious, delicate gift whose vassals were knights. Women gained the freedom to choose their husbands and the right to be defended and they were shown such consideration to the point that in the 13th Century, if a lady complained about a knight he could be excluded from tournaments. A true knight never shirked his responsibilities to a woman. Women presided over parties and courtships. They gave knights the honor of wearing their colors, and a glove, a handkerchief or any of their garments was a veritable treasure. During the siege of Cherbourg, the French and the English suspended combat to witness the duel to which an English knight had challenged all who would not confess that no one was as enamored of his lady as he was of his. The beauty of the beloved was a sacred thing that no one could blaspheme. We can recall Don Quixote who exclaims when he is defeated by the false knight of the White Moon, "Dulcinea of El Toboso is the most beautiful woman in the world, and I am the most unfortunate knight on earth, and it isn't just that my weakness should discredit this truth. Go on, knight, press on with your lance and take away my life, since you have robbed me of my honor."[67]

And nevertheless, nothing did more harm to women than knights-errantry. It made them sleepwalk through an atmosphere of adulation and homages. They became accustomed to hearing nothing more than songs of praise to them. They gave themselves up to pampering, without accepting any social responsibility, like creatures that were only suitable for love, precious dolls that fulfilled the words of Lord Byron: "All they require for happiness is a mirror and some toasted almonds." And so, we see that they did not go to school, did not coexist with men, had no access to careers—those who seemed to grant themselves everything, actually denied themselves everything. The same Code of Alphonse the Wise[68] decrees that a woman "cannot outfit a knight, even though she be a queen or an empress."

---

67   This translation of the Cervantes quote is by Walter Starkie, from *Don Quixote of La Mancha*, New American Library (1964).

68   Alphonse X of Spain (1221-1284), known as "*El sabio*/The Wise One, was an important king of Castile and Leon renowned for his erudition. The *Partidas* were written during his reign.

Part of the vindication of feminine culture comes from Italy. The woman Christine de Pisan, the daughter of Thomas de Pisan — who played such a great role in the Courts of Charles V and who was widowed at a young age — was able to live and support her children through her literary endeavors. In her work *The Treasure of the City of Ladies* she put forth the novel idea that instead of invoking the saints and theological virtues, as was the fashion then, she entrusted her emancipation to *Reason, Law* and *Justice*. In 15th Century Italy there was no great lady who did not speak at least two or three languages and who did not write poetry. They were the protectors of the poets, the driving force behind wise men. For a long time, they continued to excel at the liberal arts. Victoria Colonna, the widow of the Marquis of Pescara and Michelangelo's platonic love, was a great poet, and the beautiful Julia Gonzaga was an inspiration for Juan de Valdés. A veritable court of artistic, wise ladies of noble birth were followers of this Spanish philosopher and listened to his words in the shade of the laurel trees in the gardens of their marble palace. The theories of Luther and Erasmus had proselytes among the Italian ladies, although Luther mistreated women with his crude country manner. In Wittenberg, the Lutheran bishops and theologians presented fifty theses in order to deny that women were humans, and Erasmus wrote two pamphlets that harked back to Plato and questioned whether women should be classified as what he called "an inept, crazy animal, although attractive and graceful," or as rational beings.

France accepted women's influence, despite the fact that they were treated so poorly in Rabelais's satires. In 1499 Anne, Duchess of Brittany, trusted a Norman humanist to write the biographies of all the women who had distinguished themselves in any branch of science or art. Catalina of Medici was a feminist under whose influence theories favorable to women were promoted. Montaigne confesses that "men and women are formed in the same mold" and Pierre of Bourdeille, seigneur de Brantôme, requested that women be given full rights. Margarita of Navarra had influence over Guillaume Pastel, and in the book she wrote, she not only defended women's right to succeed to the throne, but also believed women to be superior to men "because woman was God's last creation and thus His most perfect." The popular *Queen Margot* said that women "possess that which is transcendental of the things that were created." Simmel uses similar language when he affirms, "In spite of disregard and mistreatment, from primitive times women have always been the objects of a peculiar sentiment: the sentiment that they are not just women, that is, beings that are the correlative of men, but even something more." He believes that this is why women are assumed to be Sybil priestesses and witches, as "beings who are capable of conferring the blessings and curses from the distant cosmic bosom." The reigns of Anne of Austria and Maria of Medici favored women. The Gnostics proclaimed female superiority and Ruscelli prostrated himself before women's beauty.

The 16th and 17th Centuries were the time of wise women. Ladies worked in the fields of science and literature. In Italy, female archeologists were predominant. In the French salons, algebra problems were solved and platforms for public speaking were opened. In Sweden, Queen Christine was a notable mathematician. In Portugal, Princess Maria, the daughter of Don Manuel I and granddaughter of Queen Isabella, had a court of wise men and poets in which the principal Portuguese authors flaunted their ingenuity, and where Camoens wrote and recited madrigals to the beautiful Lady Catalina of Atahide, who was the *Natercia* immortalized in his poetry. Among the ladies were the daughters of Gil Vicente and the Spaniard Luisa Sigea. The latter was so well versed in the Humanities that she could write correctly in Latin, compose verses, and was not unaware of philosophical ideas. In the courts of the Catholic King and Queen, Lady Beatriz Galindo, Lady Francisca of Lebrija and Lady Luisa Medrano flourished. Later, in Spain we had Lady María de Zayas, who was immortalized by Lope de Vega. In Mexico, we have Saint Teresa and Sor Juana Inés de la Cruz. Cornelius Agrippa inspired the *Fronde* and dedicated to Lady Marguerite of Austria, the governor of the Netherlands, an exaggerated homage to women. According to him, Eve took no part in the fall of Adam, because the prohibition had been established before she was born. He said, "If Christ became incarnate in the shape of a man it was because men are inferior, and he wanted to humble himself."

But then the female cause became a literary tournament in which friends and detractors abounded. One person wrote the "Alphabet of the Female Sex's Imperfection" and another wrote the "Alphabet of the Female Sex's Perfect Traits." There were some who declared women to be good, chaste, prudent and faithful. Others said that they are perfidious, greedy, lying and vain. The ancient controversies from the time of Don Juan I were repeated and "satires against women" and books that defended them were abundant.

When it proclaimed the rights of all men, the French Revolution seemed to be the dawn of women's liberation. Abandoning the theoretical ground, women met at clubs like men and created the "Fraternal Societies" that aided so much in the victory. But it cannot be denied that the Revolution was ungrateful to women. The political leaders who had applauded the *generous French women* were unsettled by their conduct, and so they ordered that women's clubs be closed and marginalized women in the law. The most progressive of them, such as Robespierre, Marat, Montagne, Herbert and Chaumette, were hostile to women. They began to state that women were "degraded beings that wanted to break the law in order to go to the public plaza and rabble rouse from the grandstand." They said, "Nature has given them breasts to feed our children." La Rochefoucauld and Saint Evremont showed women no mercy and called them vain and capricious. Only Condorcet, the wise, noble, martyred philosopher, asked in 1792 that women be given the right to citizenship. In his "catechism of the human race," Boisse proclaimed the liberation of the female gender so broadly that he surpassed present-day Russian leaders.

Rousseau wanted women to be just wives and mothers. Men should command and women should obey. *Julie, or The New Heloise* is an old-fashioned woman who just takes care of her home and family. His *Repose in the Village*[69] influenced the movement for a return to the countryside, to patriarchal life and the family. *Emile* is a portrait of maternal education. For Rousseau, any woman who is involved in Liberal Arts and politics, and who has a salon and frequents men's society, is "A poisonous flower born in the dung heap of civilization." Taking that same path, Restif de la Bretonne wanted the teaching of women to be limited, and Silvan Marechal tried to prohibit women from learning how to read. Diderot painted a vivid picture of female bondage, saying that "In every custom the cruelty of civil law has conspired against women, it treats them like imbeciles." In *The Spirit of the Laws* Montesquieu wrote of the paradox that "it goes against reason and nature for women to be owners of their homes, because their weakness does not grant them preeminence, although it does grant them sweetness and moderation." And later he said that "they work out well in government, be it moderate or despotic."

Voltaire also contradicted himself. On the one hand, in his *Philosophical Dictionary* he declared that "women are generally inferior to men because of their bodies and natures." On the other hand, he made an energetic defense of them when he condemned the Salic Laws,[70] the presiding laws concerning marriage, and all those that enslave women. Voltaire described them as "ridiculous,

---

69   It seems that the author has misnamed this work by Rousseau. The correct work is likely the opera *Le devin du village* ("The Village Soothsayer").

70   These laws, codified in the early Middle Ages, excluded females from the inheritance of

odious Laws." In his letters to Madam de Chatelet and in his work about the opera *Geniuses*, by Mme. Duval, he revealed himself to be in favor of cultural equality for women. Voltaire, who was taught by Nino de Lenclos as Socrates was taught by Aspasia, who was a friend of Queen Christina of Sweden and was in love with Mme. De Chatelet, he, precisely, had good reason to develop a positive opinion of women, since these three women were representatives of ingenuity and beauty, wisdom and strength, as well as tenderness and talent.

Descartes would accept nothing as truth except that which could be proven through reason, and he served the female cause by wanting to debunk prejudices. In "The Education of Ladies" and "The Equality of the Sexes," his disciple Poulain de la Barre asked that women be granted full rights. On the other hand, in his "Ridiculous, Precious Things," Moliere[71] satirized women's aspiration to have a scientific and literary education.

As a logical consequence of the insults directed against them, a lamentable tendency to create obstinate women came about, women who were the enemies of men and, thus, far removed from true feminism, which is a collaborative effort. There were such women in Italy, like Modesta Pozzo, the Patrician of Venice. In her book *The Worth of Women* she included a scene in which seven beautiful noblewomen are departing from the terrace of a palace on the banks of the Grand Canal, under the night sky. Some of them were of the opinion that women were not made to serve men, some affirmed that in marriage women lose their freedom and gain a master, and one exclaimed, "Wouldn't it be better for us to buy a pig rather than a husband with our dowries?"

In France, Jacobini,[72] an Italian theater actress, responds to men's diatribes. With great knowledge of the male gender, she says, "Men never desist from indulging their whims and passion. They are ridiculous and inconsequential." This school of thought is followed by Madeleine Peletier[73] and a number of others, among the many women who wrote and thus immortalized their names. Like Madam de Sevigné, Madam Galien, and Madam Gacon Dufaur y Cocy,[74] who maintained that women are capable of performing any function in

---

a throne or inheritable lands.

71 The stage name of Jean-Baptiste Poquelin (1622-1673), who was a masterful French playwright and actor.

72 Maria Jacobini (1892-1944) was a popular silent movie film star.

73 Peletier (1874-1939) was a French physician, psychiatrist, feminist and activist.

74 These would appear to be the names of French women born well before the 20th Century

society. In her book *Corinne,* Madam de Staël[75] showed women the path to success in the arts. The great George Sand, who was detrimental when it came to feminist work—her heroines in the novels *Indiana, Lélia* and *Valentine* were the daughters of Rousseau's *Julia*—confirms her worth as a brilliant author. In her lies the proof that women conceive heroines that have the same restlessness as their own natures, which does not coincide with the nature of the community at large. Simmel says that "the profound understanding of the souls that belong to another depends on the soul of the individual who apprehends them."

Success did not take long to make the effort worthwhile. Today women produce every genre of literature with great success. There is a profusion of poets, novelists, essayists and dramatic authors. A great number of women dedicate themselves to journalism as feature writers, editors and reporters. One must remember that the first daily newspaper that appeared in the world in London in 1702 was founded by a woman. And in Spain, at the beginning of our newspaper age, a woman whose name, "Carmen Silva," recently served as the pseudonym of the Queen of Romania, directed and edited *The Spanish Robespierre* in Cádiz with great merit, enthusiasm and talent. In France, Marguerite Duran[d][76] waged battle through a daily political newspaper called *The Sling*.

At present, here are many magazines that women run in every country in Europe and America. Thanks to the power of journalism, the chorus of insults and stupid jokes that were being directed at women has been quieted down a bit. Women have found that this has given them a platform for their voices to be heard as they defend their rights. But let us not forget that women cannot run newspapers in countries where their political rights are denied them.

Generally, women are relegated to a special type of literature. A revealing literature like the sort that the great artist Colette unfortunately initiated is what is desired. She was influenced by Willy, who did not allow her to completely exhibit her own nature in her books. Instead he wanted her to exaggerate feelings that are not characteristically feminine.[77] Some people want to find that which modesty makes unmentionable in feminine books. The cries of carnal

---

(e.g. Mme. De Sévigné was a 17th Century writer who lived at Versailles).

75   Anne Louise Germaine de Staël (1776 – 1817) was a Swiss aristocrat who lived in Paris. Her first novel, *Delphine*, dealt with the limits to women's freedom in an aristocratic society, and was so controversial that it prompted Napoleon Bonaparte to exile her.

76   Durand (1864-1936) was a French suffragette leader as well as an actress and a journalist.

77   Sidonie-Gabrielle Colette (1873-1954) was a French novelist and performer. The

desire that seem beautiful in the poetry of Juana de Ibarbourou[78] because they are so close to her heart, so deeply connected to her body and soul, that they come to acquire an almost mystical purity. But those cries do not a movement make.

Perfection is demanded of women. Except on rare occasions the critics, who are usually men, treat them with disdain or with a gallantry that is even more harmful. In almost all critiques, in every interview with a woman, the man exercises his masculine tendencies and praises her for her beauty, which diminishes the value of her opinions and her intellect. Or, if she is not young and beautiful, he ends up mortifying her through ridicule. The critics do not distinguish between the actress and the writer, who does not require this public exhibitionism, but rather maturity and talent.

Women's work is normally treated harshly, without keeping in mind men's greater ineptness and propensity for social climbing. This is not because of men's inferiority, but rather a result of the greater number of men who participate and the greater number of chances they are given. The desire is for all women to be compared only to men of their own intellectual ability. Inept, mediocre men are never compared to brilliant women. For each worthless woman writer, there are a thousand men of equal worthlessness. The Academies[79] obstinately shut their doors to women. The French Academy does not have members who are as illustrious as some of the women it rejects. The Countess of Noalilles has been inducted into the Belgian Academy, while that honor has been denied her in her own country [France]. Madam Aurel presented her own candidacy and then considered founding an Academy for Women.

Doña María Isidra de Guzmán y La Cerda was allowed entry into our Royal Spanish Academy, protected by the King and Queen. She combined talent and elegant speech with charming youthfulness and beauty. But after that the entryway for women has remained under lock and key. It is an oddity that the Academy modifies its rules in the face of male demands. But it did not modify them when it came to honoring Doña Gertrudis Gómez de Avellaneda, the great Spanish poetess, who was born in Cuba. Meanwhile, the eminent Doña Emilia

---

Claudine series of novels that she wrote using her first husband Henri Gauthier-Villars's nickname "Willy" as a pen name scandalized *belle époque* French society.

78 Juana Fernández Morales de Ibarbouorou (1892-1979) was a popular Uruguayan poet whose early work was highly erotic in nature.

79 In Europe, it is common for countries to have academies, institutions that promote art and literature, the sciences, etc.

Pardo Bazán[80] was too soon forgotten. Both of these women had the silly idea of petitioning to occupy a seat on a platform where many of those who were seated were less worthy than they. Posterity always reveals the stain of injustice in the Academies that deny women a place, although in the future other more fortunate women may be allowed in. We have already seen that there are countries where this prejudice does not exist, such as Portugal and Belgium.

But women succeed not only in literary pursuits but also in all the fine arts. There is a multitude of women who are theater and film actresses, dancers, singers and musicians. They also practice the plastic arts—painting, sculpture and architecture, in spite of the deficient, unequal training they are given, since for reasons of their gender, they are not allowed access to an education that is not limited. There are some very distinguished artists among us who are women: Luisa Roldán, *La Roldana*,[81] to whom are attributed the famous statues in Seville, which come up to the standard of those sculpted by Montañés and Alonso Cano.[82] When it is argued that not as many brilliant women have stood out in the art field as men have, Tarde responds, "The slaves did not invent anything and they had the same abilities as free men; but they did not have the freedom to use them." Helvetius[83] agreed with this opinion when he affirmed that lack of education was the cause of the supposed inferiority of women.

In the field of architecture, which is a blend of science and art, it has been said that women are failures, but at present there are some very talented women architects. Mrs. Guarino Fiecher,[84] from Uruguay, says that since women love the home out of habit and because of their own natures, they had to come up with a way to build homes that are pleasing. She asserts, "A man can amuse himself making a blueprint without including the corner of it that will bring happiness to the lady of the house." And women have not only excelled in the field of art; there are numerous examples of women of science who have been able to refute the assertions made by Schopenhauer, Boileau[85] and Proudhon, who all deny that women have scientific aptitude.

---

80 Pardo Bazán (1851-1921) was an eminent Galician author and scholar.
81 She was the first woman sculptor in Spain (1652-1706).
82 These were two important 17th Century Spanish sculptors.
83 Claude Adrien Helvetius (1715-1771) was a French Encyclopedist philosopher.
84 Julia Guarino Fiecher (1897-1985) was the first woman architect in Uruguay.
85 Nicolas Boileau-Despréaux (1636-1711) was a French poet and critic. For Proudhon, see chapter 3, note 46.

Catherine Descartes did honor to her uncle as a researcher; Maria Kirch was a great mathematician and Liebig himself introduced her to the court of Prussia. Lavoisier's wife edited and published the scientific memoirs of the great chemist. Linnaeus' daughter made important botanical discoveries. Sofia Kovalevskaya, Clémence Royer, Madam Curie, who discovered radium, and Madam Curie's daughter, who continued the glorious research of a family of geniuses, were all great mathematicians. Simmel says that in his opinion there are scientific roles that are specifically feminine. Moebius injects some truth into his misogyny when he says, "Whether we desire it or not, exceptionally gifted women will be born, and it would be a pointless cruelty to put obstacles in their way to keep them from developing their true talent as women."

Teaching was the first career to which women were given access. Two factors contributed to this: the tacit recognition of women's mission to guide and protect children, and the scant appreciation that has been given such an important mission—anyone was trusted to do it. We have examples of distinguished women who held university chairs, such as Hipatia of Alexandria, the "Glory of Women,"[86] who taught at the University of Bagdad without great difficulty.

Among the Greeks, Plato confessed that women had the ability to dedicate themselves to Medicine. A half century later, the Pythagorean Theano attempted to reclaim for her gender the study of Philosophy and Medicine, with the aid of Phintys. Before all Athenians, Agnodice succeeded in making the practice of Medicine available to women. Perhaps this was considered to be a merciful occupation and so did not prompt loud protest.

In France, before the fall of the Empire, women were already admitted to study the Baccalaureate degree in the School of Medicine, which had the honor of admitting the famed doctor Miss Mary Putnam,[87] who had been denied that right by the English university in 1868. But England did not take long in repairing its mistake and creating a special school of medicine for women in London. These schools have multiplied quickly, as have special

---

86 Hipatia (355 or 370-415 or 416 B.C.E.) was a Greek teacher and philosopher who distinguished herself in the fields of math and astronomy.

87 Mary Corinna Putnam Jacobi (1842-1906) was an American physician and suffragist who was the first woman admitted to the French School of Medicine. Before attending the French school, she already had a degree from New York College of Pharmacy and an M.D. from the Female Medical College of Pennsylvania (1864). We are unable to confirm that her application to study was rejected by any English schools.

schools in higher education. In the vicinity of Cambridge and Oxford, centers for female students were established. Women were authorized to attend classes at the University. The first of these has become the great Girton College, where women can earn a medical degree. Today there are women hospital administrators in London and a large number of women doctors, nurse practitioners and registered nurses. Nevertheless, there is the odd case at the University of Oxford where the number of women is restricted. This is the result of the campaign waged by the male students, who have declared that "women study more than men and they raise the average level of knowledge, which makes the exams more difficult." It is deplorable that that selfishness continues to place such immoral obstacles in the way of women's development and that a battle of the sexes has ensued, in which both sides lose. This celebrated English university is a sad example of the times—only one woman is admitted for every four men. So, they will be able to continue to employ the usual argument that the number of outstanding women is lower than the number of outstanding men.

In Belgium, Holland and Switzerland, women doctors enjoy high esteem, above all those who specialize in women's and children's medicine. In Portugal, a woman doctor is the head of a department at San Jose hospital, and in Scotland, mental hospitals are run by women. In Italy, Mrs. Catani has been professor of Pathology at the University of Pisa. The first woman to receive a doctorate in Medicine studied in Boston at a school that was founded for women in 1848. She was Miss Elizabeth Blackwell. Fifty years later, 4,555 women with university degrees were already practicing Medicine. In 1861 a woman was the administrator of a hospital for women in Boston, and in 1865 women were the administrators of similar hospitals in Philadelphia and Chicago.

Since 1890 it has been customary to have a woman doctor in each mental hospital for women. Recently the School of Medicine for women in New York had fourteen female professors, and a woman was the dean. In the Philadelphia School of Medicine, 15 of the 20 professors there were women. Among oriental women, who do not allow themselves to be seen by men, women doctors have played a beneficial role, and in Europe, their work during the war was truly admirable. Simmel confesses that women doctors are equal to men and that they exceed them when it comes to treating other women. In these cases, their diagnoses are more precise—female nurses interview other women more freely because they understand them better.

On the other hand, greater obstacles stand in the way in the field of law. Even though among the Spartans, who were educated in the spirit of Lycurgus,[88] no exceptions were made for either of the two genders, a woman mother and educator was valued as much as a man. The Dorians of Peloponnesus and Crete considered women to be equal when they established their form of perfect communism — they gave their property to the State, and the State saw to the support of everyone. It was always women who presided over the Common Table and who directed the orators' debates. Plutarch said that these women wielded such authority over their husbands that husbands called their wives *Miladies*, but even so women could not practice law.

Athenian women were shut up in the *gynaeceum* [89] as if in a prison due to the laws of Solon. We note that when Hector said his farewell to Andromache, "she of the white arms," he entrusted the care of the home and the servants to her, telling her that these things were her responsibilities just as it was his burden to go to war. Telemachus said to Penelope, "Keep to your distaff;[90] man is the sole owner of the spoken word. A woman's role is to keep silent."

But during the brilliant age in Rome that I have described, famous women educators such as Grachus' wife, the daughter of Scipio and Cornelia, were achieving great things. At this time Hortensia, the daughter of the great orator Hortensius, was born. She was so learned and eloquent, and defended before the Senate the cases of 1,400 matrons whose interests were being harmed by the taxes imposed by the triumvirate. All the historians uniformly praise her beautiful, harshly eloquent, coldly ironic speech. It was steeped in doctrine and devoid of sentimentality and moving tones. It contained words that would be appropriate for our day: "Women are on the sidelines of political life, they are deprived of public honors and duties. Why must they endure these charges? Civil wars have never favored them, and it is unjust that they must suffer the wars' consequences." So much truth and justice resonated in her words that the triumvirs overturned their decisions. Hortensia, a true lawyer, won the case.

Although this defense might be considered more political than legal, there are many other examples of women who defended cases for themselves. A very famous one was Amasia Sentia. Another,

---

88 The legendary law giver of Sparta who established the military-oriented reform of that society.

89 A portion of a house reserved for women.

90 A tool used with a spindle for the task of spinning thread.

Afrania,[91] earned great fame for her talent and would win all the cases that she defended, even though she was blamed for putting such passion and excessive vehemence into her speeches that it bewildered the Court. Whether it is true or not, her influence has been detrimental for the entire gender, because upon her death women were prohibited from being defense attorneys. Her name became an insult, used as a synonym for scandalous. The famous *Calpurnia's Reason*[92] is still remembered: when the celebrated lawyer was angered that the Court would not hear her case, she slapped the judge. Since Roman women could not serve as defense lawyers, they had to content themselves with being legal consultants.

Even among the Arabs there were women who were notable for their knowledge of legislation, such as Takyale and Zemab, who earned degrees that were equivalent to our Bachelor of Law degree. Arab women's thirst for education is revealed by the fact that when enslaved in the Harem, they learned to read and to interpret poetry. In Persian literature, we see that all of them, from slave to princess, knew how to pluck the gusla[93] and improvise songs. Zobeida, the favorite wife of Harun al-Rashid, was a poet and Scheherazade was a novelist and Chokdah is placed among the brightest lights of Islam.

In France when they were granted the right to practice Medicine, women also tried to put the legal robes back on. In the famous trial of Madam Lafarge,[94] she demanded that one of her woman friends be allowed to defend her, because "she could not have confidence in any man." But women continued to be denied this role until 1901, when Madam Jeanne Chauvin[95] was admitted to the bar. Since then the number of women practicing law has grown, and they show signs of being truly talented. In Germany, Austria-Hungary,[96] and Russia women were allowed to study law but could not practice it, as was the case in Spain until just recently, when the right to practice law was granted to women. In Belgium, the Courts ruled in 1889 that women were incapable of being lawyers even if they

---

91   Amasia Sentia and Gaia Afrania were two famous women lawyers of Ancient Rome.

92   This was the reason given for not allowing Roman women to argue cases.

93   A single-stringed musical instrument used to accompany epic poems or legends.

94   Marie Lafarge (1814-1852) was a French woman convicted of poisoning her husband in 1840, after a trial that raised was followed intensely by the press and public. The controversial decision, one of the first based on forensic toxicology, attracted the attention of such people as George Sand.

95   Chauvin (1862-1926) was the first French woman allowed to practice law.

96   The Austro-Hungarian Empire was established in 1867 and lasted until after WWI.

held a Juris Doctorate. This prohibition was sanctioned in Italy when Lidia Poët,[97] a lawyer from Turin, was denied the right to practice law. In Portugal, there are notable women lawyers who practice law with the same rights as men.

Even in America women's entry into the field of law was controversial, until in 1879 a federal law established that women who had tried cases before a Superior Court of a State or territory for a period of three years could be allowed to practice their profession before the Supreme Court of the United States. At the beginning of the century, close to two hundred women were practicing law. Today, in New York and Chicago alone, there are more than a million women lawyers and eight thousand one hundred women with Juris Doctorates. The latter have access to judgeships, and they serve on every Court. The fact that in Wyoming they have managed to bring gambling and drinking under control is due to women's influence. In Washington, mixed juries have been serving since 1893, and women jurists can boast of having voted against the acquittal of "Fatty"[98] during that famous trial. Women are particularly needed in trials involving so-called crimes of passion, in which men always absolve men—for those cases in which a man makes a journey to kill his unfaithful wife, plotting his crime with premeditation, without appealing to the law; and for those cases protected by the shameful article 438[99] that absolves a man who kills his wife, perhaps having entrapped her. That man keeps control of the couple's estate and the state takes authority over the children born of the assassinated woman. A jury of women would not condemn to a jail term any woman who adopted a little girl abandoned by her mother, for having forgotten some formality of written law. During one such case not long ago in Mexico, the intelligent *Loreley* requested a *Jury of Widows*, and in Cuba, the illustrious writer Aida Peláez de Villa-Urrutia waged a similar campaign. Both countries have a multitude of talented women: doctors, lawyers and writers. In Cuba, they even serve as Justices.

In all the other countries in America there are many women who practice medicine and law and who are successful for their

---

97 Poët was the first woman lawyer in Italy. Her disbarment prompted a movement to allow women to practice law.

98 Roscoe "Fatty" Arbuckle (1887-1933) was an American actor accused of raping and killing a young actress. He was eventually acquitted by a jury.

99 Author's note: The author has led an active campaign against this article. See her short story "Article 438," which is published in the second edition of the collection *My Best Short Stories*.

talent in the Sciences and the Humanities. In Colombia, Georgina Flecher has distinguished herself as a noteworthy herald in the fight for women's rights. In Bolivia, there is a prestigious female Athenaeum.[100] In the United States more than five million women work in commerce and industry, on an equal footing with men. There is a large number of women civil engineers, miners, mechanics and chemists. There are women police and detectives. No profession is off limits to them. Within some religious sects, women even have the right to the priesthood.

The profession of business woman already existed in Rome, where women took an active part in finance, money lending, societies dedicated to the operation of certain industries, and banking. Terencia, Cicero's wife, was very successful. This profession has gathered great momentum in the United States, where there are women bankers, head tellers, and leaders of commercial associations. In Ohio, there is a business run by a woman that produces 100,000 tons of iron each year. A women's association administers the *Texas-Pacific Railway*, which brings in 300 million dollars each year. Women employed in Banks and offices are also numerous in England and Sweden. At the beginning of the 19th Century, French women demanded the right to be stock brokers and to work in insurance and other financial sectors. They were denied these rights, and were limited to participating in the business world as office workers.

In North America, numerous women are merchant marine officers, and in England women have officially been declared capable of occupying the post of ship's captain, as long as they fulfill the established regulations. Miss Victoria Rammond has made the voyage from England to Australia as a mechanic on board a steamship. In Brazil, Miss Anesia Pinheiro Machado and Miss Teresa de Maozo have earned their pilots' licenses from the International Aviation Women's Association. In France, there have been notable women aviators and not long ago a French woman flew over the Andes. There are coach women and women drivers everywhere. Victor Hugo's granddaughter served as an ambulance driver between the hospitals and the trenches during the Great War:[101] the movement is common the world over.

In Sweden, there are such outstanding women writers as Fredrika Bremer, Baroness Sophie Adlersparre, Anne Charlotte Edgren, Ellen Key, Selma Lagerlöf and the noble Ana Vicksen, were

---

100 A literary or scientific association.
101 World War I.

exemplars of the internationalism of the women of their country. They defended Finland against their own country when justice demanded it.

Because of female influence schools of agriculture, gardening and gymnastics have been founded. The historic Uppsala and Lund Universities, and the College of Humanities in Stockholm, have opened their doors to women since 1870. In the College of Humanities, women have held chairs in Arts and Sciences. They are banned from no profession, and they even hold the posts of sacristan and organist in the church. Norwegian women are their sisters in every way; Finnish women offer us the exemplary woman Mina Silonjee, who began as a working-class woman and cook and has become a great writer, orator and chief editor of a newspaper. Danish women, who have such illustrious precursors as Clara Raphael,[102] and Russian women during the last period of Czarist Russia,[103] have been exemplary lovers of culture. They have dedicated themselves to the study of Sciences and Liberal Arts with true zeal. The awakening of the nation's consciousness against slavery is in large part due to them.

Balkan women are cultural models. The now deceased Queen Elizabeth of Romania achieved much deserved fame as a poet. Thanks to European influence, which made possible the opening of the first teacher training college during the reign of Abdul-Hamid, Turkish women have made great progress. There are now women doctors of medicine, and worthy novelists and poets. In China, thanks to the efforts of the woman lawyer Su-Han-Sangs, the fortunes of young enslaved women have improved. They are no longer treated as beasts and they have the right to demand a place to sleep, to educate themselves, and to marry according to their own wishes. Japanese women travel to Europe, get an education and have careers. Three of the Universities in their country now admit women under the same requirements as men.

Indian women suffered culturally under the influence of the English Government.[104] Many of them studied in Europe and North America and predicted that there would be independence upon their return. So today India has such writers as Sarojini Naidu,[105] whose

---

102   She is a partially autobiographical character in the novel of the same name, written by the feminist activist Mathilde Fibiger (1830-1872).

103   This period lasted until the Communist Revolution in 1917.

104   English incursions into India began in the 17th Century, and English colonial authority lasted until independence in 1947.

105   Also known as the Nightingale of India, she joined Mahatma Gandhi in the Indian Independence Movement.

poems have earned the praise of critics like Goss and Simons, and Mrs. Ghosal, the sister of the famous Rabindranath Tagore,[106] who writes novels in Bengali.

We will now turn to the state of affairs in Spain. Our Constitution of June 30, 1876, as well as the Constitution of 1812, granted civil rights to all without regard to gender. In reality, women are equal to men. They have the same privacy in their home and correspondence, their assets may not be confiscated, nor can they be discriminated against for their religious beliefs. They are free to choose any profession that they please and to practice that profession as they see fit. Just like men, they are not obliged to pay more taxes than what the Congress or legally authorized Corporations have voted on.

The Constitution recognizes the political rights of men and women equally, as well as the right to express ideas orally or in written form, without being subjected to censorship. They have the right to peaceful assembly, the right to address grievances, freedom of association to earn a living, and may apply for any employment opportunity or responsibility. They can only be tried and convicted by a judge in good standing and according to the laws established for the crime. They have the right to practice any profession for which they are granted a degree from the State in accordance with the State's rules for granting them. And they have the duty to take up arms to defend the Homeland when necessary, as well as the duty to pay national and provincial taxes in proportion to their income.

In spite of these strict guidelines, the Civil Code has interpreted the principles and articles of the Constitution in an absurd way that goes against their spirit, denying women rights that they really have and immobilizing itself with the inflexibility of written law. It has not been revised since 1888, but since it is based on social customs, it should be flexible and evolve with them. Women are only deemed equal to men with regard to financial and tax issues. Here there are no gender differences. When it comes to paying taxes and surcharges, the Constitution considers men and women to be equal. The constitutional principle of the right to work is so categorical for both genders that there is no proviso made with respect to skills or trades. The same is true of public positions.

But legislators have resorted to the subterfuge of distinguishing between *profession, industry* and *job.* The Constitution says, "The State

---

106   Tagore was the first non-westerner to win the Nobel Prize for Literature, in 1913.

has the duty to issue professional titles and to establish conditions for those who apply for them, as well as the manner in which they must prove their aptitude." The outrageous practices that place women outside of common law came in through this doorway. And so, even though Spain's spirit is progressive, it is backward thinking because of this unfair interpretation. For this reason, Spain has advanced so slowly and with so much difficulty. In 1836 the Conservatory of Music and Oratory, which admitted women into its classrooms, was founded. In 1857 the law of Public Instruction recognized the degree of midwife, with a qualifying exam and prior experience. Until 1858 there were no Teaching Colleges. At that time, the Madrid center was opened, under the supervision of the Ladies of Honor and Merit, which also had a Lancastrian school for children.[107] In 1877 Teaching Colleges were opened in the provinces. In 1885 women were allowed to join the Customs and Excise Corps.[108] And in 1884, women were allowed to be Telegraph assistants and wardens at prisons for women.

The women's penitentiary in Alcalá and the women's prison in Madrid are served by the Daughters of Charity, who are in charge of all services (except for those that require official documentation; those services are performed by employees) through a contract with the State. The law gave women access to official professional Institutes, Universities and Schools, but it banned them from three liberal professions: lawyer, solicitor and pharmacist. The first two were banned based on the absurd Partida laws[109] that denied women the right to a profession, saying, "It is neither desirable nor honest for a woman to take a man's office, since she would be publicly involved with men in order to argue a case for another." And they quite specifically banned the practice of lawyering, alleging that "when women lose their modesty it is a terrible thing to listen to and compete with them." The famous Code does not add what happens when a man does dishonor to the robe, because "when a man has lost his modesty it is a terrible thing to listen to and compete with him."

But it is not justice that prevails when it comes to the Partidas' treatment of women. The 3rd law of title VI insistently says, "No woman, no matter how wise she may be, can be a lawyer at a trial on behalf of another." Women are only allowed to represent offspring or

---

107　Joseph Lancaster of England designed a learning system at the beginning of the 19th Century that became popular in Europe and the Americas.

108　In this capacity, they were charged with searching other females who were suspected of carrying contraband.

109　See chapter 3, note 65.

parents who are old and sick or infirm "when there is no other person whom they can trust for their defense or if the case involves trying to free them from servitude or death." The tradition of the "Novísima recopilación"[110] was opposed to the pharmaceutical profession. It banned women from owning a pharmacy "even though there be a certified pharmacist employed there."

Only very recently have women been allowed to enter Bachelor's degree or Doctoral programs in Philosophy and the Humanities, Medicine, Pharmacy, or Sciences and the Law. Next, they were issued degrees, even though they could not work in the field. In our times women have been allowed to practice law, but they are denied the right to be Notary Publics or hold Judgeships. This is logical in a country where women cannot be witnesses. Today there are women Medical doctors who are truly talented. There are women working as Resort directors, ophthalmologists, dentists, nurse practitioners and registered nurses, as well as worthy lawyers. Women serve as Postal workers, Telegraph operators, Bank tellers, and work in private offices, etc. There are women typists, women officials working in departments of the State, etc., etc. But there are always limits, pay differentials, denials of promotion and a great number of injustices. This exclusion of women has nothing to do with ability but rather, with gender, in such a way that it results in an annoying situation of privilege for men.

With regard to private instruction, women have been extremely neglected. Instruction for girls was completely routine and consisted of reading, the religious doctrine and rules for being demure, cleanliness, modesty and composure. The usual tasks of sewing, embroidery, crocheting and knitting were essential. And even so schools were in short supply. Spain has much to be thankful for in that private initiatives and the Economic Societies and Friends of the Country[111] helped out during the age of home schooling, when only official teachers were required to have a degree. Today one needs a degree to give private lessons, and the State reserves the right to inspect private schools, as stipulated in the Law of the Count of Romanones, to which we refer when dealing with teaching in convents.

---

110 Author's note: 3rd Law, 13th title. [See chapter 3, note 68, for an explanation of Novísima Recopilación.]

111 These were private organizations established in various cities of Spain and the American colonies during the Enlightenment to help stimulate economic and intellectual development.

Little by little special schools are being established: for Governesses to learn Home Economics, for the Blind, Deaf and Dumb, Business schools, Language schools, Advanced teacher training programs, Fine Arts schools, and Trade schools. Women have access to all of them. The Committee for the Expansion of Scientific Study and Research, informed by a truly progressive, liberal spirit, gives grants to women so they can study abroad, the same as they do for men. And the future University Campus that they plan to build in Madrid includes facilities for women. Nevertheless, women have not yet been allowed to take part in art competitions to study fine arts in Rome. Given that women's education has been so limited in Spain, that coeducation does not exist, and that schools for boys are more numerous than schools for girls, it is strange that the Census of 1900 showed that the majority of illiterate people were men: 64% of women, and 38% of men, could read and write.

Until recently, only middle-class women studied at official schools, and they were the only ones who had a profession. With rare exceptions, aristocratic young women were educated in convents, in schools abroad, and with private tutors at home. Even today an education that is merely decorative is preferred for rich women. Fleury was outraged by the limit of feminine education, saying, "It is paradoxical that women are only taught catechism, sewing, housework, singing, dancing, dressing fashionably and making curtsies. It has been deduced, as if based on a true experience, that women are not capable of studying, as if women's souls were from a different species than men's. It is as if women had no reason to act of their own free will, no passions to combat, no health to preserve, no goods to manage, and as if it were easier for them than for us [men] to satisfy all their needs without learning anything." When Fénelon laments that children's education is so mishandled by their mothers, what he is really lamenting is that mothers do not have sufficient knowledge to be educators.

Supposing that women had nothing more to occupy themselves with than their homes and families, that would require an amount of knowledge superior to that needed to hold the most difficult of posts. Being the head of a household and a companion and educator for men requires the broadest, superior amount of knowledge. Soy affirms that men's education must begin through women. Richard adds, "If the vast sums of money that every town spends on horse racing were dedicated to the education of a particular number of youths, two invaluable benefits would result: there would be more sensible women and fewer consumptive horses."

Colorado recognizes well the harm caused by a lack of education when he exclaims, "We raise women to be ignorant in hopes of keeping them virtuous; we hide evil from them fearing that they will become corrupted, and so without becoming dishonorable, they will fall into it more easily. We teach them to covet beauty and we do not take care that they learn to love that which is good; in this way women allow themselves to be carried away by their feelings, more instinctively than reasonably, more through nature than spirit, with more desire than understanding." But the antifeminists do not give up and they say that "when women are possessed by the Demon of Equality and become engineers, doctors, and furniture or soap makers, this makes it impossible for them to be homemakers and lovers."

There are even women who sadly go against their own gender's education. Mme. Lambert[112] has said that "women should have the same bashfulness with regard to science as they do with regard to bad habits." She thinks as Moliere does that "it is not honorable, for many reasons, for a woman to have knowledge and study." Colette Yver,[113] whose books have become outdated so quickly because at the time that she wrote them, it was still rare for women to have a profession, puts these words in the mouth of the woman lawyer in *Love vs. Law*: "I have two parts within myself. One belongs to my husband, the other I reserve for myself, it is my secret domain. Marriage has not weakened it. I keep my freedom and my personality as a single woman intact. My husband has no control over it. He knows it and allows me to defend myself on my own."

The woman physician in *Princesses of Science* says, "Don't you think it praiseworthy and useful to associate identical purposes with two equal beings: to be lovers and friends, to remedy the conjugal troubles that derive from intellectual disproportionality?" When her husband complains, she sensibly replies, "You don't recognize my tenderness. Not expressing it with silly remarks does not diminish or weaken it. My unfettered heart is capable of a superior love. I tell you without boasting that few men are loved more nobly and absolutely than you are. You doubt the immensity of my affection? It is the precious essence that raises us above vulgarity. Admit that you're often more pleased with the energy and sincerity that I put into my work than with aggravating, physical caresses." And the lout replies, "I want the timeless lover that all men dream about, for whom tenderness is her sole religion."

---

112   The Marquise de Lambert (1647-1733) was a French author and salonnière.
113   Yver (1873-1954) was a popular French author.

When saying this, men forget that women's sorrows, pleasures and pettiness rob them of their spirit and tenderness more than do Science and Art. It is shameful to demand that women only exist for sexual love. If this is the only thing that women are extolled for, let us not hope to find good spouses and mothers. Colette Yver wants to prove that women whose brains are dominant are heartless. But the brain (intelligence) and the heart (sensitivity) always march in step with each other. To prove her thesis, Yver paints the portrait of a *cerebral woman* who does not nurse her son. On the other hand, Jules Bois paints the portrait of a woman doctor who has three children and raises them without neglecting her profession. Collette's character is a literary fiction, while De Bois' woman, as he assures us, is taken from real life. De Bois was one of the most generous and selfless champions of women who always defended the female cause in the French press, as does Cristóbal de Castro in our country.

But on the other hand, all misogynists are antifeminists. Strindberg[114] is one of the most rabid of them. He adored women and treated them badly because he did not know how to make them love him. Nietzche conceives of women as "an arid plain" and calls them "cats," "cows" and "monkeys." Without a doubt, certain men have feared seeing themselves belittled by educated women and have said that "men prefer beautiful women to erudite ones," and adding, "The value of women does not consist of their having intellectual vigor, but rather, that they serve as men's guides in the arduous battle of life." These are two laughable assertions, since there is nothing that says that a beautiful woman cannot be erudite. Intelligence does not diminish beauty, but rather it increases its value and makes it more expressive. Max Nordau[115] stated that intelligent women maintained their youthfulness for a longer time.

With regard to the second statement, it does not make for a blind man to be another blind man's guide. The woman who is only good for perpetuating the species thanks to her physical vigor, but is not endowed with intellectual vigor, will never be "that guide that men need in the hard battle of life." She will not even be a decent partner. It is precisely because of this lack of education that women are more detrimental to men. We celebrate Book Festivals and Book Days, try to establish libraries and organize the National Book Conference. For what purpose? We must promote education and love of reading for the sake of the most important factor: women.

---

114   Johan August Strindberg (1849-1912) was a Swedish writer and artist.

115   Nordau (1849 - 1923) was a physician, a Zionist leader, writer and social critic. His *Degeneration* (1892) attacks contemporary artists as "degenerates."

In the last National Book Conference, the topics dealt with were exports, tariffs, the price of raw materials and labor, all that which is material, external and secondary. The problem is for women, who have more spare time, to instill a love of reading in their husbands and children. We cannot forget human beings' paramount obligation to perfect ourselves, as well as the right we have to honestly seek spiritual satisfaction by quenching our thirst for knowledge and wisdom.

In *A Doll's House* and *The Revolt*, Ibsen and Villiers de l'Isle Adam, respectively, were able to represent this responsibility that women have to themselves. Their heroines have the same moral standing to proclaim *the right to learn*. The first heroine is victorious because of the strength that comes from being a Northern woman; the second is defeated because of her weakness as a Latin woman. The second argument, the necessity of taking care of *House* and *Home* (which serves as the receptacle for all vital content) is immediately trotted out. Just as the ant carries away the grain from the threshing floor and the bee takes honey from the flowers to its hive, men and women take home all their personal, religious and social interests. Simmel said, "The home is a part of life, but at the same time, it is also a special way to condense life, reflect upon and express our existence."

Everyone recognizes that women's great cultural achievement is having created the home. Simmel declared, "Here we have an objective product whose very nature is comparable to no other; it [the home] is imprinted with the feminine stamp by the particular abilities and interests of women, by their typical sensitivity and intelligence, by the entire rhythm of their being." But it would not be fair, as a reward, to turn the home into a jail that results in women becoming like the silk worm that weaves its own tomb. The home would be converted from a delight into a prison for its very creator.

It has even come to be said that mothers' educational attainment puts their children at risk. People assure that "if Bacon and Goethe's mothers had been as learned as they were, they would not have been able to bear those brilliant sons." I have no idea why people could believe that maternal erudition could harm their children. The maternal influence on great men is frequently studied: Saint Augustine and Saint Francis of Assisi owe even their sainthood to the two remarkable women who gave them life, Saint Monica and Magdona Pica of Provence. Chateaubriand proclaimed that he owed his talent to his mother. Leopardi and Figaro were unfortunate because they had vulgar, uneducated mothers. The most notable men are very frequently heard saying, "My mother was educated, intelligent and good. Without her I would not be where I am today."

A legislator like Manu, from whom we can still seek inspiration, said that "a father was more venerable than a hundred teachers and a mother more venerable than a thousand fathers." He added, "We owe our existence to our fathers; to our mothers, we owe who we are." There is an abundance of modern philosophers who are of the same opinion. In *On Women*, Diderot exclaims, "Do whatever you please with the man and leave the woman to me. I will raise her, I will educate her, I will teach her and she alone will be capable of regenerating the world."

Anatole France, who owes his mother so much for his brilliance, summarizes what should be true education, whose purpose is not only to instruct in a dry way, but rather to awaken the spirit to sensations and feelings, at the same time as learning. He tells us, "If you were to entrust a girl to me I would make her a creature that is superior in intelligence and life, in whom all things from nature and art would be reflected in sweet splendor. I would have her live in harmony with beautiful landscapes, ideal scenes from poetry and history, and with nobly emotive music. I would make her as loveable as you would like her to be. I would not neglect to teach her about needlework, the beauty of cloth, the tastefulness of embroidery and the shape and style of guipure lace.[116] I would give her a dog and a pony to teach her how to control her children; I would give her birds to feed so that she would learn the value of a drop of water and a breadcrumb. In order to give her a bit more happiness, I would want her to be joyfully charitable, and since pain is inevitable because life is full of misfortunes, I would teach her the Christian wisdom that raises us above all misery and that even gives beauty to pain. This is what I understand a woman's education to be."

---

116 A type of French embroidery using heavy lace.

CHAPTER 5
THE RIGHT TO WORK

Women's work. — Labor that is gender appropriate. — The guild's enslavement of women. — Work in the shop and factory. — Work in the home. — Blood wages. — The spiders. — Damages caused by poorly understood protections. — The harmony necessary between both genders in the workplace. — New aspects of work, capital and the consumer. — The legal situation of working women in Spain. — Labor unions and egalitarian laws.

We have noted that the first feminism to show itself was working class, although feminism had been incubated in the so-called *middle class.* The great mass of working class women felt more acutely the need to seek a way to earn a living and proclaimed the right to earn it through their own efforts, in equality with men. The right to work has been a victory for feminism; even those tasks that are called "women's work" that women were consigned to by the town councils as if they were professions, required that women fight hard battles to get them. In "The Badly Paid Worker," M. P. Gemhäling records that on March 30, 1676 in France, seamstresses needed to be protected from the tailors' monopoly on the trade that did not allow women to make suits. The royal edict decreed, "It is favorable to women's modesty and decency that people be allowed to make suits for their own gender, when they judge it to be advisable."

Later, in 1789, women delivered a petition to the king in which the following curious paragraph is found: "Your Highness, to alleviate ourselves of so many hardships we request of you that under no pretext may men be allowed to perform the tasks that pertain to women: seamstress, embroiderer, clerk in a women's clothing store, etcetera, etc., and that men at least allow us to keep the needle and the spindle, and we will promise never to pick up a compass or a carpenter's square."

In some regions of Spain women did not have the right to work, and in others they were subjected to unfair limitations. In Castile, the guild denied membership to women and denied them even such tasks as spinning, weaving, passemonterie,[117] etcetera. The same exact

---

117 The French word used in English to refer to the making of ornamental fringe for curtains, furniture, etc.

thing happened in Aragon and Valencia, where the guilds professed the principle of excluding women: "Women at home and men in the square." Women were not granted employment either through legal means or through customs. Only in Catalonia, which is freer, were women able to dedicate themselves to some crafts, but not if they required entering a bachelor's house. No law prevented men from entering a woman's house.

The laws passed down to us from good King Charles III[118] and the construction of the Seville Tobacco Factory were the first steps toward women gaining the right to work, although they had to fight many customs and prejudices that remained. The first thing that Charles III had to do was declare that the trades were *Honest* and *Honorable,* and that the women who practiced them were *authorized to be employed.* This erased the dishonorable status that manual labor had. Law 12 by the same monarch proclaimed that men and women had the freedom to work in the art of spinning silk, *at home or in the workshop.* Law 21granted to widows of craftsmen the right to keep their shops and Law 14 declared the *right to work* of all women in all trades that were *gender appropriate,* in spite of the guilds' ordinances. To clarify the obscure name "gender appropriate trades," Law 15 added that "all women have the authority to work in the thread factory as well as other pursuits as they choose, provided that these are compatible with the decorum and strength of their gender." It is curious that since ancient times, while sociologists have not been shocked by the enslavement that women's work as domestic servants implies, since it forces them to *completely* abandon the home, they are so shocked when women spend a few hours away from home to go to the factory or workshop.

Maids, assistants, seamstresses, laundresses and clothing pressers who work in customers' homes abandon their own homes without anyone protesting. In all of antiquity women have worked without this hullaballoo rising up all around them, sometimes out of compassion for their powerlessness, at other times out of pity for the abandonment of the children. Nor is sympathy felt for the children of the nursemaid who entrusts their care to a stranger during her lactation period. They say that necessity forces nursemaids to seek a way to make a living, but what forces the working woman? Women have worked at all times. Penelope wove cloth, Omphale was a seamstress, and Nausicaa washed clothing at her father's palace.[119]

---

118   An Enlightenment monarch who ruled Spain from 1759-1788.

119   These are three famous women in Greek mythology.

Suetonius[120] said that the Emperor Augustus Caesar's daughters and granddaughters sewed his clothes. The highest praise that could be given to Roman matrons, who, like Aquillace Amimone, were famed as workers, was "she knows how to spin wool." Among us women's work was praised. Queen Berta was a renowned spinner and Isabel I sewed her husband's smock. Since antiquity on, women in small towns turned millstones, made cloth and carried large bundles on their heads, as we see in Greek and Roman artwork. Roman paintings show that women dedicated themselves to all types of work.

Among the Germanic tribes and other early Spanish inhabitants, women did more work than men. Gothic women tilled the land, and at the court of the Omniades slave women did the toughest jobs. Saint Isidore[121] allowed servant women around the convents, and women workers were mistreated to such a degree that in the Council of 1020 it was prohibited for "a woman to be forced to knead dough for the King if she was not his serf." The social arrangement that divided citizens into castes based on their trades differed little, since it was ruled that these be perpetuated *according to the type of work:* fishermen, shepherds, laborers, servants, craftsmen, etcetera. Servants were true slaves; even the *Novísima recopilación* [122] established that when they are fired by one Lord, they may not work for another in the same area.

At the same time that these laws and guild ordinances prohibited women from working, no one was concerned that they were already doing the most difficult agricultural work in every region. On the roads of Andalusia, it is common to see women on foot carrying a bundle or a child, behind the horse upon which their husbands are happily mounted, and women herd for the men so they do not have to do even that. In the countryside women are the ones who get up in the middle of the harshest winter nights to give fodder to the animals, while the men stay snuggled in bed. It is women who collect the esparto grass and shoots[123] in the hills, dig potatoes and pick fruit in the orchards, harvest wheat in the fields and grapes in the vineyard; and they thresh the grain. In some places, they still practice a custom that Strabo[124] *(la curade)* talked about: husbands stay in bed and eat chicken while their wives give birth.

---

120 Gaius Suetoniius Tranquillus (ca.69-130 CE) was a Roman historian.

121 St. Isidore (560-636 C.E.) served as the Archbishop of Seville for three decades.

122 See chapter 3, note 68.

123 Esparto grass was once used widely in rural Spain. It was dried, processed, and made into rope and other articles for both humans and animals.

124 Strabo (64 B.C.E.? -21 C.E.?) was a famous Greek geographer who, among other things, noted that the world was round.

And so, it is clear that what inspires the protest movement against women in the workplace is not feelings of pity for the ill-treated weaker sex, nor for their children or homes. It is formulated on the one hand by daily routine, and by selfishness on the other. Spanish customs had been shaped by the ancestral criterion expressed by Fray Luis de León[125] in *The Perfect Wife*: "And as fish when they are in the water swim very lightly about in it, but if per chance they are taken out of it, they lose the ability to move, so the good wife, when she passes through her doors, must be swift and nimble, just as outside of the home she must be seen as crippled and slow. And so, God did not equip women with the ingenuity required for serious business or with the strength needed to fight wars and work the fields. They must measure themselves for what they are and be contented with their destinies, and be understanding in their homes and wander there, since God made them only for the home." The dominant idea was that there was no other course of action for women than to stay in the church, in the kitchen and the nursery. Wilhelm II later synthesized this notion with his three Ks: *Kirche, Küche, Kinder.*[126]

But beset by necessity, women were forced into the workplace. For country women, this is barely a problem. The agricultural system is basically communistic. Everyone works, eats and lives with the same interests. Working women in the city are the ones who suffer neglect and misery because of the despotic, unequal family situations. Work in factories or a shop is more beneficial for these women than work in the home. Now that the workday has been limited to eight hours (we remember with trepidation the campaigns waged to reduce them to twelve!) and there are laws on the books that require that premises be inspected, the workplaces are more hygienic than homes. While they are working in the shop, women have no other concerns, and they earn a higher daily wage than they would by spending the same amount of time working at home. Once their workday is done, they still have sixteen hours left. If they manage their time well, they have time to rest, tend to the family and avail themselves of entertainment.

The laws protect working women but they cannot protect those who hide the fact that they work. At the same time, laws also damage

---

125   Fray Luis Ponce de León (1527-1591) was a Spanish lyric poet and theologian of the Golden Age.

126   These words (lit. "church, kitchen, children") are attributed to the aforementioned German Emperor Wilhelm II (1859-1941), pronounced in a diatribe against the German suffragist movement.

feminine work the most. Women working at home earn less than they do in the workshop. In a report presented to the Congress, the French Secretary of Finance stated that for a female florist to complete three African violet arrangements in his home, earning seven francs *per week*, she needed to get up at six in the morning and did not go to bed until ten at night. In a workshop with eight hour days, she could have made 24 francs a week.

There are many working women who prefer to take in work at home because of their desire not to neglect their families and daily chores. These unfortunate women *take care of everything* and to be more productive, they work more than the standard number of hours. This results in what in England is called a *Sweating-System*[127] ("regimen of exhaustion and sweat"), and what Doña María Domenech de Cañellas, the spokeswoman for the Board of Trustees for women who take in work at home, refers to as the *Daily Blood Wage* (Doña Domenech de Cañellas was awarded the Silver Medal for her activism in Barcelona). Making higher earnings without neglecting the daily household chores is done at the cost of women's health and lives. Jules Simon portrays this type of woman in the pitiful working-class characters of his books that die of exhaustion and hunger.

The stiffest competition comes from the *lady workers,* middle class women whom we could call *shamefaced workers.* There is one longtime prejudice that has not yet disappeared: if economic conditions make it necessary for the women of a *good family* to work, they sew, do embroidery, make candy and arrange flowers. But they do this secretly and with great caution so that no one finds out. In the majority of cases, these families still accept the work that has a certain veneer of intellectuality, but they hide that they perform manual labor. This lowers wages in a pernicious way, even for the women themselves. They are paid so poorly that they barely make the minimum daily wage, even after fourteen hours of hard labor that prevents them from going out, breathing the open air and uplifting their spirits, which seem to become asphyxiated and immobile due to the monotony.

In some jobs, women who are experienced with the work that they are contracted to do are preferred, while in others preference is given to those ladies who work in secret, because they are believed to be better prepared and more careful with delicate tasks. And do not believe that because of the variety of work produced in the home,

---

127   The author means "sweatshop," of course.

its artistic merit rises above that made with the uniform production of the workshop. The majority of women who work in the home are tired, worn out, poorly rewarded, hungry and sick, they have neither pleasure nor dreams, nor do they have any incentive that moves them to do a job that is anything but mechanical and routine.

The work outside the home that receives the most criticism is that done by married women. The opponents of women in the workplace have published statistics to establish a connection between infant mortality and women's work. But the statistics of child mortality in Spain are horrific and higher than the rates in other countries where women work more. Almeria is at the top of the list for infant mortality in Spain and it is not an industrial city. Except for a scant number who work at the esparto grass factory, women are only busy harvesting grapes and performing a few other jobs. Many men emigrate from Andalusia and Galicia, where fewer women do factory work, which proves that female competition does not create a scarcity of work.

The viciousness directed at working women reaches such a degree that they are blamed for all of society's ills. In *The Social Power of Women,* Georges Deherme[128] has said that in homes where both parents work, children grow up to be depraved and immoral. To justify this absurdity he writes, "Men and women work and become respectable because they have lived past the age at which dangerous adventures are attractive to them, and they deem it to be more advantageous to be respectable. But among themselves and their children they show their true natures, with particular ideas that can sprout from their dead souls, remorseful that they have not been able to take advantage of good opportunities. Their hope, their only ideal, is to amass wealth in order to laze about and enjoy themselves. In the midst of all this the question that Baudelaire posed to a Bourgeois father, regarding which one of his children was destined to be a swindler, would not shock anyone." This idea is so absurd, and conceiving this notion about respectable parents who work and serve as a moral example to their children is so illogical, that there is no need to refute it. And this antifeminist book concludes with the hypocritical phrase: "Through the sweet splendor of the feminine soul the world will be reformed."

Campione says the words *"Woman and Work"* are conflicting. He maintains that in women the source of the strength that affects

---

128   See chapter 1, note 23.

the ability to work is weaker; but the facts prove that in everyday life, all women without exception endure a heavier daily workload that requires more energy than men's work. The housework that women of modest means have to endure requires constant effort. Additionally, the greater effort that motherhood demands over that demanded of fatherhood reveals that Nature had the foresight to make females stronger so that they can hold up. It is an obvious fact that women who physically exert themselves are stronger than men who do not work or who spend their time playing sports. So, we see country women doing jobs that require great strength, taking care of the toughest agricultural chores, loading and unloading cargo at seaports and train stations. By developing their strength women can even become circus performers, and we have women who are *boxing champions*.

We must not forget Lamarck's theory:[129] "Its function creates the organ." All the physical elements can be trained and are capable of development: the voice, physical strength, and hearing. Nature gave men mammary glands, perhaps just in case they would have to feed a newborn in some circumstance. The lack of usage made them atrophy. Scientific authorities assure us that milk can be sucked from a man's breast by a child. The influence of atrophy can even be seen in the follicle system. Men of today do not grow such long beards as those that El Cid Campeador and Alphonse de Alburquerque[130] were forced to braid up. In the same vein, men and women are no longer as tall, and their bodies are no longer capable of bearing the weight of the suits of armor, or of unsheathing the swords, that are on display in museums.

There is much adaptation that species undergo. In his admirable study *Gender, [Work and Sports]*, Marañón[131] says, "Upon becoming domesticated, cows lose their musculature and become incapable of exerting effort; all of their energy is expended in gestation and milk production." Additionally, Darwin believed that muscular superiority is an adaptation that occurred even before birth, an effect of the law of heredity, as mysterious as the determination of gender. This law goes so far as marking the dimples on the earlobes of newborn baby

---

129   Jean-Baptiste Lamarck (1744-1829) was a French zoologist credited with being a forerunner to Charles Darwin.

130   El Cid was the nickname of Ruy Díaz de Vivar (1043-1099), a vassal of Alphonse VI of Spain who participated in the Reconquest. He is immortalized in the epic poem that bears his nickname. Alphonse de Alburquerque (1453-1515) was the Portuguese nobleman who established the Portuguese colonial empire in the Indian Ocean.

131   See chapter 2, note 24.

girls where they are pierced for earrings. Adaptation and heredity was caused by so many years of women's servitude, which atrophied a large amount of their musculature. But the fact that women need to make use of their strength is proven by the women who do not work and take up sports, in an attempt to substitute them for fruitful labor.

Nowadays more than half of all women are in the workforce. The number of working women is constantly growing. They are in the majority for almost all jobs: agriculture, fishing, etc. They are seen working as masons, metallurgists and they perform all tasks that require physical strength and endurance. Conversely, we see men working as tailors, designers, hair dressers and embroiderers, etc. There is no barrier, nor can there be a dividing line that sets the limits of the work that one or the other gender can do, as Georg Simmel[132] would have it. But men's intrusion into jobs that have been considered suitable for the female gender has never caused the indignation that arose when women became coach drivers, chauffeurs, shoe shiners and above all, barbers. It was considered immoral that there were women barbers and the ones who complained most loudly were the very women who go to a hair dresser every day, and all the men who sit in the waiting room while a great designer helps their wives try on a dress.

Women's work has come to be thought of as depraved. Simmel himself says, "The fact that women can live more thriftily than men is being taken advantage of, and they have provoked a reduction in salaries." It is incomprehensible that *women can live more thriftily*. For women life is as expensive as it is for men. If a woman is the head of a household and is responsible for parents, brothers and sisters, children, and at times even her own husband, it does not cost her less to support them than it would cost any man in her place. Besides, everything is made more difficult for women. Women are required to pay larger security deposits when they rent a house, and there are Electric Companies that require even women who are solvent to pay deposits that men are not required to pay—just because they are men! If Simmel believes that women need less to survive because he assumes they have the willpower to deny themselves superfluous things: tobacco, alcohol, coffee clutches and similar things, then we have to say he is right.

And it is not that women completely lack the desire for these things, but rather that custom has kept them away from those things,

---

132   See chapter 1, note 26.

and they have not become a necessity. For that reason women are more punctual, they arrive at work more rested, their minds are more lucid, and they do the work with great zeal and care. The director of an important Book Publishing House has spoken to me about the vast difference he noted between men and women employees when they came to work, above all on Mondays. He told me, "On Sundays men tire themselves out and women rest."

I have heard many heads of ministerial departments and public offices, both official and private, praise women's work. Why, then, do women earn less if life is not cheaper for them nor their work inferior? This is a new abuse of women by men. Employers, who take advantage of the needy and the employees who allow them to do so, are equally as abusive—even when the employer is the State! The anecdote of the Russian woman who went to work dressed as a man is well known. She worked this way for many years without anyone noting that her work was any less worthy than that performed by her male coworkers. When asked why she disguised her gender, she responded, "Because passing for a man, *I make three times more for the same work.*"

A short while ago in Seville, another woman disguised her gender in order to earn a living, earning a salary as a Security Guard. In Madrid, a young woman who was desperate to find work was employed at the continental Madrid Post Office delivering letters dressed as a boy, thus avoiding starvation. The reduction of daily wages that causes men to fear competition from women is disastrous for women themselves. I repeat, it is not the fault of women in the workforce, but rather, of those who do the work at home for any price at all, just to help themselves a little bit, without depending on this work alone. These are the women I have called *shamefaced* workers, and they make use of intermediaries. In their shadows, the so-called *spiders* make their living. The *spider* is a woman who takes work from the shops and sends it into homes. She agrees with an employer on a price for each dozen undergarments, shirts, pants, handkerchiefs, etc., and farms it out to other women at half the price agreed upon. It tends to happen that a second *spider* catches others in her web, so that women complete the work for less than what that *spider* is offered. Sometimes the contract goes through four to six different hands, each *spider* an exploiter of the only one who does the work.

And nevertheless, even though these contractors are primarily out for their own profit, they do not reduce the cost of labor for the merchants as much as the *Charity Centers*. They commit the more or less real altruistic act of taking in abandoned women, feeding them a frugal diet and making them work from morning until night for the shops. Since workers here produce more than they cost and the Centers have their own resources needed for their philanthropic mission, they take in work at any price. The women wash and iron clothes, embroider, sew… everything, at implausible prices that do not allow for competition. These Charity Centers take for themselves all the work that is produced, to the detriment of the women laborers, and they lower the cost of labor in a deplorable way.

For that reason, at the 10th Feminist Congress, Margarita Durand requested regulation of work that is carried out in prisons, convents, secular or religious orphanages, and all establishments where the cost of labor is almost free, resulting in harmful competition for both genders. But instead of helping their women partners to retain their rights in the face of the hoarding of these clandestine jobs, working men turn against them, wishing to ban them from working. There are examples of this, such as the case that happened in Madrid, where women typesetters were opposed, and in Portugal, where working men went so far as to hurl bombs into the bakeries that hired women. That deplorable spectacle occurred in a country where the Republic gave working people every freedom, from free competition for work to the right to go on strike. You cannot say precisely that it is the advanced groups that want to impede the work of women, their companions and comrades.

It is precisely the working men who need to lean on their female companions in misfortune. The vindication of women and the proletariat go hand in hand, to the point that socialism, the brother of the French Revolution, proclaimed political and civil equality as well as equal salaries, training and education for men and women, and women's equality in the laws and customs. This was done at the Socialist Workers' Congress in Le Havre in 1880, and at the congresses held in Austria Hungary, Brussels and Erfu[r]t in 1891. But at the Socialist Congress at Bourdeaux held in 1882, citizen Marty asked for the abolition of women in the workforce. At the same Congress, Roussel said to Michelet, "Men work for the sake of women, and they [women] do not have to leave their homes." And Michelet bought it and defended the poetic deception that claims that women continue to be rocked to the sound of that fake lullaby that causes them to sleepwalk in servitude, not allowing them to gain independence. Michelet's opinion did much harm to the female cause.

Karl Marx did not sympathize with women's involvement in collective work, considering them to be a source of corruption that capitalism introduced, enslaving not just men, but the whole family as well. It did this through mechanization, which obviates the need for physical strength and accepted the fact that women, having been tossed out of their homes because of economic necessity, would resolutely join the workforce.

What was necessary was to keep women's work from becoming detrimental, for the purpose of which the triumph of this principle is indispensable: FOR EQUAL WORK, EQUAL PAY. What is indispensable is *equality*; so-called *protection* is more detrimental to women than their own enemies. Any situation of privilege is harmful. In a parliamentary session during which laws that protected women workers were under discussion, Jules Guesde[133] said quite correctly, "As a consequence of the law of 1892, which prohibited women from working at night, today thousands and thousands of respectable women are found living in poverty." The Feminist Congress of 1896 declared that women's work must be free, as long as men's work is not regulated. Mlle. Schumacher asserts that those who ask for a prohibition that keeps women from working at night are the same working men who want to suppress competition with them; in that way women cannot work for newspapers, operate printing presses or work as typesetters, etc.

At the Catholic Congress, Marie Mangeret[134] stated that freedom to work should be established, with no more regulation than the strength and needs of the workers, which only they should control. At the Congress of the Center for Women, Marie Martin[135] exclaimed, "We demand that all adult women have the right to judge the conditions in which they control their work; we want free employment in a free country." At the Congress of the Feminist Left, Marguerite Durand[136] declared that humanity's first responsibility was to eliminate difficulties for women who work. The so-called law meant to protect women in reality does them harm. The best interpretation of the laws is the one that accurately adapts them to needs.

Speaking of time off for working mothers, Marie Martin said, "Women will be more and more frightened if the idea of being a mother is linked to the idea of losing their way of earning a living."

---

133   Jules Basile Guesde (1845-1922) was a French socialist, journalist and politician.
134   Mangeret was an important Catholic suffragette in Paris and one of the founders of the Christian Feminist movement.
135   See chapter 1, note 10.
136   Durand (1864-1936) was another important French suffragette, a stage actress and a journalist.

In Russia mothers are protected to such a degree that they are almost banned from the workforce, harming them in such a way that they cannot find work, since no employer will employ working mothers who are given four months of time off at full salary: two months before and two months after the birth, and nine months more at a fourth of their salary while they raise the child.

The 10th Feminist Congress voted that the laws that exempted women from work be abolished and replaced by an equitable system that protected both women and men. That is what would be fair and just. True feminism does not wish for special privileges. The standard prevalent in Spain was also *equal* protection for both genders, although this has not been made into law as it was formulated.

In 1891, Don Vicente Santamaría de Paredes[137] presented the plan that he had been charged to draw up that would establish rules to organize women's employment. He was inspired by principles of mercy and took the benefits of hygiene into account; for that reason, his plan was filled with prohibitions. It banned women younger than twenty-three years old from working at night, regulated women's hours, prohibited them from undertaking any occupation that might harm them physically and from all work performed underground, and ruled that after giving birth women should return to work, without four weeks having passed.

But the typical standard for Spanish politicians and economists was that the freedom of people who found it necessary to resort to the legal system must be respected. Many denied the ability of legislators to limit the freedom of adult women and prohibit them from any kind of employment. Others, like the Catalan employer Mr. Ferrer y Vida, were against regulating women in the workforce. He said, "When women are already adults, of an age at which the Civil Code has given them complete freedom of action, and if they are not under parental authority, I understand that the State does not have the right to impose new obstacles in their way with regard to employment." And if this opinion may seem not to be impartial, we have the vote of the notable sociologist Segismundo Moret,[138] who maintained that the State did not have the right to coerce or prohibit women women's employment, even by invoking health or gender concerns, unless such measures were compensated. The illustrious politician

---

137 Santamaría de Paredes (1853-1924) was a Spanish writer and legal scholar who held professorships at the universities of Valencia and Madrid.

138 Moret (1833-1913) was a Spanish politician who helped draw up the constitution of 1869, and served two terms as president.

said, "As unhygienic as some professions may be, there is nothing as unhygienic as hunger." Mr. Sanromá had excellent judgment when insisting that limitation on women's activity should not be the object of special laws, but rather a general law for women and men, in all that pertained to hygiene.

These expert opinions correspond to the spirit of justice that inspires true feminism, which does not want special privileges. Women do not deserve more protection than men and the health of the former and of the later are equally worthy of respect. I felt great pity upon seeing a mason's apprentice, almost a child, who was lugging stones on his back while climbing the wooden ladder attached to a scaffold on the second floor—his back bent, completely exhausted, his breathing labored, under the weight of a cross that no one helped him carry down that Street of Endless Bitterness. What our Institute of Social Reforms has done is fine: prohibiting women from performing work for which they do not have the physical strength and making laws to regulate the weight of the bundles they carry on their heads. But that law should also be applicable to men. Neither of the two genders should perform tasks that endanger or ruin them.

There are companies that look out for their own interests by not letting sick employees work and having them undergo a medical exam. Likewise, the State should also make sure that women and men who are unable to perform certain tasks not be allowed to perform them, by taking the necessary precautions. Prohibitions should be mandated taking into account *individual* ability, not making them *generalized*. Protecting one half of humanity means protecting all of it. Men and women have the same rights; the wellbeing of fathers is as important for the species as that of mothers. It would be absurd to suppose that during infancy only girls should be cared for and boys should not be given equal care. That would seem as monstrous to us as the crime Arabs commit [sic]: killing newborn girls.[139] Both genders should be equally protected from the crib to the grave. The State that constitutes the great national family must be inspired by the family of which it is made up, in the noble, respectable abodes that fortunately exist, where boys and girls, men and women in the prime of life, and elderly men and women are all equally well cared for, all wrapped in the same loving embrace, everyone working, without exception, according to their abilities.

---

139   The author is referring to an ancient practice not heard of in the modern era. It is true that in the pre-Islamic Arab world, some tribes committed this type of infanticide, but most likely it was not widespread.

Additionally, the jobs women were prohibited from doing were not the most dangerous ones, but the ones that provoke jealousy and lead to competition. Among other things, women are allowed to work washing clothes, which has victimized many of them in the large cities: the ironing that exhausts women with its fumes, excess heat and physical demands; flower making, which poisons them with arsenic laced dies; sewing, which is perhaps the most dangerous of all, especially if done on a machine. It causes heart palpitations, kidney pain, fallen uteruses, lung conditions, vertigo and even stupor; and the dust from tobacco manufacturing causes eye conditions and tuberculosis.

It is not necessary to keep pointing out the dangers that lie in wait for both men and women workers on the painful road they travel. But how can people who work to survive be prohibited from working? When a woman needs to choose between work, hunger or indignity, there is no doubt about the choice she should make. In no situation should the State prohibit her from working. The protective role of the State consists of ensuring that work is performed under the best possible conditions. Above all, we must end the hypocrisy of *protecting* women from those jobs in which they can compete with men, and not restricting them in all the others, no matter how dangerous they may be. Referring to ourselves, we must now erase the phrase "feminine work." Neither exclusionary employment for one gender nor protection or prohibitions for the other alone. We should give special importance to these issues, since as Franklin [K.] Lane,[140] the United States Secretary of the Interior, said, "The work in which we engage ourselves keeps our flag stitched together."

Until now the struggle between workers and capitalists has divided society more and more into two antagonistic factions, however much socialism has already managed to provide some advantages. Members of both groups look at each other with hostility. Workers justifiably complain about inequality, since "wherever capital risks its money, workers on the whole risk much more, since they risk their very lives." Capital and workers need each other equally as much. The former cannot survive without the other: but the latter justifiably demand adequate wages, sufficient time off, and job security. Women's employment is caught up in this same debate.

Karl Marx assures us that members of the modern working class survive only as long as they can find work and that they can only

---

140   Lane (1864-1921) was Secretary of the interior during the Woodrow Wilson presidency.

find it when their labor increases capital. He said, "This, and women who compete in the work force, are the causes of the scarcity of jobs." Bernard Shaw[141] states that "competition between the industrialists themselves leads to disastrous overproduction, making it impossible for workers to find permanent work." The great humorist is extremely pessimistic regarding the matter. He can see no salvation. And so, he adds, "Instead of shedding light on the matter, education instills the idea of the sacredness of private ownership and brands as criminal any State that seeks to redistribute wealth… Commercial unionization is one stage of capitalism, since it applies to the worker the principle of selling in the market to the highest bidder, paying the least possible amount."

But more than any of these theorists, Henry Ford, who through his practice as a businessman turns out to be a great sociologist, synthesizes them remarkably. He presents a new phase of capitalism, stating that "capitalists, workers and the consumer public are none other than one and the same people." Henry Ford did not start out by expounding doctrine, but by carrying out actions. More than twenty years ago, when the average wage fluctuated between two and three dollars a day in the United States, he raised it to a five-dollar minimum, and shortly afterward spontaneously established the eight-hour workday.

Ford approached the labor question differently than the other skinflint employers who try to cheat workers into accepting the usual wage by not providing them with job security, and who think that their profit depends on the pennies they save in wages. They all predicted Ford's ruin, thinking that doubling the daily wage and reducing the work week by one third was madness, and accused him of carrying out socialistic, revolutionary, anarchic work. But his methods produced excellent results: the productivity of his satisfied workers made up for the shortened work week and corresponded to the higher wages. Still not satisfied, Henry Ford has just declared a five-day work week. His workers will be able to rest for forty-eight consecutive hours. And do not think that charity is what motivates Ford, but rather his spirit as a far-sighted industrialist, and his experience. He assures us that these advantages given to the worker enrich the nation. Ford begins with the premise that the differences between workers, capitalists and consumers are empirical, and he believes we are all those three things at the same time. Thus, if

---

141 George Bernard Shaw (1856-1950) was a Nobel Prize winning Irish author and playwright.

workers have low wages and most of their time is occupied, they can neither consume nor make purchases. Since the working class makes up the majority of the people in all countries, commercial exchange is weakened because there are no consumers. But if workers are well paid and have two or three days off each week, they will buy clothing, food and a thousand other things, and therefore they will consume more, to the benefit of industries. Ford says, "Unless industry can come up with a way to keep salaries high and prices low, it will destroy itself, since it limits the number of its customers." Under his system, workers are realizing their dreams of a good wage, time off and work security, and capital assures the survival of industry. It can be said that in an indirect way, workers give back what employers have given them, but multiplied.

Now this system is being implemented. Garvin, the defender of American capitalism, confesses, "Since socialism first lodged its charges against capital there has been a shocking change in the improvement of salaries, work hours and health precautions. In America, high salaries are considered to be a vital principle of creative ability in a way that Europe is beginning to understand." Ford's theory has to be extended to women, who, with good pay and sufficient time off, will increase consumption, and that way will give a greater number of workers the opportunity to participate in production. Industry should not exploit women, giving them lower wages, and with the same stinginess destroying working men; women do not compete with men, nor is there a lack of consumers. Industry should be able to employ everyone.

There is no doubt that the Great War was a powerful consciousness raiser. The warring nations were obliged to take advantage of all their reserves and then the value of women and their importance to the life of society was demonstrated in a practical way. Women replaced men in all workplaces. At least through this example they put an end to the discussion of whether or not women were capable of holding down jobs. Women themselves felt satisfied. They moved with the unconscious pride of a child who discovers a truth all by himself for the first time and gains the self-confidence to take his place at the table with the grownups. It is not true, as Barrè asserts with obvious ill will, that when the war ended women abandoned the workplace as happily as children leaving school. The strengthening of the International Federation of Unions in Amsterdam gives the lie to this idea.

At the Roman Congress in 1922 the issue was not resolved and it was decided to continue the relationship of solidarity between working men and women and to begin a campaign to create a joint system, the basis for unions. In England, working women have organized themselves into *Trade Unions,* through which they have managed to improve their working conditions. The *Confederación Regional Obrera Mexicana* [The Mexican Regional Confederation of Workers], commonly known by the name formed with the first four letters of the words that make up its title (*CROM*), is worthy of special mention as a model organization for women workers. I have had occasion to observe the good sense with which the Mexican women who belong to the organization work. The Secretary of Labor himself, Mr. Morones, is the president of the *CROM*; thus, they will be able to implement their program more easily by benefiting from wise and fair legislation.

In Spain, the spirit of modern laws is to establish women's right to do any job that is suited to them. An analysis of all our laws reveals this right to be clear and conclusive, and for some time they have given no conditions or allowed any exceptions with regard to women's employment. There are regulations that are favorable to women, established by the Institute of Social Reform and the Department of Labor. This year women's employment in the home and work at night have been regulated.[142] A minimum of twelve hours of time off between two consecutive workdays has been established for all women without regard to age, for those employed in factories and workshops and all other industrial and commercial operations and establishments. Women who work as domestic servants, those who bring work into the home and those who work in family businesses are exempted from this rule.

Time off should always include the night time hours, that is, the hours between nine in the evening and five in the morning of the next day; but there are numerous exceptions made for cases of work stoppages that are impossible to foresee, in the interest of avoiding the loss of perishable materials in the agricultural industry, and to keep hospitals, clinics, mental hospitals and any other such charitable organization staffed. There is also a so-called Law of the Chair, sponsored by the noble Don Eduardo Dato,[143] which sounds like a poetic refrain in the midst of our set of laws. According to this law, anywhere that women work, the employer is obliged to provide a chair for each one, so they do not have to stand up for too long. There

---

142 Author's note: by Decree of the Department of Labor. August, 1927.
143 Eduardo Dato e Iradier (1856-1921) was a Spanish political leader who served as Prime Minister until his assassination in 1921.

are also laws to protect mothers, and the Mining Police Regulation prohibits women of any age from working in a mine. In general, the plight of women workers is gloomy, and they are warned more and more of the need to join the General Workers Union.

In Catalonia, where labor unions are strongest, employees can rely on important Workers Federations, and now other provinces are following their example. Declaring the principle of women's freedom to work and to earn equal pay serves no purpose if it does not have the strength to make employers respect it. Mrs. Elvira Santa Cruz Ossa,[144] who gave a beautiful speech at the Inter American Women's Congress held in Panama in 1926, mentioned the curious case of the Department in her country that passed the Contract of Employment law, which establishes the equality of both genders. They set a salary of 15,000 pesos a year for the head of the Bureau of Labor Oversight, in the General Office of Industry, and only 9,000 pesos for the woman who is head of the Bureau of Labor Oversight for women, which is in the same office. So, it is not only the industrialists who evade regulations that are favorable to women, but even the selfsame Government that decrees them.

And nevertheless, working women continue to fear unionizing. They have been led to believe that organizations for working women are revolutionary and the enemies of employers, and many fear losing their jobs. Working men should help resolve this issue by supporting the standard set at the conference held in Vienna by the International Workers Federation. The standard upheld there would prevent any type of exclusion for either of the genders. One must only notice that there are more than one hundred million women currently working on all the continents to realize what strength they would have if they formed a homogenous mass instead of being separated.

Women workers need to unionize, if only they would recognize this, in order to have, among other things, free access to a salary, as we will see when we deal with the rights of married women in different countries. It is necessary for women to be granted the same rights as their fellow men: pensions, insurance, back up workers, and freedom of employment, as well as an equal workday and equal pay. It is in men's best interests to help them. Humanity has only one cause.

---

144   Cruz Ossa (1886-1960) was a Chilean author, journalist and educator.

Chapter 6
Marriage and the Family

The organization of the family. —Marriage. —Subordination of women. — Causes that determine subordination. —Different types of marriage. — Unwedded partnerships. —Religious and civil marriages. —Sacrament and contract. —Love, the foundation of the home. —The advantages that marriage gains with feminism.

Women's subordination to men is not an inevitable fact because of its historical precedents. Bachofen,[145] the wise German, assures us that all societies have passed through a matriarchal phase during their history. His publication of the book that supported this theory was quite scandalous, but after all the controversy was over they had to admit that, if not in all of them, in the majority of societies the existence of matriarchies is proven. Primitive societies organized themselves around the mother figure, as do all animal groups, realizing from the beginning that "maternity is a proven fact and paternity is just a conjecture, as long as it is not proven."

Women dominated the clan and relegated men to second place. It was women's voices that were raised during tribal councils to resolve the most serious issues. As with all groups, economic interests were always taken into account and for that reason it was usual for a woman to wed all the brothers of her first husband, who shared their only wife without jealousy; the wife would assign them work, guide them and watch over their common interests.

The shapes that human groupings have taken are innumerable, from promiscuity to polyandry[146] to polygamy to patriarchy, etc., we arrive at the family that we know today. On occasions, the family was not a private right, but a political arrangement. The *Father* has had jurisdiction over his own family; at the time of the Roman Empire, there was even the case of a husband who demanded the right that he, and not the ordinary courts, be the one who sat in judgment of his wife, when she was accused of a public offense. The family cannot be considered an institution that has been in existence since the dawn

---

145   Johann Jacob Bachofen (1815-1887) was a Swiss professor of anthropology who studied prehistoric matriarchy.

146   Polyandry is a form of polygamy in which one woman has more than one husband.

of man on earth. As Stuart Mill[147] says, it is a moral conquest that has gone through profound transformations and will be called to undergo others, since it is a living organism that cannot crystalize into a definitive shape. There is no reason for marriage not to continue to evolve.

The loss of female dominance was due to religious transformation, in the first instance, when the principle of female divinity was no longer worshipped. So, we see that Egypt was free at the time of Ramses,[148] but was enslaved in the time of Ptolemy.[149] The invasion of the barbarian tribes and the advent of Christianity ended up depriving women of the freedoms that remained to them. The Germanic tribes brought with them the cult of strength, barbarity, militarism and the principle of patriarchy. They introduced the law, the physical yoke, while Christian theology supplied the moral law.

Christianity had not yet broken away from Judaism — it was a continuation of it, and Moses, like Manu, Confucius and all the religious lawgivers of antiquity, considered women to be *impure* vessels, the cause for the downfall of humankind. They have contempt for the *daughters of Eve,* as if Eve were not the mother of everyone. Christ's doctrine is not opposed to the liberation of women. He wraps both genders in the same love; He desires freedom for all the oppressed, and justice and happiness for all. He does not deprive women of culture, since He teaches the parable of the Samaritan woman. He does not disdain them, since He makes room within his friendship for Magdalena and the sisters of Lazarus. He does not subjugate them, since He submits himself to his own mother. When He addresses her, He calls her *Woman* as an honorific title. But Christian theology has developed in the Germanic spirit and has its roots in Judaism, a religion in which marriage was not monogamous, homes were established based on polygamy, men enslaved women and repudiated them with the greatest of ease. There is no doubt that monogamous marriage was a step forward, but marriage suffered from two fatal flaws: the enslavement of women and indissolubility.

---

147 John Stuart Mill (1806-1873) British philosopher, economist, moral and political theorist, and administrator, was the most influential English-speaking philosopher of the 19th Century. Among the things for which Mill campaigned most strongly were women's rights, women's suffrage, and equal access to education for women.

148 Ramses II (1303-1213 B.C.E.), also known as Ramses the Great, was the third king of the 19th dynasty of ancient Egypt.

149 Claudius Ptolemy (90-168 C.E.) was an Egyptian mathematician, astronomer, geographer and astrologer.

It was a terrible moment for women when Saint Paul said, "Wives, submit yourselves to your own husbands," [Ephesians 5:22] [150] and Germanic law added, "No woman can live independently under her own authority. Her entire life must be under the authority of her husband or of the Prince." Upon examining these precepts, Boissel[151] was outraged by the subordination of women within the family, because he considered male arrogance to be a heresy against the creator, who made everyone equal. Men tried to justify this through the myth of the original sin, agreeing with Tertullian[152] that "because of women, evil has come into the world as if through an open door."

There are times when Saint [Peter] himself proclaimed equality: "Husbands, in the same way be considerate as you live with your wives, and treat them with respect as the weaker partner as heirs with you of the gracious gift of life" [I Peter 3:7]. But actually, equality is that gracious gift of which they speak, and women are made to wait to enjoy it in heaven. Saint Paul said, "The husband should fulfill his marital duty to his wife, and likewise the wife to her husband. The wife does not have authority over her own body but yields it to her husband. In the same way, the husband does not have authority over his own body but yields it to his wife" [I Corinthians 7:3 – 4]. But then he added, "For man did not come from woman, but woman from man" [1 Corinthians 11:8]. So, it turns out that women "shall be called 'woman,' for she was taken out of man" [Genesis 2:23].[153] In their eagerness to be dominant, men go so far as to claim maternity for themselves. According to that view, Adam was the first *Mother*, and Eve only the first *Woman*.

As Saint Peter expounds on his theory, he increases its strictness: "For the husband is the head of the wife as Christ is the head of the Church [...] [Ephesians 5: 23]." "[...Man] is in the image and glory of God; but woman is the glory of man" [1 Corinthians 11:7]. The epistle's precepts order the following: "Wives, submit

---

150   Unless otherwise noted, bible quotes are from the New International Version.

151   François Boissel (1728-1807) was a French philosopher, writer and a pioneer of feminism.

152   Quintus Septimius Florens Tertullian (c. 160 – c. 220 C.E.) was an early Christian author from Carthage.

153   In her original citation, the author uses the term *Virago*, from a Spanish translation that attempted to be faithful to the Greek and Hebrew versions of this verse ("woman shall be called *Virago* because she was taken from the *vir* "). In modern Spanish, *Virago* means "mannish woman."

yourselves to your husbands, as is fitting in the Lord" [Colossians 3:18)]. At times, there is kind advice that favors women: "Husbands, love your wives and do not be harsh with them" [Colossians 3:19]. Fearing husbands would abuse their authority he added: "I give you a wife, not a servant" [Ephesians 5:25]. But the damage was not avoided. Male dominance was proclaimed in all the religious orders. They would say, "The hen cannot sing in the presence of the rooster," and women were like hens, like furniture purchased by men. The abuse reached such a degree that it was necessary to clarify the true situation, as we see in the dialogue that Bertold of Regensburg[154] wrote in the 13th Century:

"Brother Paul, you say that women must submit to their husbands. So then, I can do with mine whatever I please and treat her any way I see fit?"

"No, no. Your knife belongs to you, but would you use it to slit your throat? Your ham belongs to you, but would you eat it on Fridays? Your wife belongs to you, but according to divine law, if you commit an offense against her, you will not enter into Heaven."

Nevertheless, the idea persists, all one need do is listen to Petruchio from Shakespeare's play *The Taming of the Shrew*: "I will be the master of what is mine own: / She is my goods, my chattels; she is my house, / My household stuff, my field, my barn, / My horse, my ox, my ass, my any thing." In 1880 Leo XIII[155] was forced to proclaim women's rights in marriage without breaking with the principle of marital authority established by the Church. He said, "The man is the prince of the family, the head of the wife, but she is flesh of his flesh and bone of his bones and should not serve him as a slave. She is his submissive but respected companion."

Although the Church elevated matrimony to the level of a sacrament, it always held it in less regard than chastity, which is not a sacrament. Saint Jerome said, "Let us take the hatchet and cut out by the roots the infertile tree of matrimony, for although God has permitted it, Jesus and Mary have consecrated virginity." Regarding marriage, the Church supports the absurd theory of the *necessary evil*, which is used as an excuse to avoid chastity without sinning, and for the sake of convenience and health. Saint Paul himself advises that only those people should marry who have the gift of continence, because in this case "it is better to marry than to burn

---

154   Bertold of Regensburg (1220-1272) was a German member of the Franciscan order.
155   Pope Leo XIII (1810-1903), born Vincenzo Gioacchino Raffaele Luigi Pecci, was leader of the Roman Catholic Church from 1878 to 1903.

with passion."[156] For the sacrament of marriage, the Church does not require the intervention of any minister or, to more accurately use the language of the theologians, in this sacrament, each spouse will serve as the minister to the other. For a long time, the Church did not reject the practice of free union, that is, a union entered into by consent only, without a public official, a priest or witnesses. The presence of a priest to insure the validity of the marriage only became essential at the end of the 16th Century, when the Council of Trent[157] and the ordinances passed at Blois proclaimed that marriage is an act that benefits the whole society and should be consecrated and subject to strict laws that definitively establish monogamy.

But the Church had a tolerant nature and desired to promote marriage. According to Baluze's testimony,[158] Hadrian II[159] wrote to the bishop at the diocese at Chalons Sur Marne to ask him to validate a clandestine marriage, and Alexander III[160] went so far as to officially approve *consensus et copulam*.[161] In the 11th Century at the Council of Melfi, the marriages that were strictly prohibited under penalty of excommunication were those involving priests, which had been tolerated up to that time. The most devastating condemnation fell upon the poor wives of those priests, whom Pedro Doniceu called "the devil's marrow, the poisoners of intelligence, whores, wolves, owls, fat pigs" and other such niceties.

Promoting marriage became more and more tolerated. It was allowed between patricians and plebeians, between relatives who were thrice removed (after a Church dispensation), and between people of different religions, in the latter case, only if it was determined that the spouses would not enter the church through the main door or receive the nuptial blessing at the main altar. These practices were not observed when the heir to the Belgian throne married a protestant Swedish princess who did not want to recant her religion and violate her conscience in order to gain a throne.

The Church compromised on many types of marriage: when the bride or groom is on his or her deathbed, secret marriages, elopement, marriages that happen the moment the celebrant gives

---

156 Authors note: I Corinthians [7:9].

157 Author's note: 1561.

158 Étienne Baluze (1630-1718) was a French scholar and historian.

159 Pope Hadrian II (792 – 872) served as pontiff from 867 until his death.

160 Pope Alexander III (c. 1100 – 1181), who served from 1159 to 1181, laid the foundation stone for Notre Dame de Paris.

161 Lit. "agreement and coitus."

the benediction during mass, etcetera. In spite of the fact that freely given consent is one of the indispensable conditions, there have been verified cases in which brides have been forced to wed. Enslaved in this way, they had to submit to taking a husband whom their parents had imposed upon them. The daughters of nobility would marry at the whim of the monarch, while the daughters of serfs had to endure the humiliating *droit de seigneur*.[162] Moratín's *El sí de las niñas*,[163] in which a woman dares to exert her own free will, was considered to be outrageous even at the dawn of the last century. There was not a big difference between European women and those poor Chinese and Japanese women who committed suicide in order to escape the torment of a loveless marriage.

And none the less, even in those places where civilization had not penetrated due to their isolation, vestiges of primitive society were preserved. For example, in Bareges, [France], a remote village in the Pyrenees Mountains, until the time of the revolution,[164] women were the heirs to the exclusion of men. A woman also chose her own husband, who did not have the right to stipulate anything. It is quite true that husbands had the right to give their wives a beating, just as Don Alphonse de Aragón had the right to *lay his hands and feet* on his wife Doña Urraca's royal person, in spite of the privileges she enjoyed as the Queen of Castile.[165]

Since ancient times there have been institutions in Spain that have infringed upon the institution of marriage, one of which was the acceptance of *barraganía*.[166] The word *barragana* came from two Arabic words *barra* (outside/out of) and *gana* (profit). According to the first Partida[167] law, title XIV, this meant "profit gained outside of the authority of the Church." In spite of this the arrangements were tolerated, to the extent that in the Middle Ages they became so common that only single men and lay clergy did not have *barraganas*.

---

162 This was the right of the feudal lord to take the virginity of the new bride. There is no historical evidence that this "right" ever existed.

163 *The Maiden's Consent* was a neoclassical play written by Spanish playwright Leandro Fernández de Moratín. It debuted in 1806, and challenged the prevalent thinking about arranged marriages of the time.

164 This is a reference to the French Revolution (1789 – 1799).

165 Urraca of Castile (1079 – 1126) had an arranged marriage to Alphonse I of Aragon, which ended in separation after Urraca accused Alphonse of abuse.

166 This was a contract for a relationship outside of marriage between a man (*abarragonado*) and a woman (*barragana*) that formalized their relationship to a degree. It was accepted in parts of Spain but never sanctioned by the Church.

167 See chapter 3, note 57.

Men could only have one b*arragana,* joined together in the presence of witnesses, in front of whom the men declared their intentions. In these unfortunate circumstances women were required to be single and of good character. Distinguished gentlemen could have a relationship neither with a *barragana,* a woman minstrel, a tavern girl, a servant, nor generally with anyone from the so called "inferior" classes. No man could have more than one *barragana,* in keeping with the principle of monogamy. The law also required that the *barraganas* not be younger than twelve years of age or be relatives less than four times removed, and *abarragonados* had to be single laymen. The children from this type of relationship] were considered to be "natural"[168] because the *barragana* had to "declare friendship and faithfulness to the man, dedicated to him alone."[169] When the *barragana's* situation was not stated, it was presumed that the couple had a "clandestine marriage,"[170] based on the fact that they lived together. This type of relationship was very common at the time, and in fact, the principle proclaimed by Saint Just[171] prevailed in unions out of wedlock: "All those who love each other are husband and wife."

These unions were considered to be a type of marriage, not a sacrament, but certainly a contract for the benefit of the children. The *Partidas* explain their tolerance [for such relationships] this way: "The wise ancients agreed that some men could have *barraganas* without penance, for they held that it was better to have one woman than many, and because the paternity of the children that they gave birth to would be more certain." Don Rafael María de Labra[172] had this say about it: "The certainty is that in Spanish society and in our system of jurisprudence, the *barragana* occupied a perfectly defined position between a spouse and a woman who, either by chance or only fleetingly, had relationships with one or more men."

Thus, we used to have three types of union: formal and legitimate public marriage, *a Yuras* or clandestine marriage, and *barraganía.* The latter form survived for a long time, in spite of the

---

168   See chapter 3, note 50.

169   Author's note: Title XX, *Partida* IV.

170   This was a type of marriage that took place without benefit of clergy and with no witnesses, also called an *"a yuras"* marriage.

171   Louise Antone Léon de Saint-Just (1767-1794) was a French revolutionary leader and the author of a number of proposals for a communal and egalitarian society.

172   Rafael María de Labra Cadrana (1840-1918) was a Spanish politician, a prolific writer, and an abolitionist.

prohibitions and punishments aimed at the *barraganas* who were not the partners of a single man. Those who were in a relationship with a clergyman [i.e. a priest] were sentenced to wear a red cloth "brooch," among other penalties, in order to distinguish them from good women. There was no punishment at all for their partners. The law passed by Don Juan I[173] at Briviesca established that "when the concubine of a priest or a married man continues to err in her ways, she shall be publically flogged." But it does not order that her partner be flogged. The laws passed down in the [Royal] Ordinances of Castile or Montalvo by the Catholic Monarchs[174] dealt with bigamists and priests' concubines, in which it is decreed that anyone who committed "adultery with the queen or a daughter of the king, even though they are not married" would be accused of treason.

Today we have canonic and civil matrimony. The former is valid due to the effect of compacts between the State and the Holy See, but requires the presence of a State functionary and entry in the Civil Registry. As for civil matrimony, all the legal regulations are in effect without the need for the canonical ones. This was difficult to implement, since those who considered sacramental matrimony to be legal did not agree that matrimony by contract should be legal. Don Rafael María de Labra said this about the proposal: "The law of civil matrimony is the consecration of a legal advancement, already widespread in the civilized world and an irrefutable consequence of the principal of freedom of religion that was proclaimed in Westphalia and sanctioned by consecutive progressive processes. These have given civil matrimony the quality of an inescapable supposition in moral life, government and social behavior." Every day we are making more progress toward this type of goal.

There are political doctrines for which marriage holds no importance. Bebel,[175] the advocate of socialism, said that the union of a woman and a man is merely a private contract that need not be legalized by any functionary and that both parties should have the freedom to choose and the freedom to break up. The anarchists contend that relationships should be free and that society should not concern itself with them.

---

173   This was King John I of Castile (1358 – 1390), whose reign began in 1378 and continued until his accidental death in 1390.

174   Queen Isabella I of Castile (1451 – 1504) and King Ferdinand II of Aragon (1452 – 1516) were the Spanish monarchs known for completing the Reconquest of Spain and funding the voyages of Christopher Columbus.

175   See chapter 1, note 19.

With the experience he gained on the Juvenile Delinquent Court of Denver (in the United States), Judge Lindsey says that marriage is postponed too long and the intervening period between the end of schooling and starting a family is excessively long. During this time, young people fall into bad behavior. To resolve this problem, he proposes a "preliminary marriage," which would not produce children and so could be dissolved without serious consequences. Or it could be converted into a "permanent marriage" and become a family. He believes that this would improve the moral environment by putting an end to illicit affairs. The respectable judge's opinion has created quite a scandal; leading the charge in the fight is Father MacMenamin, who supports indissoluble holy wedlock.

The great English novelist H. G. Wells says this about it: "The majority of people are unreasonably frightened by many respectable pacts or agreements and by the idea of men and women establishing relationships freely, because they do not realize how natural and necessary it is that men and women living in the working world — that is, in a world in which both go to work each day — be allowed to associate with each other. It is something that can very well be left up to everyone to discover and appreciate for themselves. If everyone were at complete liberty to act as they pleased and to take their own initiative, they would very happily and with minimal effort do almost the same things society makes such an effort to force them to do. They would partner up the same as they do now, and what is more, the unlucky and the misfits would not feel compelled to suffer for their misfortune or peculiarities. In a word: human beings should not be forced to act in a certain way with regard to these matters. There would be less dishonor and persecution because of these reasons. All sorts of mistakes could be rectified; everyone would find their significant other more quickly and there would be a large reduction of prostitution and secret criminal sexual disturbances. In general, I believe that people's thinking and desires are moving firmly and constantly toward rationality, candor and charity when it comes to sexual matters, and they are becoming distanced from emotion, secrecy, coercion and repression. The Denver dispute is surely only one of the incidents that reveal the extremely broad progressive movement that favors revising and modernizing matrimony."

But no matter what type of marriage one wishes to accept, the foundation of the home is "love," as Élisée Reclus[176] points out.

---

176   Jacques Élisée Reclus (1830 – 1905) was a French geographer and anarchist.

If both genders are educated within the same moral code with pure tendencies—so that marriage is no longer a depraved thing that is confused with love—homes would be built on a solid, indestructible foundation. Very soon mutual interest (that comforting element of wellbeing found in happy homes) would be added to love, which would cause the couple to defend what they have. There is nothing as maligned as a love that is not solely the "chosen relationship" that Goethe mentioned, nor the mission imposed upon the individual due to the nature of the species, as Schopenhauer would have it. Both are no more than signs of the libido that drags one sex toward the other with desire. This is what Stendhal[177] has called "physical love" that becomes impulsive and turns into blind, rash "passionate love." Stendhal himself distinguishes two shades of meaning in it, which he calls "pleasurable love" and "vain love." Neither one of these terms offers a solid foundation for the happiness of the married couple.

For a human couple, love cannot be "abstract," no matter how pure it may be. "Platonic love," which exists in its own essence, without the need for reciprocation, only concerned with the happiness of the person who is loved, is the love parents feel. It is a humanitarian love, the love that Saint Francis of Assisi dedicated to brother bird, sister beast, sister water and even sister death, but it cannot constitute a home. The ability to love everything gives us a greater capacity to be happy because love is the source of pleasure and allows pleasure to predominate over pain. There really is no such thing as suffering for love because in love there is always joy. The idea of hell is admirably portrayed in the saying that "it is a place without love" and the portrayal of the three austere virgins who cannot love even in dreams and who were turned into furies.

No manifestation of love can be detested except for the paradoxical "love hate" relationship to which Bourdeau [178] refers, which is different from love and is the product of tortured nerves that are brought together by desire but repelled by reason. It is only produced in excessively sensual relationships. Aside from this, as Lacour declares, there is also the right to "all love," pleasure and passion. The distinguished author[179] of *Lay Down Your Arms*, who won the Nobel Prize, wrote, "Oh, damn the ineptness of your dualism, of

---

177   The pen name of Marie-Henri Beyle (1783 – 1842), an important French realist writer.

178   Jean Bourdeau (1848 – 1928) was a French writer who wrote about philosophical issues and socialism.

179   *Baroness Bertha Felicie Sophie von Suttner* (1843 – 1914) was an Austrian writer who won the Nobel Peace Prize in 1905.

your ridiculous disdain for nature. This is the origin of so many evils and of your hypocrisy and cruelty! What! You are ashamed that the basis of your purest, most elevated sentiment is an instinct that you share with the animals, and therefore you at least want to deny it, if not stifle it altogether? But then why are you not ashamed of the need to nourish yourselves, a need also shared with animals? Why don't you hide your aspiration to enjoy the sunshine, which all the plants share with you? Haven't you discovered the sacred connection that unites you to the universe? You stubbornly persist in the belief that you are above all of this, able to manage without nature. For that reason, you have violently split your essential being and have invented an abstract love, which you judge to be noble and pure. With this love, you deny someone the right to aspire to a physical relationship, and the more you experience the loftiness of your love, the more you try to pull it from the carnality in which it is rooted… You do not understand that by destroying ideal love you create the vice of licentiousness, since licentious behavior consists specifically of the seeking of the pleasures of love but *without love*."

No one who speaks sincerely and thinks honorably can question the existence and the necessity of this love in relationships between the sexes. Feminism is slandered when someone says that its goal is to exterminate love. What it seeks is not for couples to be content with physical love, since we know full well how easily quenching one's desire puts out true love's flame. Physical love has to be controlled and channeled, to be connected to another type of love as real as it is. Ideal love is born when moral character is valued, just as physical love is born when only looks are considered. This is what Faguet[180] calls a "love habit" and a "love friendship." Along with physical love, which is necessary in a relationship, another love that is sensible, based on friendship, tenderness and understanding must be joined to it. This other love must have pleasures and ideals that will keep happiness in the home. H. G. Wells says, "When it comes to matters of sexuality, human beings do not have a simple physical desire, there is always something that speaks to the imagination, and that something has its own demands. In order to be successful, all relationships have to be based on true love with all its nuances, and also on mutual honesty and good faith that can overcome the problem of monotony, which prompts us to seek new emotional experiences."

---

180   Émile Faguet (1847 – 1916) was a French writer and literary critic.

The will plays an important role in love. Victor Hugo said, "One loves a woman as one discovers a new world, always thinking about her." The will manages to transmit its intentions to the emotions and makes love all the more noble, profound and delicate. Men and women have been able to make love last and have found in love a source of happiness that makes life become marvelous and creative. In love, the danger lies not in loving too much, but in loving too little. If a couple marries without love just on a whim, the wife will find the same faults in her husband as she would if they only cohabited, but with the aggravations of indissolubility and subservience imposed by law.

Ellen Key,[181] the Swedish intellectual who recently passed away, tried to redeem love in all its forms, and was able to find the essential formula for a perfect family. She says, "Men long to find partners who will share life's burdens. True love is only born when the desire to form a relationship with someone of the opposite sex is joined with the affection that inspires and the understanding that lets us know that the other is worthy of our love and can understand us." In *Delphine*, Madame de Staël[182] harshly attacks marriages without love, and George Sand said that a marriage arranged without love was "legal concubinage and legalized prostitution." Far from endangering marriage, as people of bad faith have claimed, feminism favors it. As the degree of morality increases, marriage acquires a more sacred nature. "Facile love is moveable capital that is quickly squandered. On the other hand, serious love is an asset, a plot of land whose value increases as it is cultivated."

Educated, emancipated women will not cease to feel love, all the more intently the stronger are their personalities. To believe that no theory or doctrine can extinguish that which is typical and fundamental is to ignore nature. No sensible, wholesome woman without mental or physical abnormalities will deny that love is sublime, nor will she try to close the doors of her heart to it. George Sand said that "love is the voluntary slavery that women accept because of their own natures," but in reality, where there is true love, there can be no slavery. Trying to extinguish love in someone's heart would be impossible, and would be like committing a sacrilege against "the sacred spirit of life." If women today are suspicious of marriage, it is not because they do not have the capacity to love, the desire to love, or love itself. It is just that they are fearful because they know of the lack of virtue and justice in our society.

181　See chapter 3, note 48.

182　See chapter 4, note 75.

Furthermore, feminism favors marriage from the economic point of view, which is another of the legal purposes for a relationship. When women cease to be a burden to men, marriage is made easier and a guarantee of choice is brought into the home, since a woman will not marry the first man who woos her, forced by necessity, if her economic situation is assured. Educated free women will choose wisely and the marriage will be made with the necessary requisites of love, respect and comfort.

But the types of homes are being transformed: the home in which the woman works and lives as a servant to her family, content with what the man gives her and held accountable to him, is disappearing. A new type of home will be established upon new economic efforts that will constitute a superior type of family relationship. This will serve to reinforce family ties. Because it happens that all the institutions that seem to be waging battle against marriage are actually in favor of it. Divorce has done nothing more than increase the number of marriages. The Bolshevik Code,[183] which made things easier, shored up the family structure that was so harshly embattled and kept it from being brought down.

Sensible women should be found in the home, not the "reflection of a woman" that Confucius had in mind when he said that "man is to woman as the sun is to the moon, and she needs to be his reflection so that harmony reins." These antiquated ideas have been the cause of a great deal of our problems. As long as the family is based on laws that conflict with the fundamental principles of nature, it will only favor the procedures that civilization fights against and will continue to be the force that endangers the law. Matrimony is not a relationship that only aspires to legalize sexual desires, nor a business arrangement in which love is completely absent. But a little bit of everything is needed: desire, love and comfort. It has been shown that matrimony is either a signed contract that grants equal rights and freedoms to both parties or that it is no more than the legalization of the law of the strongest. Without love and freedom for both spouses, there cannot be a happy home and the "sanctity" of matrimony does not exist; "monogamy" and "indissolubility" will be reduced to mere words.

---

183   After the Bolshevik Revolution in Russia (1917), the 1918 Family Code was introduced as part of a larger reform movement. The code established civil marriages, in order to reduce the power of the church, simple divorce which could be requested by either partner, and the legalization of abortion, which was also made free on demand.

CHAPTER 7
MARRIED WOMEN IN THE CIVIL CODE

Married women in the Civil Code. —Women's standing within the family. —The eternal minor. —Married women's situation with respect to their assets. — The Fruits of Labor. —Literary copyright. —Commercial law. —The progress of Civil Rights in all nations. —The emancipation of Argentinian Women. —Movement in Spain.

The subordination of women is stated in our Codes. In a reasonable plan of emancipation, it is necessary to begin with equal rights. Feminism does not desire a position of privilege for women; it is not a revolutionary doctrine. Feminism only tends to recognize all of women's rights, without freeing them from any of their responsibilities. Marriage should not diminish the civil capacity of married women since the Code states[184] that "being underage, having dementia or imbecility, being a deaf mute, profligacy and civil action are the only restrictions of legal status." And so, matrimony is not included among the causes for the diminished capabilities that women suffer in general, but which are accentuated for married women, turning them into "eternal minors."

The spirit of our laws has favored equality. The *Novísima Recopilación*[185]says that the law is the same for men as well as women of whatever age they may be or the status [they may have]. The Constitution that consecrates men's rights, that admirable Constitution, a flower of peace and good sense, watered with noble blood and scented by great spirits, gives guarantees to citizens with complete disregard to gender. To create a fair system of law, it would be enough to observe this Constitution. Transgressions and misinterpretations of the spirit of the Constitution are the cause of the proliferation of regulations that get embroiled in complicated legislation. It is already known that [having] many laws in a nation is like having many doctors at the foot of a sick person's bed: it is an indication of a gravely ill social state.

Customs are also at odds with the Code's regulations, which grant greater rights to single women and widows than to married

---

184   Author's note: Article 32.
185   See chapter 3, note 58.

women. On the other hand, married women enjoy greater freedom in their social lives. Marriage is like a rise in social standing and women gain more freedom in their habits. Society is more lenient with and tolerant of a married woman whose morality is questionable than with young unmarried women. It even seems that marriage erases the mistakes of the past and restores honor in many cases.

But the Code closes the door on this apparent freedom. A married woman, whose praises are sung in this sweet litany — "Chaste wife, loving Mother, Model of virtue," etc., etc., etc. — is more disadvantaged by the laws than women of ill-repute who stay single. The majority of marriages in Spain have suffered from two people getting married without knowing each other. The education of young girls is zealously guarded. Coeducation does not exist, nor is there contact with men — girls are taught to see them as enemies who must be feared and deceived. They arrive at marriage without knowing men. As far as men are concerned, their unsociable nature makes them avoid dealing with women, and they do not learn to understand feminine nature either. Engagements tend to be brief and lack intimacy. Even if an engagement is long, the couple does not learn about each other's temperaments and tastes. A woman gets married to make her future secure. Until recently, it was said that women "have no other careers than marriage." A man gets married for the comfort of having his house, his wife, his domestic service and social representation. It is usually said that "It [getting married] is something that must be done."

Generally speaking, people get married too young. Nearly all countries require engaged couples to be older than in Spain. The Swiss cantons of Berne and Vaud, as well as the countries of Holland, Portugal and Germany, require men to be eighteen and women sixteen in order to marry; in Sweden men must be twenty-one and women fifteen. Even in India a law has been enacted that does not allow women younger than fourteen and sixteen years old to marry, nor does it allow disproportionate marriages in which the man is more than twenty years older than the woman. Only Italy and Spain do not require men to be older than fourteen and women older than twelve, an age at which there cannot be the discernment necessary to make such a transcendental and indissoluble contract. Nietzche said, "The age of marriage arrives before the age of loving one another." This gives one the impression that women are betting their happiness on the toss of a coin. Everything depends on them discovering "by chance" the companion that suits them. Nevertheless, there are those who think that a couple should marry at a young age, for the good of the race and morality, because their characters will not yet be formed, they will have no ingrained habits, and they will adapt better to each other.

Another problem is that matrimony is not preceded by a medical report that reveals any defects that put the descendants, and the spouses themselves, at risk. A distinguished woman doctor maintains that this type of examination would be immoral and that in some cases would make lovers fearful of losing their happiness, when faced with illnesses that can be cured, to commit suicide. This possibility should not preclude examinations. The cure should precede the marriage, and in any case, suicide would be preferable to the crime that an infected husband would be committing against his offspring. With regard to such a delicate matter, between the abstention of the State and prohibition, we could follow a middle path, such as the one followed when parents deny permission or advice. A period of time that allows for reflection. Surely couples who truly love each other would more easily renounce a harmful marriage than those who are dragged into it in a fever of desire. In any case, there should be no deception on the part of the other spouse.

From the start wives are at a disadvantage. To begin with, if a woman marries a foreigner she loses her citizenship. It is curious that if her husband is English or North American, the wife stays "stateless" until taking the nationality of her husband, since in those countries women do not lose their citizenship when they marry, nor does a foreign woman gain citizenship by the mere act of marriage. Our Code[186] says: "A married woman maintains the citizenship of her husband. A Spanish woman who marries a foreigner will regain her Spanish citizenship, if the marriage is dissolved, by returning to the Kingdom [Spain] and declaring this to be her will before the manager of the Civil Register of the location of her choosing, so that there is a relevant entry, and by renouncing the protection of the flag of the other country." That does not happen in the United States, where the "Cable Act" gives women the right to defend their citizenship.[187] The Act, signed by President Harding in 1922, stipulates that any American woman who is the wife of a foreigner will not lose her citizenship, unless she renounces it in a court of law. A foreign woman married to a North American must be naturalized in her husband's country if she wants U.S. citizenship.

186　Author's note: Article 22, 1ˢᵗ book.

187　Actually, the Cable Act had the opposite intent for certain nationalities. It denied U.S. citizenship to any American Caucasian woman who married a Chinese, Japanese or Philippine man, since they were not considered to be eligible for naturalization. It was repealed in 1936.

Think of the difference that exists between Spanish and American women when it comes to having recourse to courts of law. The former cannot seek protection from their Spanish ambassadors or consuls so they can uphold their rights, while the latter do have recourse to theirs and are protected by their laws. The fact that, after marrying, women have to suffer whatever changes of citizenship their husbands please, without their will being taken into account, is also unreasonable. In order for a husband to change his citizenship, he should be obligated to get his wife's permission and the same goes for when he avails himself of the jurisdiction of another region. The distinguished legal scholar Don Ángel Ossorio[188] describes the case of a Castilian who was able to cheat his wife out of their shared possessions by the mere act of living for two years in Catalonia and declaring his intention to be a Catalan before a judge, without honoring the laws under whose protection the marriage took place.

Additionally, women follow the social position of their husbands in everything, according to a precedent in the Partidas,[189] that stated, "Women have the honors and positions of their husbands and because of them [the husbands], so even a commoner who marries a king or count should be called queen or countess," and women even continue to suffer the penal consequences of their husbands' actions, because they also stipulate: "the wife of a traitor should be exiled from the Kingdom because of the treason of her husband." The Civil Code[190] states that women enjoy the honors that their husbands receive, except for those that are strictly and exclusively personal, as long as they do not contract a new marriage. So, women assume the noble title of their husbands: countess, duchess, etcetera, but they do not take on the husbands' positions: general, cabinet minister, etcetera. It is also customary for men to use the titles of their wives.

In Spain, women retain their maiden names and add a "de"[191] that expresses that they belong to their husbands. So, for example, when Doña Juana Pérez Martínez marries Don Pedro Sánchez Rodríguez, she becomes Juana Pérez de Sánchez. But in no instance does the husband become Pedro Sánchez de Pérez. He keeps his entire personality, while she is an object that belongs to him. She is marked

---

188 Ossorio (1873-1946) was a lawyer and politician, member of the Conservative Party, mayor of Barcelona in 1909, an Economic Minister in 1917, and was elected to Parliament in 1931.

189 See chapter 3, note 57.

190 Author's note: Article 64.

191 In this sense, "de" is the Spanish preposition that indicates possession, lit. "of."

with her husband's name, just like his handkerchief or his sheep. In France this is taken even further—women take both the first and last names of their husbands. When Mlle. Adele Lasarte marries M. Adolfo Charles, she becomes Madame Adolfo Charles. Nevertheless, there have been cases there in which men assume their wives' last names. When Ines de Sully married Guillaume de Champagne, he adopted the Sully name and coat of arms.

The Bourbons also have a last name that was transferred from a woman, Beatrice of Burgundy, who gave to her husband the Bourbon Barony. Assuming the husbands' last names has caused men and their families to think that they are authorized to more zealously control their wives' behavior, in order to uphold the integrity of their names.

In divorce, the husband maximizes the penalties against the one who "takes his name and who he does not want to dishonor it." There have been lawsuits brought when a woman has continued to use her husband's last name when a divorce petition has been started but the divorce has yet to be granted, until she takes back her maiden name once the divorce has been granted. There was a case in France in which the woman made her husband's name famous through her art and losing it was prejudicial to her. In Spain, distinguished women have used only their own names as signatures: Avellaneda,[192] Pardo Bazán,[193] etc. There have also been cases of women who have exploited their husbands' distinguished names in order to get a contract for the stage, not because of their talent, but rather due to the mercantilism of impresarios who wished to benefit from the scandal.

In Spain, filiation is always paternal. There are nations in which it is maternal, as in Portugal, where in addition to this, an anarchy of last names rules, since anyone can arbitrarily use the first or last name of their father or their mother.[194] The Code establishes that spouses are required to live together and "that women are obligated to follow their husbands wherever they decide to take up residence." The only condition made is that "the Courts can exempt women from this requirement when their husbands move overseas or to a foreign country." When under the protection of these regulations a husband is abusive but does not perform an action which the law

---

192 Gertrudis Gómez de Avellaneda (1814 – 1873) was a Cuban Romantic poetic and writer who gained great fame in Spain.

193 Emilia Pardo Bazán (1852 – 1921) was an important Spanish novelist, short story writer, literary critic, journalist and university professor.

194 In Spain, the first surnames of both the father and the mother are the only ones that a child inherits.

considers to be sufficient motive for divorce, his wife has no means to liberate herself. The husband chooses the house of his liking, in the place that he wants, he furnishes it according to his own whims, sets up the household management as he sees fit, and imposes the company whom he pleases on his wife.

In one case, relatives of a husband who were jealous of his wife tormented her to such a degree that the poor woman escaped and took refuge at her parents' house. The husband protested and the Courts forced his wife to return to the conjugal domicile. Getting along poorly with the husband's family is not a cause for divorce, and the wife is obligated to live with them. In another case the husband was opposed to letting his wife's parents, friends and brothers and sisters come into his house and he prohibited his wife from going to see them and writing to them. He kept watch on her and kept her as a kind of kidnap victim. The desperate woman escaped, but the law forced her to return to her domicile.

The law stipulates that husbands have the right to see their wives' correspondence, that letters and telegrams sent to husbands' post office boxes or homes should be delivered to them, and that husbands can intercept anything their wives write. In one of these cases, at the Public Hearing of Nimes, it was decided that husbands had the right to intercept the letters that their wives wrote to their parents if they believed that the parents could exert a negative influence on their daughters' attitudes and disturb the peace of the marriage. Husbands are granted the right to keep watch on their wives and to prohibit any relationships that are not of their liking. Imagine a husband trying to exert this right when his wife is a doctor or a lawyer and he wants to keep an eye on her in her clinic or office.

And this continuous vexation, this disguised slavery, this hidden martyrdom, this clash of characters that is a torment day and night, is not legally considered to be a motive for divorce. For married women to take a trip they need permission from their husbands to obtain a passport. On the other hand, husbands can go abroad and abandon their families without the wife even knowing and without encountering any legal difficulties in getting their passports. Women constantly protest against this irritating difference established in the Code, which states:[195] "the husband must protect his wife and she must obey her husband."

In this way women are placed in a situation of obedience

---

195   Author's note: Article 57.

and servitude within the home, which, among other things, has the disadvantage that the children see their mothers as inferior, and by extension, all other women as well, thus growing up with injustice and lack of respect for women. In this situation women cannot be good citizens in the full sense of the term, nor create dignified, happy homes. The moral principle of every domestic or political administration results in there being no legitimate authority, if it is not a beneficent, fair and egalitarian instrument. The words of absolute monarchy cannot be parodied within the family. Husbands say "I am the State" and "I am the Home," as they tend to do when smugly stating, "In my house there is no master but me," or more crudely, as if wives deserved no courtesy, "I'm the one who wears the pants around here."

When discussing in the Spanish press whether the inequality of this article of the Code should disappear, the same thing has happened as with all controversies—there is always more invention than serious arguments. Some say that if the Code did not mandate that women be protected, husbands would mistreat them more. But what we are attempting to do is establish equality and situations of mutual support, because at present, as Mr. Os[s]orio says with true irony, "When one spouse—the husband—holds the purse strings, the other—the wife—can only hold out her hand like a beggar and can give little help."

Recently, the Anglican episcopate has abolished wives' promise to be submissive, in the knowledge that only compromise can save ancient institutions. With respect to fidelity, our Codes favor men to such an extent that the phrase "law of the funnel" is inspired by them, in the sense that the narrow part always goes to women. Without permission from their husbands women can appear in court neither for themselves nor through an attorney. They can only do without their husbands' permission to defend themselves in a criminal court or to sue or defend themselves in a lawsuit with their husbands, as stipulated by the law of civil trial. Without the permission of their husbands, neither can they purchase for gainful purpose or good and valuable consideration, transfer their assets nor bind themselves. All actions that married women implement are null and void, and even though only husbands and their heirs have the right to appeal those actions, since their insolvency is well known, no one dares to make any kind of contract with married women, neither renting a house to them nor making any sale to them. Only the purchases made of things that by their nature are meant for a family's daily consumption are valid. The purchase of jewelry, furniture and valuable items purchased without the husband's permission are only valid when he has granted the use and enjoyment of them to his wife.

The only thing women can do without the permission of their husbands is give testimony and exercise their rights, or fulfill the responsibilities that they have with regard to their legitimate children, or the natural children they may have had with another man,[196] and with regard to the assets of those children. In the case of adoption, both spouses have the same rights. Neither one can adopt without the permission of the other—both of them must do this jointly. The husband is the head of the conjugal partnership, even if he is a fourteen-year-old boy and his wife is thirty. It is preferred for such husbands to have guardians rather than to allow their wives to manage the household. When young husbands turn eighteen they no longer require guardianship, but until they reach adulthood they cannot accumulate debts or mortgage real estate. They can do this when they reach adulthood. Women never reach adulthood.

Here is a case that proves that it is not because women are considered incapable that they do not manage households. If the husband is under the penalty of civil interdiction or is declared to be prodigal[197] overnight, the wife becomes the head of the household. When her husband dies his wife, who the day before was unqualified to manage the household, now finds that she has the full right to do so. If a husband is found to have abandoned the home, his wife also has full rights with regard to their property[198] and children. A wife can also act as the guardian of an insane husband if they are not legally separated. Madam Oddo Deflon[199] rightly states, "Notice the immorality of some laws, which sentence women to fulfill their hopes only when their husbands die or go crazy."

Couples who are engaged to be married can sign nuptial agreements regarding the conditions of the conjugal partnership in relation to their assets. After the marriage has been performed the

---

196 See chapter 3, note 56.

197 Civil interdiction is placed upon someone who proves to be incapable of administering their estate, e.g., due to mental incapacity. Someone is declared to be prodigal if they waste their assets, thus proving themselves to be incapable of managing them. A curator is appointed for them by the court.

198 Author's note: She may not sell, trade or mortgage her property without legal authorization.

199 Mme. Oddo Deflon was the secretary of the legal section of the Women's National Council of France who criticized the Code Napoléon, which left wives no control over their property, thus ruining many families.

contract cannot be altered. Gifts on account of the marriage must be given before it is performed, cannot exceed ten percent of the value of the property held, and are no longer revocable after the marriage is performed. Donations given between husbands and wives are null and void unless they are the gifts that are customarily given on saints' days,[200] birthdays, etc. Neither can either spouse make donations to the other one's children nor to anyone who may be a presumptive heir. Since married women have no control of their property, they cannot make donations or post bonds. Without the permission of their husbands, they cannot accept them either. The Laws of the Partidas stipulated, "Women are naturally covetous and avaricious and it is never assumed that they will make donations." So it is that the Partidas do not even deal with women's donations.

Nuptial agreements tend to protect wives' interests, but a seed of discord always appears within them for the home that is being established. If her generosity prompts a wife not to make any stipulations, she usually has something to regret. For that reason, instead of nuptial agreements there should be a joint regulation: "All married women shall have ownership and oversight of their property and the fruits of their labor." In marriage, the most common arrangement has been that of community property. But this co-ownership has existed in name only, since women have nothing available to them, not even their day's pay, and husbands are the ones who control their joint property, which they can squander as they please. It is a system with a deceptive name that sacrifices the interests of women to the whims of men.

Ascollas says, "Community property is the greatest swindle that exists in the law. It is abusive and deceptive, and within the system women contribute all that they own and all that constitutes joint funds and they have nothing available to them without the authorization of their husbands, whom they enrich, sometimes while they end up deprived and in ruin." Without a contract, it is understood that the marriage is arranged under a social system of shared possessions, which begins with the marriage and only ends when it is dissolved. When separating the personal property of each spouse, those that may serve to increase their fortune, because of the industriousness, work or salary of either one of the two, are considered to be shared possessions. Husbands can dispose of the couple's property and legally bind it for good and valuable

---

200   Traditionally in Spain, the day of the saint a person was named after was widely celebrated, considered to be more important than a birthday.

consideration without their wives' consent, but the latter cannot do this without their husbands' consent. So, when the Code says that property of an arrangement of shared possessions is to pay for the debts and obligations of both spouses, it should be understood this only pertains to the husband's property, since women cannot owe money or bind themselves to any obligation.

In marriages between Spaniards and foreigners, if the husband is Spanish nothing relative to property is stipulated; it is assumed that the couple is marrying under the joint property arrangement. If the husband is a foreigner, the couple is married under the system of joint rights of the country of his citizenship, without affecting what the Code stipulates with regard to real estate. Sales of property between a husband and wife are not allowed unless they are married under the arrangement of separation of property. This was the first step for updating the institution of marriage.

Co-ownership derives from Germanic law. Ancient legislators were inspired by the idea that spouses "should live on the same bread and eat from the same pot." If this were true and in marriage there were "a single purse and a single heart," all regulations would be good, but experience teaches that men are the ones who eat all the bread and all the contents of the pot when they take control of the purse without any concern for the heart. "Earnest money and dowries" also tend to guarantee the property of women, whose situations are known to be precarious. This institution has gone through many stages throughout history and sometimes husbands have used it as if they were purchasing their wives, and other times wives have used it as if they were purchasing their husbands.

So it is that even in modern times the dowry has had many detractors. Monsieur Lintilhac[201] said that "it demeans husbands and corrupts wives." Madame Marsy, the president of the Ladies' Club, said that the dowry is a "humiliating custom for women." In ancient times, on the other hand, it was believed to be humiliating for men. Plautus[202] said, "No dowries. Women suffocate you with dowries. They sell you for a dowry." The Goncourt brothers[203] condemned the dowry system, which turns marriage into a business agreement. They said, "Parents hand over their daughter's body, health and well-being

---

201 Eugène Lintilhac (1854 – 1920) was a French educator and politician.

202 Titus Maccius Plautus (c. 254 B.C.E. – 184 B.C.E.) was a Roman playwright of the Old Latin period.

203 Edmond de Goncourt (1822 – 96) and Jules de Goncourt (1830 – 70) were French naturalist writers who wrote all of their work together.

to a husband without reservation. They only insure her wealth." We know that dowries are the assets that women contribute at the time a marriage is arranged and those received during the marriage through donations or inheritances of a dowry-like nature. Authorities or those outside the family can set up dowries before or after the marriage. Husbands can only set them up afterwards.

Parents have the obligation of providing their legitimate children with half their expected inheritance, except if they marry without consent before reaching legal age. But this regulation is easily evaded because investigating the parents' fortune is prohibited. Additionally, parents have the right to pay their daughters a yearly income in place of a dowry. In the case of an "estimated dowry" husbands are required to return the amount, guaranteeing it with a mortgage. In the case of an "unestimated dowry"[204] husbands are required to return the same assets and objects that they have received, if these are not fungible.[205] Husbands administer and enjoy the usufruct[206] of the property that makes up a not estimated dowry and are not required to give financial backing to the joint usufructuaries. With the consent of their wives, men can transfer property in order to invest the amount in securities that are equally as safe. But if by some accident husbands do not proceed in this way, they are not responsible for anything. They return real estate however it is left, and if they have transferred the property, they return the price of sale or…nothing.

With the permission of their husbands, women can encumber or transfer property from an unestimated dowry. This is in response to the normal family expenses that are the result of the wives' actions or resulting from their orders with their husbands' indulgence. It is easy to appreciate what scant protection the dowry system gives women. The only advantage is that during a husband's bankruptcy proceeding she enjoys the preferential right to recover her dowry. Don Ángel Os[s]orio says, "In all honesty and provided there are

---

204 In the Spanish Civil Code, article 1346, the dowry could be either estimated or not. In the former case, the property of which it consisted was appraised, and when the ownership was transferred to the husband, he was obligated to return its value. In the case of the latter type, the wife retained ownership of the property, whether appraised or not, and the husband was bound to return the same property.

205 These are the types of things that, due to their nature, can be exchanged or substituted for something equivalent.

206 This is the temporary right to make use of and derive profit from a possession one does not own, such as property, without causing damage to it or changing its substance.

no unusual limitations, husbands can do whatever they see fit with their wives' dowries, because though husbands are prohibited from making some transfers without their wives' consent, we all know how wives' freedom is limited when they are dealing with violent husbands who are capable of terrifying them with threats directed at them or their children."

He adds, "It is certain that husbands are required to guarantee their wives' dowries by mortgaging their property. But this is…when they have estates. If they do not have estates, since the law does not require other types of guarantees, husbands hide behind the saying 'the King sets free the man who has nothing,' and they can ruin their wives with impunity. Legal experts may say that it is possible to avoid this with such and such an article. I, on the other hand, could cite millions of cases in which husbands have used up their wives' dowries, leaving them destitute, in spite of all the articles and Codes."

Paraphernal assets,[207] which do not form part of the dowry that women bring to the marriage, have a better guarantee. The law says that women retain the right to administer and control these assets, but in reality, they form part of the jointly held assets of the conjugal partnership, and the profits derived from them are subject to being used to pay the couple's debts. This provides the benefit that husbands' obligations outside the family cannot be fulfilled using those assets, unless they can prove that this will result in a benefit for the family, something that can be proven through any number of subterfuges. Husbands have the right to deposit or invest paraphernal assets so that it becomes impossible to transfer or use them as security without their consent, since without their husbands' permission or a court order, women cannot encumber, transfer or mortgage their paraphernal assets, nor can they litigate concerning them. And so, the statement that women retain their right to administer and control these assets turns out to be completely false.

Moreover, there is the contradiction that in order for women to acquire property, even if it is through inheritance, they need the permission of their husbands. And if a husband denies his consent, a judge will not authorize the acquisition without extremely long and costly proceedings in a divorce suit carried out through annulment, which is worse and more expensive than a civil trial. But the cruelest, most outrageous and least comprehensible thing is that if a wife is given a favorable ruling against her husband that results in his

---

207 This is property acquired before the marriage over which a wife (or a husband) has complete control.

insolvency—which happens frequently—the wife is obligated to pay the costs for the man who always acted in bad faith, doing as much harm as he could to her. This is explained in the Code with the absurd name of "court costs."

The Literary Property Law of 1847, renamed the Literary Copyright Law in 1879, granted women authors and translators the same rights that their male counterparts enjoy. This is a recognition sanctioned by all prior analogous laws, with the exception of the civil marriage law of 1870, which established that women may not publish writings, scientific or literary works for which they are the authors or translators without the permission of their husbands or relevant authority, if there is no husband. This restriction was lifted by the present Code, but husbands are still the owners of their wives' writings.

Working women need the authorization of their husbands to be able to work. Actresses cannot sign a contract without their husbands' consent, since the latter can prevent them from acting. There was the case of the actress who was working to earn a living for herself and her family whose husband shot her to death while she was onstage. He was acquitted by the court. There is no lack of people who have reacted against this type of thing by trying to value women's work in the home. But far from emancipating women, this is the recognition that wives are slaves to whom husbands would have the right to say, "Serve me, since I pay you." It is an immoral principle.

Local laws, which are born of custom, are more favorable to the defense of women and are in force in some of our provinces such as Aragon, Catalonia, Biscay and the Balearic Islands, but none of them goes so far as to completely emancipate women. There are places in Spain where customs rather than laws prevail, and where some primitive customs are preserved that prove that the family has lost in purity what the marriage may have gained through laws and official regulations. There are towns in Galicia and Asturias where children continue living with their parents in the same house, even though they are married. The father is the administrator and head of the household and the children work. And so, the father dies, and the siblings separate, each one taking their own belongings. In Valencia de Don Juan and in Sahagun it is customary for husbands and wives to each spend the day at their parents' houses and to rejoin each other at night. The parents share their property with the children that help them.

It seems that married women merchants have more freedom, but this is not so. They may only work in the profession with *the authorization of their husbands,* recorded in a public instrument, which is then inscribed in the Trade Register. It is presumed that women are authorized to do business when they work in the profession with their husbands' knowledge. If her husband is not opposed to it, when a business woman gets married she may continue doing business as legally authorized by him. As we see, married women are not at liberty to do business, since they need the *express* permission of their husbands or the *tacit* permission that their tolerance implies. If a husband wishes for his wife to cease practicing her business at such a time as it is flourishing the most, he has the right to withdraw his authorization and to revoke the public instrument granted to her, without needing to give any reason whatsoever. The Trade Register enters and registers this decision and it is advertised in the official papers and announced to the correspondents by way of letters. Naturally, revoking this permission does not jeopardize the rights obtained by the people who did business with the woman before her husband's decision is published. But the woman must resign herself to abandoning her profession, which at times means her ruination and that of her children.

While a woman is involved in commerce, with the *essential* permission of her husband, the assets from her dowry, her paraphernal assets and all the assets and property rights that the married couple have are subject to her commercial obligations. That is, the woman may sell or mortgage her own assets as well as jointly held property. If the husband's authorization is extended to the assets that belong to him, the wife can also transfer or mortgage them. A married woman above the age of twenty-one may engage in business when she is separated from her husband by means of a final judgment of divorce, or if her husband is under guardianship for reason of wastefulness or dementia, or if he is declared to be missing or if his assets have been garnished. In these cases, the woman's own assets and those of the married couple that have accumulated as a result of the business activity are subject to her commercial obligations, since the woman is able to sell and mortgage them.

If the marriage has been made under the joint property regime, the husband and wife cannot become business partners. But they can form a partnership if they are married under the separation of property regime. Under this regime, the husband is not responsible for the obligations of his wife's business activities, and she is also protected from claims made by her husband's creditors. In the case of the regime that allows joint property of assets acquired before and during the marriage, the husband is accountable for his wife's obligations, since the benefits that she derives from her business are jointly held. But as we have already said, the husband's responsibility is as a *guarantor* and not as a *partner*. His responsibility is civil, not commercial, and he cannot be declared bankrupt.

It is easy to see how ludicrous and absurd this situation is. The husband and wife really are partners, since they share the responsibilities and earnings equally. But the Code refuses to recognize this as a partnership, since in that case both spouses would be declared to be legally equal. This would be incompatible with the exercise of marital power that article 1316 of the Civil Code always protects. A married business woman cannot enter into a partnership either, without another special authorization from her husband. And a woman does not have recourse to the Court to appeal against a decision by her husband to keep her from operating a lucrative business, nor can she ask that the judge authorize her to continue a business if her husband outrageously revokes her license and condemns her to poverty. The Code closes the door on her when it says with total clarity[208] that "the husband will be able to *freely* revoke the license that was granted."

When the separation of assets is arranged for a just cause and pursuant to a judicial ruling, the shared partnership is dissolved. But then both the husband and the wife must each attend to their own support and to that of their children, in proportion to their assets. The husband continues to manage the assets if the separation has been arranged at his request, and the wife does not have a right to subsequent shared possessions. If the separation is arranged at the wife's request, she manages the assets and it is the husband who does not have a right to the shared possessions. The nullification of the marriage has the same effect on the couple's assets as death, but the spouse who acted in bad faith will have no right to the shared possessions. It's funny that when bad faith involves both parties, *it is rewarded*.

The reconciliation of two spouses terminates the divorce decree and does not affect the ruling; but its effects persist with regard to the children if the divorce is based on the fact that one of the two threatens them physically or spiritually, endangering their lives or their virtue. We see that our law is one of the most backward ones, when we compare it with the various laws that protect women's assets and freedom. Since our customs are modeled on

---

208   Author's note: Article 8.

Roman law, we are now frightened because the customs that attempt to break the old molds are new ones. Many believe that anarchy will reign, others that this has to do with theories that corrupt. There are those who fear for the family, thinking that the home will collapse if women abandon its [four] walls. They keep repeating, as if it were an axiom, the words of Saint John Chrysostom,[209] "Business outside the home is incumbent upon the husband, and the business of the home is incumbent upon the wife. If this order is inverted or disturbed, everything is disrupted." There is even a popular saying: "A wife in the street, a home without bread."[210]

But in order to see that this concerns a phenomenon with indisputable vitality, it will suffice to take a look around and consider the examples of the nations that at this moment are evolving. The most ancient civilizations did not enslave women in this way. The bricks of Chaldea and Assyria[211] give testimony of contracts in which married, single and widowed women had their assets at their full disposal. They bought, they sold, they wrote wills, they made donations and performed all types of juridical acts without their husbands' involvement, who were neither the owners of their lives nor their assets. In one of these contracts, the woman who arranged it said that she was "in full liberty of her will." The equality of rights for the genders can be seen clearly in official documents. Queen Shammuramat countersigned all her husband's laws and the laws of Egyptian King Cheops were countersigned by his wife.

At present, in order to see women's progress with respect to the law, it suffices to look to England. Few nations have been as influenced by the Germanic spirit as it has. In common law, there was only one spouse, not two: the husband. The wife was a shadow without juridical individuality, absorbed by the husband, annihilated. But liberty has taken great leaps forward since 1868, when the pro-feminism campaign was begun, with champions such as John

---

209   Saint John Chrysostom (ca. 347-407 C.E.) was the Archbishop of Constantinople.

210   A woman's place is in the home.

211   Assyria was an ancient kingdom of Mesopotamia (in modern-day Iraq), that ruled from the 25th Century to 608 B.C.E. Chaldea was another ancient kingdom of Mesopotamia (10th Century-539 B.C.E.).

Bright,[212] R. Lowre, S. Mill[213] and Le Fevre.[214] In 1874, women gained the right to work, in 1883, the separation of assets, and today no trace of the husband's superior authority remains. Married women's freedom is complete and the English family continues to be a model.

Women in Russia are now completely free. Married women have the same rights as their husbands, and divorce is obtained through mutual consent. In the Portuguese Republic, which amended the ordinances of King Manuel and King Phillip III, and slightly amended the Code of 1867, the husband is the *manager* of the joint assets, but one spouse cannot take action without the consent of the other, nor can they sell or mortgage their joint property except through agreement together.

In order to protect working women from their husbands' pillaging, France established that "whatever may be the regime that spouses adopt, wives have the right to keep the entire sums that result from their own work without the involvement of their husbands." This is an attempt to regulate each spouse's obligations according to the analytical notion that every matrimonial regime consists of two elements: one, determination of the share that each one of the two spouses should contribute to the household expenses; the other, the legal status of the respective assets. The share that each one contributes must be set by the law, according to their earnings, as is done today in [the case of] legal separation. Each spouse must see to the management of his/her own assets and have free disposal of his/her earnings, except for the amount set aside for the common expenses for maintaining the home.

Austro-Hungary, a conservative country par excellence, turns out to be the most liberal when it comes to legislation that gives women complete freedom. The regulations regarding the ownership of the fruits of labor are recognized in almost every country, in Holland since 1907, in Luxembourg since 1887, in Denmark since 1880, and in Sweden since 1874. In Norway, husbands cannot make donations, sell or rent without the consent of their wives. In Scotland, the law gives wives control of their earnings. In Italy, women can prevent their husbands from taking control of wages and making deposits

---

212 Bright (1811-1889) was a Quaker who consistently and passionately demanded an end to social, political, or religious inequalities between individuals and between peoples. He was elected to Parliament and occupied several posts in the British government.

213 See chapter 6, note 147.

214 George Shaw-Lefevre (1831-1928) was a British politician who advocated for women's rights.

and withdrawals at the savings bank without their authorization. In Serbia women have control of their earnings and salaries.

In Germany, article 1367 of their Code considers assets that women acquire through work and industry to be theirs to keep, but article 1356 states that women are obliged to work managing the home and in their husbands' businesses, as long as such services conform to the legal situation of the spouses. So, the fruits of women's labor, placed at the disposal of their husbands, do not really belong to them. The Romanian Code reveals its Latin origin. Rumanian women are as subjugated as Spanish women.

Swiss law varies from canton to canton. In Freiberg, Berne and Aargau, husbands have absolute control. In Neuchatel, Valois/Wallis and Schaffhouse, women have the right to shared possessions. In Basel and Lucerne women can request separate property. Husbands' authority is only limited in Neuchatel, where they cannot make donations without their wives' permission.

The Argentine Republic has taken a large step forward on the road to civilization, having granted women civil rights in 1926. As far as married women are concerned—who are always the most disadvantaged—they were given equality without any haggling. Without the need for any permission whatsoever, they can practice a profession, participate in commercial enterprises or seek employment, as well as manage and have at their disposal the profits from these activities. They can also use them to acquire any type of asset that they will manage, having them at their disposal with complete freedom. Women can also be members of social organizations, business partnerships and cooperatives. They are authorized, for valuable consideration, to manage and have at their disposal their own assets and those that belong to them in the case of a legal separation. Women can also accept inheritances with the benefit of inventory, and appear in court in civil or criminal suits that affect their person, their assets or the person and assets of minor children from a previous marriage. They can be legal guardians, attesting witnesses, and can accept donations.

A wife's own assets and the profits she earns are not liable for her husband's debts, nor are his assets liable for his wife's assets. One spouse's assets and the fruits of his/her labor are only responsible for the obligations undertaken by the other one if these came about due to the necessities of the home, the education of the children, or for the purpose of keeping joint possessions. During her marriage, with court approval a wife can have access to her husband's own assets and the earnings that she manages in order to support children younger than eighteen years of age, when the husband is sentenced to two or more years of prison, and if the wife and children have no other means of support. Married women can also retain legal guardianship over their siblings and parents. Parental authority over children of an earlier marriage is not lost when one remarries. With respect to the emancipation of married women, Argentina goes to the head of all the nations of Latin America, thanks to this law.

In the United States, the freedom that customs and laws give women is well known, but Latin America still retains the stamp of Spanish law. The husband is the head of the household in almost every country, even in free Uruguay, which has such progressive laws. And with very few exceptions, the situation is the same in Bolivia, Peru, Ecuador, Costa Rica, [El] Salvador, Nicaragua, Guatemala, Venezuela, Mexico and Cuba. In Chile, women can practice a profession or participate in commercial enterprise freely, but they cannot have access to what they produce without the permission of their husbands.

There is a certain similarity between this and the situation of Muslim women in Turkey, Algiers, Tunisia and Morocco, who are physically enslaved but have freedom with regard to their assets. They have the right to have the disposal of them without anyone's permission, but they do not have the freedom of movement to exercise that right. Something similar also happens to Japanese women, whose situation is analogous to that of Spanish women, although [the former] are more subjugated physically.

At this time, we Spanish women are demanding the reform of the Civil Code with unusual unanimity. In January of 1927, as president of the International League of Spanish and Hispano-American Women and the Spanish Women's Crusade, I presented a petition to the president of the Commission of the Civil Code in which we called for equality of civil rights, demanding that the articles that are prejudicial to Spanish women within the society and the family must be reformed. We repeated the demands that we had already presented to Congress in 1921. Here are the demands that are related to married women:

- "Amendment of article 22, by which women lose citizenship when they marry a foreigner. Women should not cease to be Spaniards except in cases in which they request it, since the motherland cannot abandon in this way the protection or sanction that as a farsighted mother she is obligated to exert over all her children."
- "Elimination of article 57, which states: 'The husband must

protect his wife, and the wife must obey her husband.' This inequality within the home is in contradiction with the spirit of orthodoxy, since the formula of the canonical marriage is 'Husbands, love your wives, even as Christ also loved the church.' In regard to these mutual obligations in marriage, only the immediately preceding article, num. 56, should remain, in this way: 'Spouses are obligated to remain faithful to each other and to help one another.'"

- "To article 58, which deals with a wife's obligation to follow her husband wherever he may establish residency, should be added these additional limitations to the rule: 'The wife can maintain her own residence when her husband does not have a known domicile or when he is suffering from a contagious disease, or [if] the wife's reputation is at serious risk in the conjugal home, or [if] the preservation and prosperity of the wife's assets is seriously threatened by [their] living together.'"

- "Article 60 and those that follow should be amended in such a way that allows wives to appear in court without their husbands' authorization, and enjoy all the rights that their husbands do for the same purposes—serving as a witness, posting bail, etc. Likewise, all articles that refer to *paternal authority* and are prejudicial to mothers if they do not figure into that authority should be amended. Judges or the Family Council[215] should be charged with resolving conflicts in cases where there is disagreement."

- "In book II, which deals with 'assets, property and their modifications,' necessary regulations should be established so that, no matter what type of marriage a woman enters into, she exercises the same prerogatives as her husband and, therefore, is able to enter into contracts, buy, sell, etc., and have full control of the product of her labor, for which she should receive the same pay as her husband for equal work. Happiness cannot reside in any home that is not based on equality, nor can the purposes of the marriage union, with all their greatness, be realized."

---

215 This is a legally appointed group of family members charged with protecting the rights a minor or a handicapped adult, especially when s/he is orphaned. This council also makes sure that the child's guardian or parent is performing his/her duties.

Chapter 8
Divorce

Indissolubility of marriage. –Adultery. –Various ways of considering it. –Article 438. –The new Russian matrimonial code. –Divorce. –Opinions on divorce in Spain.

The two great evils of marriage are the subordination of the wife and its indissolubility. In the same way as marriage has a reason for being in nature, so does divorce. Once life has demonstrated that love is not always eternal, we should not be adamant that marriage be forever binding. It is this permanent nature of marriage that gives rise to adultery.

The Civil Code, when dealing with the causes of divorce, says that these are due to: "1. adultery by the wife in *all cases*, and by the husband when it results in public scandal or disgrace of the wife."[216] The inequality already evident here is amplified in the Penal Code where the definition of adultery does not include the husband, but only the wife and her accomplice. The law states: "The married woman who lies with a man who is not her husband commits adultery, as does he who lies with her knowing she is married."[217] Later, this same article, when establishing the punishment, states: "Adultery will be punished with time to be served in a correctional facility, in medium and maximum degrees". But, since adultery is never a *misdeed* of the husband, but rather the *crime* of the wife, the law does not provide for anything with respect to him except in the case that: "the husband houses a concubine within the conjugal home, or outside of it behaves scandalously with his concubine; in this case he will be punished with time to be served in a correctional facility in minimum and medium degrees." The husband's *misdeed*, as one can see, is not deemed *adultery* in the Code, but rather *having a concubine*. Adultery is committed solely by the wife and her accomplice, the latter only if he knows she is married. What is curious is that if the accomplice is also married, he is not punished for *the misdeed* he commits against his wife, but rather for *the adultery* that harms the husband of his lover. A husband is never disciplined if he is skillful

---

216 Author's note: Article 105, section 4, title IV.
217 Author's note: Article 448, chapter 1, title IX.

at varying his lovers, because it is not the infidelity that is punished, rather the concubinage that is scandalous. What is desired is that it not leak out into society; the wife's suffering due to the misbehavior of the husband does not matter. What the law attempts to save, by maintaining marital authority, is hypocritical.

The Partidas[218] already established that the wife could only be accused of adultery by the husband with the following exception: "if the husband were negligent and she persistent in her immorality, then, her father could accuse her, then her brother, her uncle and, in the final instance, the other residents of the town."[219] The statute of limitations for accusing an adulterous woman was five years. Then the law proved itself more benevolent with the woman than with her accomplice, since it established the death penalty for him, but for her only a sentence of lashes, imprisonment in a convent, and the loss of her dowry. If the husband surprised her in flagrante, he could kill her accomplice, but not her; she had to be turned over to the authorities. On the other hand, a father could kill his adulterous daughter, as long as he also killed her accomplice when he surprised them in flagrante.

The Fuero Real[220] instituted some curious peculiarities in this respect. In this code, illicit relations between family members and in-laws, or the marriage of a guardian or his son to the orphan placed in his charge are also considered adultery. The accusation of the delinquents, in this instance, was public; but if it had to do with a married woman, only her husband could accuse her. In the case that the woman could prove that her husband committed adultery before she did, she could not be pursued by the authorities. The law placed the adulterous pair at the offended husband's disposal, he also inherited all property belonging to them, and had the right to kill both, but could not kill one without the other. The same Royal Forum resolved that the married woman who committed adultery "should be placed under the power of her husband along with the adulterous male." The husband could not kill them, but, rather, use them as servants.

---

218 See chapter 3, note 57.

219 Author's note: Law 2ª, title XVII, Partida 7ª

220 The Fuero Real was also written by order of Alphonse X. It is believed to have been completed toward the end of 1254 or 1255. It contains 550 laws that establish the norms for peaceful coexistence in the land, and define what is a crime and how it should be punished.

The Law of Ordenamiento de Alcalá[221] generalized the Fuero de Segovia[222] that established that an adulterous pair caught in flagrante should be subject to the death sentence, which should be carried out by the offended husband, against *both* lovers. These laws were passed on to Nueva and the Novísima Recopilación.[223]

The Laws of Toro[224] deny any excuse for adultery on the part of the wife, and ratify the right the husband has of killing the adulterers in flagrante, but it disallows his appropriating the dowry or any property. Additionally, the finding of adultery is to be settled by a court of law. The husband cannot accuse only one of the adulterers of the crime; he must accuse both or neither.

The Foral Legislation[225] established some advantages for the wife. She could only be accused of adultery by a husband who had not committed the same crime previously, and who, after knowing of her infidelity, had not shared his bed or table with her – since this would be interpreted as consent of or tacit pardon for the act. These laws deny the husband the right to kill one of the adulterers, but maintain it if he exercises it against both.

Our Penal Code preserves some of these benefits. Only the husband can seek punishment for a wife's adultery, and, at any time, with his pardon, the punishment to which the guilty party has been sentenced can be rescinded. In this case, her accomplice's sentence shall also be revoked. But the Penal Code does not treat both spouses equally in their offenses or in their punishments, and it also includes the shameful Article 438, which preserves the right to kill; it states: "The husband who catches his wife committing adultery, and kills her or her lover in the act or causes them grave harm, shall be penalized with exile. If he should cause them lesions of a lesser kind, he will be exempt from punishment. These rules are applicable as well to fathers who find themselves in the same circumstances with regard

---

221 This was promulgated by Alphonse XI in 1348. Its principal importance lies in the hierarchical order it established among the various legal codes: first in importance are the laws contained in the Ordenamiento; next, were the local laws (or Fueros), then the Siete Partidas, and finally, a consultation with the King. This hierarchy was in effect until the XIX Century.

222 Sancho VI granted Segovia its laws in 1293.

223 See chapter 3, note 58.

224 This was another attempt, ordered by Isabella I, to resolve the legislative anarchy of the reign. They consisted of 81 laws. Author's note: Number 81.

225 These were a series of laws that hark back to medieval times and could be municipal or regional. Their purpose was to regulate daily life in an area and establish a set of norms, rights and privileges granted by the king, the lord of the land or the municipal council.

to a daughter who is younger than 23 years old, as long as she lives in the paternal home, and her corruptor. Those who have promoted or facilitated the prostitution of their wives or daughters may not benefit from what is stipulated in this article."[226]

We might consider the following as attenuating circumstances: a husband who commits a murder when he suddenly realizes, with the discovery of the guilty couple, an unsuspected treason, and acts on impulse without time to reflect. But in almost all cases, the husband suspects first, spies, gathers evidence, and, instead of going to the authorities, allows himself to be carried away by rage, and commits a true murder with premeditation. He is a common criminal who should not be absolved.

There are those who say that if we are to accept the right of the husband to kill the unfaithful wife, we should also recognize that of the wife to act in the same way and kill the adulterous husband and her rival. But this is not what women want, rather they wish for the revocation of that appalling article for both wife and husband.[227] Recently, some juries in France and America have absolved women who killed their unfaithful husbands. In Brazil, a jury absolved Mrs. America Araujo Penque, who exercised her right to kill her husband when she caught him in flagrante.

Great thinkers have considered the husband's adultery to be equally as grave as the wife's. The laws of the people of Israel, who were not monogamous, forbade men to commit saying: "Thou shalt not covet thy neighbor's house; thou shalt not covet thy neighbor's wife, nor his manservant, nor his maidservant, nor his ox, nor his ass, nor any thing that is thy neighbor's."[228] It is clear that this prohibition has more to do with the right to property than with morality.

Christ was not severe with the adulterous woman: "I do not condemn you," he said, and speaking to her accusers, he added, "Let him who is without sin among you be the first to throw a stone at her."[229] And when he saw that they all moved away without daring to punish her, he exclaimed: "go, and from now on sin no more."

Seneca[230] states that conjugal fidelity is an equal duty for both spouses; he finds it shameful that a man who requires virtue on the

---

226   Author's note: chapter XIII, title XIII.

227   Author's note: The author has published a novel on this theme, titled *El Articulo 438.*

228   Tenth Commandment. Exodus 20:17.

229   John 8.

230   Lucius Annaeus Seneca, a writer on rhetoric, was born about 55 BCE in Cordoba. His work is considered to be a very valuable source for the literary history of the early Roman Empire.

part of his wife can corrupt the wife of another. He asserts that the status of women can represent either the health or death of the State. Cicero[231] in his *Republic* declares himself in favor of the civic equality of women and condemns the Vocanian Law[232] made for men. Saint Augustine[233] has said that a husband's adultery is always worse than the wife's, and Saint Francis speaks of the monstrosity that paganism committed allowing the slavery of women at the same time that it condemned adultery. Alfred Naquet,[234] that apostle of human rights who wrote France's divorce law and was able to pass it, altruistically fighting for it most of his life —altruistically, since he never wished to reap its rewards—, declared: «There should be absolute equality between both adulteries».

Felix Faure[235] speaks for those who argue that a woman's adultery may introduce an illegitimate child into the home, as he said: "Female adultery may allow entry into the legitimate family of a being that does not belong to the one who, according to the law, is considered his father." But Marat[236] had already answered this in advance: "Is it not the same for society that a man should take his heir to his neighbor's house and that a woman should receive him in hers?" It is an incontrovertible logic that takes us to natural law: man must deny himself that which he does not wish to suffer. Those who desire others to respect their home must begin by respecting those of others; to maintain the theory of two different ethics is to seek that the weakest woman be the only victim of the immorality of the couple.

Some codes affirm equality in the treatment of adultery for husband and wife. They establish identical attenuating circumstances for both, in the case of harm, in fragante delicto, etc. Germany, Hungary and several Swiss cantons do not consider adultery to be a crime, but rather a cause for separation or divorce. In England and

---

231   Marcus Tulius Cicero, a leading figure of the Roman Bar, was born in 106 BCE. His Republic discusses the best forms of government, and favors a combination of monarchy, oligarchy and democracy.

232   This was a Roman law from 169 BCE which declared that no woman could be heiress to an estate.

233   St. Augustine (354-430 CE) saw Christianity as a 'Divine Philosophy', a wisdom guaranteed by authority by explored through reason.

234   Joseph Alfred Naquet (1834-1916) was a physician, professor of chemistry and very liberal politician who succeeded in passing the divorce laws through the French Senate.

235   Félix François Faure (30 January 1841 – 16 February 1899) was President of France from 1895 until his death.

236   Jean Paul Marat (1743-1793), French physician and, later, revolutionary leader, who was well-acquainted with English, French, German, Italian and Spanish philosophers.

the state of New York, penal laws do not mention adultery. It is a private matter that can only be considered the basis for divorce. In the Caucasus, there is a town where people believe that a woman will die at childbirth if she does not confess to her husband when she is in labor. Thus, many parturient women confess without fear, since this is a matter of little importance to them. What they reject is the lie.

On the other hand, the Egyptian Parliament has approved a law that authorizes husbands who catch their wives committing adultery to kill them. It is the Latin countries of Europe that, like Spain, continue obstinately to accept the inequality of treatment in marriage, making victims of wives. But the French Code is even more tyrannical: the husband never spends time in jail, and he is only penalized by a fine. Viviani[237] presented a bill in 1894 that would have made adultery a moral offense and an abuse of trust, rather than a crime; it would have been a private affair that only concerned the spouses and whose natural outcome would have been divorce.

In reality, there is no reason to punish adultery if we do not admit divorce. This latter always existed in antiquity with the name of *repudium*, but it was a right that only men could exercise. They cast off their wives as easily as they would any servant. Even among the Copts[238] women serve their husbands their meals, and the husbands can throw them out of the house with one phrase: "Cover your face." Confucius allowed for divorce in the case of a wife's disobedience, sterility, adultery, excessive jealousy and contagious illness. The Koran accepts it in a few special cases. It existed among the Romans, and Saint Jerome testifies in Saint Fabiola's[239] life that it was tolerated in the primitive Christian Church.

Domestic violence perpetrated by the husband cannot be avoided except through a divorce. That abuse of strength acquired through habit is much too common. Jean Grave[240] states that there are revolutionaries who run their families like veritable patriarchs. In fact, there is no lack of proletarians who have just shouted, "Death to the tyrants!" at a meeting, and beat their wives on arriving home. There are model society men, courteous and gallant in the salons,

---

237 René Viviani (1863-1925) Socialist politician and premier of France during the first year of World War I. He was also a lawyer and considered to be a brilliant speaker.

238 The Christian population of Egypt.

239 Saint Fabiola was married to an extremely vicious man and obtained a divorce from him in accordance with Roman law. She then remarried before the death of her first husband.

240 Jean Grave (1854-1939) was an important French anarchist before the First World War. He edited a series of newspapers and wrote books, novels and plays.

who thrash their spouses in the intimacy of the home. Ellen Key[241] explained this, saying: "The power over women and children turns a sullen man cruel and debases a mean man even more."

There is no reason why divorce should not exist in Spain, since it is legal in all the most educated nations of Europe and the Americas, and it has not influenced life there negatively. In Portugal, I have watched its establishment and I have had the opportunity to observe that the society has not suffered any upheaval. Many poorly constituted homes became healthier, and the victims in them were able to create new and happy relationships. One can see, as well, that once the fear of indissolubility is lost, the number of marriages increases. Children's economic interests are also protected, and next to the innocent spouse, their upbringing is more moral than in a home where they would have the bad example of a fragmented family.

In some countries divorce has degenerated into a kind of free love, in which the paternity and maternity of a child born from this union is legalized. These laws admit the principle that matrimony is a private matter, and that national interest is served only by the increase in population. In these nations, there is nothing easier than marrying, divorcing and marrying again. Divorce has put an end to the crime of bigamy.

The broadest reaching divorce law has been established in Los Angeles (United States). There, the husband and the wife, upon marrying, each preserves the right of ownership of their property. The husband recognizes that he does not have the right to violate the privacy of his wife and she recognizes the same with regard to her husband. If the marriage is sterile, either spouse is free to remarry. All conjugal ties vanish the day that one stops loving the other. Enemies of divorce cited the following case to prove the harm it causes: "Mr. Cortan Wonhburne met Miss Helena Chandler on the 5th of September, on the 6th they were already courting, and on the 15th they married. On October the 5th, they had an argument, each shooting several gunshots at the other, on the 15th of the same month, they divorced." This does not prove anything other than imprudence and hastiness on the part of both people. In these cases, there is no good solution; but if divorce had not existed, would these two individuals who shoot at each other during a fight be better off indissolubly tied together?

In Europe, it is Russia that has made divorce easier to achieve.

---

241   See chapter 3, note 55.

There were cases of individuals who, in five years were married twenty-five times. The Courts were bottle-necked with requests for lawsuits and civil actions. In order to end this state of affairs, the government wrote a bill that it then submitted to a vote of all citizens, publicizing it in even the most isolated places. Workers, students, townspeople of both genders discussed this bill, had meetings on it and, at the end of this national plebiscite, the revised decree appeared in the new Code. It establishes:

> "10. –Legal protection, for those marriages that are registered with the state as well as those that are not.
>
> 20. –In the case of a divorce, regardless of whether the marriage is registered, wives have the right to a six-month pension, if they are unemployed, and a year-long pension if they are incapacitated.
>
> 30. –If illegal marriages are placed within the law in the manner stipulated, their situation will be considered legalized.
>
> 40. –Registered wives will not enjoy the same political rights as their husbands.[242]
>
> 50. –The husband is required to support his wife before the birth of a child, and six months after.
>
> 60. –In case of a divorce, both husband and wife will keep their respective property, with the exception of money and property held jointly by both spouses, which will be distributed between them according to the norms established by law."

This Code also contains an additional clarifying clause that stipulates that any children will be supported by both mother and father, unless one of them is unemployed.

Within our current customs, this Code would seem excessively radical, since we do not remember that in the old days we had what is here presented as new, since the recognition of unregistered wives is the same as that granted by the Partidas. The secret marriages that at bottom the Code consecrates, are rarely maintained this way, since it is a matter of protecting the family, legally or illegally constituted. It is evident that the recognition of "unregistered wives" can allow for men to have several wives, and this can turn into polyandry and polygamy. However, Conrado D'Kursky,[243] People's Commissar of Justice, defends this legal principle by saying: "There are hundreds,

---

242 This is incorrect. It should be that they do enjoy the same rights.

243 His real name was Dimitri Ivanovich Kursky, Commissar from 1818-1828.

perhaps even millions of women, who are virtually, though not officially, married. To leave them unprotected would be unfair and cruel. Such a state of affairs could, at any time, provoke serious conflicts, the consequences of which no one can foresee."

But radical communists are not happy with this. The new Code maintains the institution of the family, which they wish to destroy. Madame Kollontay,[244] the renowned Russian writer, requested in the Soviet press that the family be abolished by decree, and that a tax be levied among the workers of the Communist Union, to create a fund dedicated to the support of all the children born in the republic. But they have not yet gone so far, and the ease with which one can obtain a divorce, and the recognition of a marriage *that is not registered*, keeps the family intact.

Divorce does not exist in Spain. What the Code calls divorce is only the separation of property and bodies. The spouses cannot remarry. Our Code is very clear in this. Once the wedding is performed, and there are no reasons to invalidate it, it is indissoluble. Article 52 states very clearly: "A marriage is dissolved when one of the spouses dies." Separated or not, as long as both live, the bond remains.

The acceptance of divorce in some countries and not in others, allows for formidable complications in international law. There are cases such as the one of a man married in Spain, who lost his Spanish citizenship because he served in the Mexican army, and who turns to the protection offered by the Swiss law for those without a nationality. Thanks to this, in Geneva he divorces his wife legally, due to differences of religion, and remarries, thus creating a new and respected home. But his wife, Catholic and Spanish, continues to be married, without recourse to the consolation of a home or a legitimate love.

There are many cases of bigamy perpetrated by Spaniards under the protection of other countries where, after a period of residency, they can divorce and remarry or even just remarry without bothering to obtain a divorce. For them, it simply hinges on not returning to Spain, or leaving the new spouse in America and returning to the original home, with the consent of the first spouse, since this is an offense that is only prosecuted at the request of the interested party.

---

244   Aleksandra Kollontay (1872-1952) was a Russian revolutionary who advocated radical changes in traditional social customs and institutions. She was also the first European female minister as People's Commissar for Social Welfare (1917), and ambassador to Norway in 1923, to Mexico in 1926-1927, and Sweden (1930-1945).

Legitimate causes for divorce are also unequal for men and women. There is equity in those that involve battery, attempts against a child's morality, or the life imprisonment of the other spouse. A wife can invoke her husband's violence against her if he tries to force her to change her religion, or if he forces her to act in immoral ways; but when it comes to adultery, we have already seen that in the case of a male adulterer, it is only considered a motive for divorce if it results in public scandal or disgrace of the wife. Adultery on the part of the wife is in every case, a cause for divorce.[245]

The Partidas admitted a spouse's conversion to Islam, Judaism or heresy as a motive for divorce. In all other cases, they maintained the principle of indissolubility of marriage: "Spouses will never split up while alive, and since God united them it is not right that man separate them." However, it is the case that Canon Law annuls a marriage more easily than Civil Law, since it considers marriages that have been entered into without full consent as null and void. Thus, it is enough for two people to prove that this was missing for the Tribunal of the Roman Rota[246] to pronounce the annulment. Among others, we can point to the recent annulments of the duke of Marlborough with a Vanderbilt, and of Marconi with Beatrix O'Brien.[247] The British Code, along with many other Codes, prescribes legal sanctions against those who contract matrimony *in bad faith*, and, further, against the priest who blesses a new marriage while knowing the motive for which the prior one was dissolved, as an accomplice in the crime of bigamy.

A few years ago, risking the scandal and indignation that any discussion surrounding the organization of the family creates in Spain, I carried out a poll in *El Diario Universal* — the paper published by that great teacher, Augusto Figueroa —, about the establishment of divorce in Spain. Behind this survey, lay the certainty that divorce would benefit women, since men, already protected by laws and

---

245 Author's note: I deal more extensively with this in the chapter titled "The Right to a Single Moral Standard"
246 The Tribunal of Roman Rota hears cases that come before the Pope and require a judicial investigation with proof. It can hear criminal cases, but also those relating to matrimony, religious profession and sacred ordination.
247 Consuelo Vanderbilt was an American socialite who married Charles Spencer-Churchill, 9th Duke of Marlborough in 1895. They were divorced in 1920, and in 1925 the marriage was annulled by the Catholic Church. Giuglielmo Marconi, inventor of the radio, married the Hon. Beatrix O'Brien, daughter of the 14th Baron Inchiquin. They were divorced in 1924 and the marriage was annulled in 1927.

customs have it in deed, if not by law. I do not believe it pointless to reproduce here some of the most notable opinions of illustrious writers and politicians, not only republicans and liberals, but also conservatives and even of priests.

Pio Baroja[248] told me: "I am decidedly in favor of establishing this social reform. Is this because I believe that the number of adulteries in Spain is so large that they make it necessary to establish divorce? No, I do not believe this. What is more, if one could count the number of adulteries in Spain, I am sure that the number, in comparison with those of other European countries, would be insignificant. What does this indicate? Morality? No, lack of life, lack of passion. Spain is – say what they may – the coldest and least passionate country in Europe. The legend exists, it's true, that we Spaniards are terrible, that Spanish women are ardent, and have a volcanic heart; what more could we want! We are – and it is sad to have to confess this – a sickly and weak people, lacking in strong passions. The blood of the lavish, intelligent and cold Semite runs in the veins of almost all Spaniards. Just as with the Moor, the Spaniard's experience with relationships is lacking, and for women living in the provincial capitals, it is non-existent.

In Spain, men and women live as if they belonged to different species, speaking to each other through a thick veil of good manners and formulas. Men maintain that one cannot speak with women because their conversation is always about shopping; but I have heard some ladies say that one cannot speak with men because they are so stupid. I do not know who is right; the fact is that this inexperience in relationships between one sex and the other, coupled with a lack of passion, results in there being few ardent interactions between men and women, be they single or married. As a consequence, there are few adulteries and divorce would not be greatly useful in practice.

Yet, there is something else. If divorce were established in Spain for cases of adultery, the same would happen to it that happened to civil matrimony, it would be ruined and become an institution without life, a useless tool, like a microscope in the hands of a savage.

If I believe that divorce would be useless in practice, why am I in favor of it? I am in favor of it because I deem as good anything that cracks this shell of laws, precepts, customs, intangible and immutable dogmas, which do not allow us to live. I am in favor of it because I

---

248   Baroja (1872-1956) was an important Basque novelist and short story writer who revolted against the backwardness of Spanish society. He was much admired by Ernest Hemingway.

believe we must affirm that everything is revocable, that nothing is definitive, that everything can be transformed and improved. Against this progressive idea, stands the Catholic sense of the immutable, the doctrinaire and dogmatic, which we find equally in those Spaniards who call themselves more advanced as well as in those who consider themselves reactionary, both in Salmerón and in Nocedal, in Unamuno and Father Coloma.[249] We are subject to so many laws, so many precepts and orders; we are already so beleaguered by the rod of the Code, of morality, of society, of appearances, that, even if it is only a small step, one bond fewer is at least something.

To posit the question of divorce today can produce a positive result: discussion and scandal… Just the sheer mention of the problem would elicit protests from every corner of the Spanish sacristies, from all the mystical and worldly congregations, from the theater boxes, from the stages, from everywhere. To create a scandal is something; when there is absurd morality, scandal can be a form of good morality."

Blasco Ibañez[250] wrote: "I am decidedly for divorce, for the same reason that I believe in love and not in marriage. A priest's blessings, a judge's finding, social customs, are human inventions which eternal and capricious love, that sovereign of the world, laughs at. All mythologies imagine love as an undependable and fickle god. When love distances itself forever, why strive to keep the bond of marriage between two beings that hate or despise each other, like convicts tied to one chain who have to satisfy together their basest necessities? Without love, the association of a man and a woman should not subsist, regardless of the blessings that have sanctified it and the laws that protect it. Healthy and strong beings must say good bye without rancor or sadness when they do not love each other, and they must go different ways to make their lives anew."

Manuel Bueno[251] said: "The Church, with a barbaric and medieval criterion, only allows for divorce when *excapite impotentia*, [252] — about

---

249　Nicolás Salmerón (1838-1908) was a liberal Spanish politician and philosopher, and was prime minister of the First Republic for a month and a half in 1873. Cándido Nocedal (1821-1885) was a very conservative politician, journalist and lawyer. Miguel de Unamuno (1864-1936), one of the most important novelists, poets, and essayists at the turn of the century; here he represents the progressive tendency. Father Coloma, a Jesuit, was a conservative novelist and short story writer.

250　Vicente Blasco Ibáñez (1867-1928) was an important Spanish realist novelist.

251　Manuel Bueno (1874-1956) was a novelist, short story writer and journalist.

252　The Canon Law states, "Antecedent and perpetual impotence to have intercourse, which Father Sánchez speaks in his *On Marriage*—, can be proven in one of the spouses. No reason of a moral order is enough to legitimate the breaking of the bond. The Church —in this respect an accomplice of nature, for whom only the reproduction of the species matters— does not care about our happiness. It is satisfied if we do not violate the canonical mandates. Yet, since our peace is greater than the inexorable selfishness of nature and the orthodoxies of the Church, the law should be kinder to those unfortunate men and women who wish to separate from each other. To maintain a bond that would otherwise break is criminal. Many of our misfortunes are due to the impact of our parents' characters on our sensibilities. Divorce is healthy and moral. It must be established here if only so that certain men will not become too proud of their disgraceful behavior."

Don Salvador Canals[253] said: "The issue for me is very simple: In the awful realities of our lives does divorce exist among us? Undoubtedly; there is no one who does not know ample examples of marriages broken by the lack of love due to disillusion or disappointment. Thus, if the laws are to respond to the necessities of life, to social realities, how is divorce not to be indispensable in Spain?

I can clearly see the grave difficulties of this reform. Our changeable and extemporaneous character, our enormous intellectual and moral backwardness, our general condition of wretchedness. We would see that just a few years after the establishment of divorce, half the women who had left singlehood and had not reached widowhood would be divorcees with all the problems of that status in a society like ours, so unused to respecting women, and without the benefits of emancipation and independence that the social environment would make illusory, or even turn into the basis for a new and more appropriate slavery.

There lie both sides of my thinking, which could well be summarized so: Let divorce be legalized, since it is already here in reality; but let's take all the precautions elicited by the fear that people who now marry thoughtlessly, will unmarry just as thoughtlessly; and we must also face Spanish economic problems directly and as they are in the new laws and educational social action, and begin to solve the difficult and painful problem of the status of Spanish women, more beautiful than any in the world, and more unhappy than any in today's western civilized countries."

---

whether on the part of the man or the woman, whether absolute or relative, nullifies marriage by its very nature" (1084 Par. 1).

253   Don Salvador Canals y Vilaró (1867-1938) was a politician and journalist who was head of the conservative party.

Mr. Angel María Castell, editor of *ABC*,[254] said: "I am a supporter of divorce and I believe that women should be so even more than me. The indissolubility of marriage harms them more than us. When men marry they lose little of their liberty, women lose it entirely. As long as they do not have more rights and fewer duties, the marriage bond enslaves them. Now then, when they have more rights, will they have fewer worries? Stated more clearly: when a woman becomes more of a citizen, will she be less fanatical? Because, lyricisms aside, as long as legal matrimony is exclusively canonical, as long as women think that to marry one must go to church and not to city hall or municipal court, to talk to them about divorce is to waste one's time. Women, I insist, should be the most ardent defenders of this reform, because the current legislation leaves them unprotected in the civil and canonical realms. One of the legitimate motives for divorce according to our Code, is 'the wife's adultery in all cases, and that of the husband when it results in public scandal or disgrace of the wife.' Just as it sounds. For the wife, in every case, without exception. For the husband, in no case, if the man's adultery can exist without evident disgrace for his legitimate wife."

Canon law is more reasonable in that it considers that the husband's adultery is a motive for divorce in all cases. The haziness comes later when the law recognizes 'the lack of consent of the bride or bridegroom,' and adds that the consent is null when it is given in error, or coerced through violence, intimidation or pain.

When Alfred Naquet[255] defended his bill in the French Chamber, he stated that what women might not now know in their apathy, they would learn as soon as they realized that men were granted new rights that they too could enjoy. It is true that Naquet was speaking about French women, who were broader minded than Spanish women. Some say that Naquet later regretted this work. I do not know how true this is. At any rate, any leader after him would have done the same, and he could not have regretted that. His law has destroyed many homes in France. Some wrongly destroyed? Others rightly so? The good achieved for these latter compensates for the wrong done to the former. People talk of those cases that have leaked out to the public through the media because of scandals. They do not speak of the ones that remain unknown because of silence. It's well known that 20 people who gossip make more noise than a thousand who are quiet.

---

254   *ABC* was a daily conservative newspaper founded in 1903 that is still published today.
255   See chapter 8, note 236.

Some ask as the ultimate justification: And what about the children of the divorced couple? I have not seen this problem dealt with more ably than in *Le berceau*,[256] a beautiful comedy by Brieux, which has not been translated to Spanish, a fact I cannot understand since it is much better than *L'Adversaire*,[257] by Arene y Capus, so poorly understood by our audiences. Children —if they do not curb the guilty deed, which is almost always the cause for divorce—, can be the victims of this same comportment, and in this case, it is perhaps best if they live without the father or the mother than with a father or mother whose behavior harms them morally. At any rate, they can motivate the father or mother to whom the law has given custody of them to avoid a second marriage (and this is considered the true disruption of the family); but if they do not, this cannot be attributed to divorce, since there are widows and widowers that marry and give their children a stepfather or mother.

Those who argue that where divorce is legal corruption rules, forget, without a doubt, that there were also reprobates and degenerates, and immorality triumphed, along with adultery and social crime in times of intolerance. Divorce is a sign of progress. We may not be ready for this reform, but the fault is not the idea's, rather it is ours. Perhaps women are the most opposed to this; but I believe, as did the author of the French law, that due to their instinct of self-preservation and the stimulus of their noble self-interest, women will rush to take advantage of rights that are granted equally to them and to men.

Let no one say that divorce can only find supporters among those who would gladly divorce their spouses. No, those who enjoy paradise at home understand that what is more humane and even pious and good is to end the hell of others' homes."

Joaquín Dicenta[258] replied: "I believe that divorce is as necessary, as long as marriage exists, as is quinine as long as fevers exist. Of course, it would be best to vanquish both fevers and marriage; we will reach that someday. In the meantime, I agree with the doctors, on quinine, and with you on divorce."

The illustrious theologian and cleric Mr. José Ferrándiz,

---

256 This was a three act play in which the divorced and remarried mother of a sick child eventually renounces both men to care for her son.

257 This was a play about a married woman who begins to have a affair with another man, is eventually discovered by her husband, and he allows her to divorce him to save her reputation.

258 Joaquín Dicenta (1862-1917) was a popular writer, journalist and poet.

wrote: "The views of Catholics against divorce rest on the Gospel, where they believe there is legislation from Jesus Christ himself on marriage and monogamy, as a basis for the doctrines of the Church. The doctrine is incomplete, crude, and immoral. It is said to come from the Gospel; but the Gospel speaks little about marriage, and not at all about divorce; what it does speak about is polygamy and repudiation: the evidence is in the text.

Chapter XIX of Saint Mathew tells of the Pharisees who asked Jesus if it were lawful for a man to repudiate his wife. Jesus answered that God had created humans as male and female, and yoked together they would be two in one united flesh that, joined together by God, man may not separate. The Pharisees objected that Moses allowed repudiation, but Jesus responded that he did this because of the Jewish people's hardness of heart, but that in the beginning it was not this way: anyone who divorces his wife, except for sexual immorality, and marries another woman commits adultery, and he who marries the divorced woman also commits adultery." This same passage, in almost the same words, can be found in chapter 10 of Saint Mark and… there is nothing more on earthly marriage in the Gospel.

In the rest of the New Testament, there is little as well. Saint Paul, in his first letter to the Corinthians, chapter 7: 11-12 says: 'But to the married I give instructions, not I, but the Lord, that the wife should not leave her husband 11 (but if she does leave, she must remain unmarried, or else be reconciled to her husband), and that the husband should not divorce his wife.'

If we can correctly deduce anything from all this it is what follows, (otherwise there is no common sense in either the world or the New Testament): first, for Jesus the wife was the property of the husband, but once acquired, she was obligatory; second, that since polygamy was allowed among those to whom he spoke, he did not condemn it, he did not establish monogamy, what he prohibited is the discarding of women out on the street, and that no one marry the discarded ones; and third, he allowed, not divorce, but rather repudiation in the case of a carnal offense committed by the wife; with respect to adultery by the husband, one must stretch the text somewhat to include him in the same prohibition.

The vague statement that at the beginning, during some indeterminate time, there was no repudiation is simply a lie: there was repudiation during the time of the Patriarchs, as the story of Abraham shows. The fabrications invented by the theologians to reconcile the two contradictory terms, have done nothing more than to highlight them even more clearly. Saint Paul already gives a nod to divorce: a wife may separate from a husband, but may not remarry; that is all.

If the Church had wanted to keep polygamy among Christians, it would have found a basis in the Gospel, if candidly interpreted. This was not in the interest of the Church, and so it advocated the unbreakable bond of monogamy; but, clearly amending the words of Christ, without the authority to do so, it restricted the Gospel's permission to repudiate the unfaithful spouse, and it erected the current doctrine on the foundation of obligatory indissolubility. The Church states that matrimony is indissoluble; but, in fact it does allow its dissolution, and introduces arbitrary distinctions that Jesus Christ and his Apostles did not, and that therefore are not in the Sacred Scriptures. For example: if the two spouses remain chaste within the first two months of the marriage, one of them may, before consummation, enter into monastic life, even if the other spouse rejects this; but neither one can accomplish this same separation to marry another or live free in the world. Why? You ask the Church. Oh! It answers, that is a privilege of Religion; marrying or living honestly among free Christians, that is not religious for the Church! It admits divorce, not the repudiation that would come from Scripture, but only on condition that neither divorced party may remarry, and for this it only imposes a fee that amounts to thousands of 'duros',[259] and an inquiry that takes no less than four years. There is no right to divorce for the poor, and it is useless for the rich, because for each spouse to live in this way on their own there is no need to spend money and suffer four years of troubles, deposits and other misfortunes.

And while establishing this brutal indissolubility, the Church reserves the right, however, to dissolve the marriages of princes and magnates, and only those of princes and magnates, so that the stronger of the spouses can remarry for reasons of State, but not the weaker of the two – that one goes to a convent. Do not ask the Church for more; it does not have or conceive of it. Perhaps if its ministers could marry it might conceive of more; but they are celibate and at the same time polygamous, and allow or repudiate women when and how it suits them: for the people one doctrine and behavior; for the priests, another behavior and a secret doctrine. It's delightful!

Let him who has good sense say if this sociology can take us anywhere, and if we can expect anything from those who maintain such doctrines and practices nowadays, after the advances in social sciences, anthropology, physiology, medicine and all the human knowledge about man.

---

259   This was a five-peseta coin. In 1926, the exchange rate was about US $1.5 per peseta, so a "duro" was worth about US $7.50.

My thinking is favorable to divorce, when it is prudently legislated, and above all takes into account the children; divorce is a necessary complement for the indignity of being married. The two examples I cited above summarize my view. The wretches whose luck gave them insufferable spouses will say if it is Christian to believe the crude theory of the man who says: 'Let those whose marriage turns out badly put up with it; they will serve as an example for others.' No, rather they will serve as an example against marriage and as incentive for free love; because, who is the smart aleck who can tell during a courtship that a spouse will turn out to be a loser? Injustice, an injustice as large as the suffering of an innocent for another's transgression, cannot be legal."

Don Miguel de Unamuno said: "I must begin by confessing that, although I am married, or perhaps because of it, the question of divorce has never managed to interest me, nor have I been able to form an opinion about it. The latest I have read on it – and I have not read much in all – was the discussion that the Parliament of the Republic of Argentina had, and it interested me much more than for the content, for the eloquent phrasing, the rich culture, and the high tone that it exhibits, and which gives one an excellent idea of that Parliament.

What happens to me with the issue of divorce is the same that happens with novels of adultery; rarely do they manage to interest me. I have always seen everything that refers to the relations between the genders as subordinate to other kinds of problems. This is why feminism appeals little to me, I consider that some of the issues it poses have to do with the organization and regulation of work and others with education in general. A majority of the wrongs about which women complain are wrongs that we men also suffer.

More specifically with regard to divorce, I have never been able to view the family as a mere union of husband and wife, but rather aside from and even in addition to the children, I believe it has a relationship with society in general; it is a social institution and not just a contract between spouses. And it could turn out that divorce would cause more harm to social life than that subjection of those who marry to something bigger than them and the family they create. I believe, as well, that divorce is a weapon against women.

I well understand that marriage can be fought as a religious Sacrament or a legal civil contract, and the free union between a man and a woman be promulgated; but I do not comprehend that some would try to denaturalize it. 'Either shoe the horse or get out of the way.'[260]

---

260   This is a proverb related to the story of a blacksmith who asked the townspeople for

As you can see, my opinions with respect to this are the most timid, the most backward, middle class and least innovative that could be. I recognize this, but I have not been able to come up with other ones."

Azorín[261] wrote: "I am a supporter of divorce; I am divorced. I have been divorced not once, but twice, three times, four times.

I will tell you how this astonishing feat came to be. When I think often about one of those serious problems in life that continually hound us, and, fortunately, I am not facing it, I tend to ask myself: What would my behavior have been when confronting this formidable obstacle? What attitude would I have had if erratic circumstances had led my life down that path and not this one, so different, that I am now travelling down? And then for a minute, my imagination runs rampant down that other path, and while that moment lasts, I see myself as if I were another. And so: I have been married, I have adored several women, whom I loved sincerely, whom I would have gladly joined in holy matrimony (at least this is what I used to tell them). And what have the fortunes and adversities of my married life been?

I see myself on a fifth floor —one that is reached through a narrow and dark staircase—, stuck in a small, shabby room, without rugs, or paintings, or curtains, or furniture, or fireplace. I see myself in a suit bought in "El Águila"[262] for fifty pesetas, or else wearing another suit, that, if I have not bought it readymade, forces me to say every day that I am not home, when I am. I see myself writing all the time on the table of a newspaper office, subject to that gloomy sad yoke of the paper, scribbling political articles or literary chronicles, feeling excitements I do not feel or faking hatreds that are far from my soul; and then, when I have returned home, tired, exhausted, I see myself picking up the pen again and writing tasteless, bland translations or plotting stories and articles that I will take to the magazines and newspapers, in my crumpled suit, and that they will accept grumbling, with pity.

I see myself next to my wife (in one of those rare and unavoidable occasions in which we, poor writers, who are ashamed

---

permission to set up his horseshoe stand in the middle of town. When he did not shoe any horses, but rather just inconvenienced everyone, they told him to either perform the job or take away his things.

261   José Martínez Ruiz (1873-1967) was a novelist, essayist and literary critic. He coined the term Generation of '98, by which the male writers at the start of the century are known (including Unamuno, Baroja and Azorín himself).

262   El Águila was a department store. This implies the suit was cheap and poorly made.

of our wives, find ourselves forced to walk down the street with them); I see myself with her, dressed in one of those outfits that are old and that are new, indefinable, on which she has put to work her feminine skills, and which arouse more compassion than a dress that is frankly old and frankly torn. I see myself at home, on these all too frequent terrible days, in which there is no credit or money, I see me exasperated, brutal, violent, screeching while my wife screeches, cursing while the children cry, forced to move our home to another fifth floor, from which we will move in a month to another, compelled to go face another humiliation, another embarrassment, at the newspaper or the magazine that has accepted an article of mine last week, and that does not want any more...

And when I reach this point I put the pen down on the table and hold my head in my hands, thinking. And it would not be possible to imagine, with Dante's imagination, two more different hells, just as horrible, but I see another. I am on the outskirts of a grey, monotonous, desolate, waterless, treeless, town in La Mancha. Through the blackened plain wends a road, between the immense square sown fields, between the groves of grey olive trees, down this road a man comes every afternoon, after dinner in the winter, at dusk in the summer. He is neither old nor young, he does not have the liveliness of youth or the indolence of old age, but he displays profound fatigue in his appearance and his gestures.

And if you approach him and listen to his words, you will notice that this man, who once was intelligent, lively, generous, bold, enterprising, is now a wretched automaton. In days gone by, this man was a learned and clever writer: he read the old and the newest works, he wrote free and ingenious pages, he enjoyed a certain renown that encouraged his work. And now he lives locked up and silent in this town. Every day he gets up at the same time; all the moments of his life are the same; the bells of the eight or ten churches of the city toll continually; his wife has filled the house with saints and little burning candles; the pious people dressed in mourning who enter the house with their rosaries speak to him of sadness and death; the sharecroppers do not pay their fees because the crops have died; the poor tenants who live in his houses cannot pay their rents either; they need to buy a new team of oxen to replace the old one, and there is no money; building repairs are urgent, and he is forced to take out a loan...

And then, in addition to these spiritual obsessions, the details of his private and daily life exasperate him with that tame, yet ferocious exasperation that does not translate itself into screams, or curses, or insults, or blows. The rooms are dirty, messy; if one tries to clean them, all the furniture must be dragged and thrown together with a loud crash and then they are pounded, making a deafening din; from the table in his office books and papers disappear, which he cannot find when he needs them; there are diapers and a comb on the dining room table; in the morning, when he rises, he does not find water in the pitcher; meals are never ready; if he happens to sit down to work a bit, remembering the old loves of a literary artist, at the same time someone will begin to clean the room next door, or his wife will come into the office with the sewing machine – because they are cleaning the other room, as I have said – and she will spend all afternoon sewing there, while he must abandon his attempts with resignation.

And then, beyond all this —the financial anguish, the intolerable and constant private annoyances— is the spiritual and intellectual loneliness in which he finds himself. With whom can he speak? To whom can he communicate his fantasies and the memories of his soul? His name has already been forgotten in Madrid. His old comrades do not remember him. But little by little, he feels more yearning, more longing, more desire for his old free and productive life..., and then he goes out of the house, he leaves the gloomy town, and takes a walk alone down the winding road, on the huge gray plain dotted with grey olive trees.

And when I reach this point, I put my pen back down on the table again, and I hold my head in my hands, thinking. Those two women have been my wives; they have joined their fates with mine. Now I am free, in my bachelor's room, by the table that holds my paper, my pens, my books; I am happy under my cape and my bohemian hat, writing what I want, jumping from one newspaper to another, without being held back by the "children's bread," or being forced into humiliations by the need to pay rent, doing nothing when I feel like doing nothing.

So here you have it, Madam, this is how I am divorced without being divorced."

These responses, selected from many other notable ones, reflect all the nuances entailed in the issue of divorce.[263] In truth, although the power of civilization will establish divorce, feminism will resolve —with the independence of women— the problems of marriage and divorce, benefitting both so that neither will have the cardinal importance they have today.

---

263 Author's note: From the out of print book by the author, *Divorce in Spain*.

CHAPTER 9
CIVIL STATUS AND THE LAW

The exclusion of the rights of women in all areas. –Civil rights of single women. –Rights of mothers. –Various ways of considering motherhood. –Theory and practice of law. –Rights of widows. –Administrative Rights. –The most favorable Civil Code for women.

We constantly see the rights of women excluded in the entire Spanish Civil Code. Title II, which deals with the birth and expiration of civil capacity, states: "In the case of double births, the priority of birth gives the first born child the rights that the law recognizes for the firstborn."[264] It does not distinguish by sex, but one must determine carefully which child is the first born, because in case of a doubt, it is necessary to abide by Law 12 of the 7th Partida, which establishes: "that if a male and a female are born it will be understood that the man was born first. If both are male they will share equally the *inheritance* and *honor* of the firstborn," which is what in fairness should always be done, but the law treats women unjustly from their birth on.

Having daughters is almost a curse in some cultures. The Arabs usually kill them at birth; for the Hebrews, the woman who has a daughter is impure longer than if she has a son. In Persia, this formula is used as a wedding blessing: "In the name of the Liberal, Beneficent, Merciful God, may Ormud judge this to be just, may he give you love in your heart, abundant food, male children with handsome faces, who will live a long time, from parents to sons, one hundred and fifty years, like the inhabitants of Iran-Vedj." It is not desirable to have daughters. It diminishes one. War-like people want only cannon fodder.

Article 33 of the Code states that if there is a doubt as to which of two people who are entitled to inherit from each other died first, the person who avows which one died must prove it, and if there is no proof "both are presumed dead at the same time and there is no transfer of rights from one to the other." This rectifies the abuse contained in the laws of the Partidas that expressed that "the female

---

264   Author's note: Article 81.

should be considered dead first." As one can see, in case of a doubt, the laws wanted women to be born later and to die first. They have contrived to always subordinate women's rights to men's.

It is not true that single women and widows have *full rights*. Not only do they face obstacles in receiving certain types of education, carrying out particular jobs and professions[265] and exercising their political rights, but women are not even permitted to function as guardians with the same rights as men, even though this is not a public post, but rather an institution designed to be a substitute for paternal authority, to watch over the education of a minor or a handicapped person and protect his/her interests. Single women may not be guardians of younger children, and yet they can be of brothers or sisters who are demented or deaf and dumb. Brothers, half-brothers, even friends of the parents or respectable neighbors are preferred over a sister for the guardianship of minors. In this the Code considers women to be like thieves, swindlers or falsifiers who also cannot be guardians.

Another function that is of a private civil character is serving as a witness of public documents, and this is also denied women. They are not allowed to be witnesses of a marriage, a contract, a will or a death. If there is need of a witness for one of these acts, any man willing to do it can be one, at times even one who does not know the interested party or what the act is about; but a woman lawyer, a doctor or a teacher cannot do it, neither can a businesswoman nor a landowner who is renowned for her reliability and respectability. The law even accepts a man who goes around despondent, smelling of wine, maybe earning minimum wage; his testimony has weight... because he is a man.

These vestiges of ancient civilizations are incomprehensible. Manú[266] said: "The mere statement of a man is decisive, but the official report of a multitude of women, even if they are honorable, is not useful because of their garrulousness." And the Ottoman Code said: "the testimony of a man is worth that of two women." But the strangest thing is that regardless of this view of women, they are allowed to be witnesses in criminal matters, where their testimony can determine the fate of the accused in terms of his/her reputation and life. Women are granted the graver act and denied the less important one. Additionally, their inabilities disappear in

---

265 Author's note: See the chapters on The Right to Work and The Right to Education.
266 In the Hindu religion, Manu is the legendary first man and lawgiver; his laws appear in the *Manu-smriti*, or *Laws of Manu* which dates from the 1st Century BCE.

times of epidemics, when they are allowed to witness wills without any other requirements. Moses,[267] whose laws harmed women so much, based his opinion on the belief that women only testified to what their fathers or husbands permitted. Therefore, the falsity that women are blamed for, if this is true, would not be their doing, rather it would be that of men. At most, women would be weak, but it is men who turn out to be the liars and abettors. The rights of even an adult woman are eroded in all possible ways before she is emancipated, since she cannot leave the house of the father or mother with whom she lives until she turns twenty-five years of age unless the parent remarries or she changes her civil status by marrying or becoming a nun. They say that single women, widows and those legally divorced have legal capacity because they can buy, sell and administer their property, enter into contracts, be executors of wills, choose and adopt a residence, and have it and her correspondence be inviolable. They have the right to assembly, association and freedom of speech that the Constitution guarantees all Spanish citizens, but in reality, their legal capacity is limited, it is not true that they have full rights: they are banned from certain posts, professions and trades; they lack military and full political rights and the civil rights we have listed.

With regard to our obligations we are the same. Women pay the same taxes as men, have the same duty as they to help pay the financial burdens of the State, and that of feeding their legitimate, natural[268] or illegitimate progenitors and descendants, and even their husbands.

The law does not overdo the severity of its sentences when punishing crimes committed against women. Abuses against modesty are only punished with temporary imprisonment and time served in a correctional facility in the medium and minimum degrees.[269] The corruption of minors is only punished by the latter sentence, even if it involves a sister or offspring, and if the woman is older than twelve years old the offender is only punished with arrest for a period from one to six months. Kidnapping is only punished with temporary imprisonment in the minimum and medium degrees, unless the kidnapped woman disappears or dies. The progenitors, guardians, teachers or any persons who abuse their authority and collaborate as accomplices, are punished in the same way as the authors of the crime.

The Code stipulates that "those convicted of rape, rape of a

---

267   See chapter 6, note 170.

268   See chapter 3, note 57.

269   Author's note: chapter II, title XI.

minor, or kidnapping will also be sentenced to provide compensation: 1) to give the injured party a dowry if she is single or widowed; 2) to recognize the offspring if the quality of his/her origin does not prevent it; 3) in all cases to support the offspring." These crimes are not prosecuted without the request of the interested party or her parents, grandparents or guardians, unless she is helpless, has no family or guardian and has no legal status due to her age or moral standing. In this case the district attorney or the public prosecutor acts for the public good.

The explicit or presumed pardon of the injured party halts any penal action or sentence and can only be established through the marriage of the injured party with the perpetrator. A betrothed that is kissed by her fiancé will have the right to half the gifts the husband would have given her if the marriage does not take place. The leniency of punishments is the cause of the abuse and lack of respect suffered by women; the frequency with which women sue in Court for having been publically insulted or slandered shows a people's lack of civility. In France, a jury absolved Mrs. Caillaux, who killed someone in defense of her wounded honor.

Respect for women is scant in our customs; the Novísima Recopilación[270] already tried to protect them in public places by stipulating that the punishment for whistling at or insulting a woman in the streets of the kingdom be six months of work in the Prado or banishment from royal lands for four months "if the offender was a prominent person."

Current laws fine those who make *flirtatious comments* (which are almost always crude utterances); the laws show that not much has changed from the time when the *tapadas*[271] were pursued on the streets to our days. We have already seen how women are hardly respected in the family. The husband who causes his wife injuries that keep her from working for one to seven days, or necessitate medical assistance during the same time span is punished with a month of jail time. The one who abuses her in word or deed without causing injuries is only arrested for five days. This is little better than it was among the Franks, when the death of a woman was fined 33 sous, since the homicide or assassination of a woman is always surrounded by attenuating circumstances, such as: "acted under the power of an irresistible force" or "acted under such a strong impetus which, naturally, produced rage and obfuscation."

---

270 See chapter 3, note 58.
271 Women who walked alone in the street would often cover their faces with their shawls so they would not be recognized.

All murderers of women avail themselves of these attenuating circumstances, invoking the love they say they professed for them. But the majority of the times these *crimes of passion* are not born from the pain of a heart that breaks on seeing the love that once was the center of his life lost forever; rather, they display the basest of passions: rage, selfishness and pride. The feigned irresistible violence of jealousy is usually no more than hurt self-esteem, male vanity and excited sexual jealousy. They refer to the solemn words of soiled honor, shattered happiness, etc., etc., to find a legal excuse for an act of arrogance and barbarity.

Recently there have been *crimes of compassion* carried out to avoid seeing a loved one suffer. The absolution of a Polish student who killed her sick boyfriend to free him from pain was a bad precedent, since there has been no lack of imitators. That honor, love or charity can serve as excuse for a crime is the biggest of absurdities.

The laws of dissociation and the current Code have made the rights of both sexes to inheritances and bequests equal, but when it comes to titles of nobility preference is given to males, even though the owner of several titles can distribute them among the males, since we have not reached the point of *confiscation and sale* of titles. Some lineages preserve nobility through the womb, that is whoever marries a noble woman acquires the nobility that she transmits to her children, while in other lineages it is only the man who is ennobled. Until recently one needed a record of *pure bloodline* that proved he was not a descendent of Moors or Jews to embark on a military career or several others: the prejudices were so great and so disgraceful that the laws even prohibited Christian women from raising the children of infidels.

Male privileges circumvent birthright even when it comes to the succession to the throne. Alphonse the Wise's Code[272] already stipulated that women could only reign when there was no male heir: "That only a male child should have the lordship of the Reign after the death of his father... and that if there were no male child the eldest daughter should inherit it, and if the eldest son died before inheriting it, if he had a son or daughter from a legitimate wife, he or she should have it and no other."[273]

Felipe V [1683-1746] established the Salic Law which dictated that only males had the right to succeed to the throne: "Females, even if they are of better lineage and degree than males, may not

---

272   This would be the *Seven Partidas*.
273   Author's note: 2nd Law, title XV, Partida 2.

succeed to the Crown of Spain if there are males, even if these come from other lineages."[274] This was the greatest injustice in a country where there exists a tradition of queens who have eclipsed the glory of male monarchs, such as Doña Teresa, guardian of Ramiro III; Doña Elvira, guardian of Alphonse V of Aragón; Doña Sancha of León, Doña Mayor of Castille, Doña Berenguela of Barcelona, Doña Berenguela and Doña Blanca, daughters of Alphonse VII of León and Castille, who reigned in their respective states; Doña María de Molina, guardian of Fernando IV, Doña Catalina, guardian of Juan II and Doña Isabella I of Castille; additionally, there were Spanish princesses of universal renown such as Doña Blanca, mother of Saint Louis of France, and Saint Isabella, queen of Portugal.

Carlos IV repealed the Salic Law in the Cortes [Parliament] of 1789, but the Decree was only enacted by his son Fernando VII in 1830. This weak, and tyrannical, monarch – obvious proof that the women who surrounded him were worthier than him – reestablished the Salic Law only to repeal it in 1832. The evils wreaked on Spain by the fickleness of this monarch are well known, as he left behind the sad memory of a civil war[275] that plunged the country into mourning in the 19th Century. Next to him the figures of women of liberal and energetic dispositions, such as Princess Carlota and Queen María Cristina, stand out; this latter one knew how to fulfill the duties of a wife with extraordinary selflessness as she preserved the throne for her daughter and created a home filled with love.

Finally, the Constitution of 1812 reestablished the rights of the Partidas and the law of June 30, 1876 established the succession to the Crown.[276] It gives preference to the descendent line over the ascendant one, and the closest kinship over the more distant, the male over the female and if both are of the same sex, to the eldest.

We have closely examined the situation of married women as wives, but we must study their situation as mothers. The mother's authority is unknown. The Code never says *the father and mother jointly*, rather it says the father or ABSENT HIM the mother.

As we have seen, the husband chooses a residence, determines where and in what way a child will be raised in the religion that he [the father] chooses, has him enter into the career or trade that

---

274 Author's note: *Novísima*, 3rd law.
275 This is the first of the Carlist Wars (1833-1840) which was waged by Fernando's brother, Carlos, against Isabella II and her mother, the Queen Regent María Cristina, for succession to the throne.
276 Author's note: Article 60.

he thinks best or decides he should not have one. If the mother is better educated than her husband, wants to watch over her child's upbringing and take it on a different course, she cannot do it, not even if the child agrees with her. The husband rules due to the *merit* of being male.

The father exercises parental authority with respect to the persons and property of legitimate, unemancipated, natural, recognized and adopted, minor children. He can correct them and punish them moderately or implore help from the authorities to do so in certain cases. The father administers the goods and property of the children who are under his guardianship, and is entitled to any interest earned from it. When the time comes that the child wishes to marry or enter the Church, he needs permission if he is a minor or counsel if he is an adult. ONLY the father grants these. In his absence, the mother concedes them. It is necessary for him to die, go mad, be sentenced to jail, or abandon the family for the mother to exercise parental authority. It is only when the child is illegitimate that the legally recognized mother or the grandparents can exercise their rights.[277] This is an advantage of a single mother over a married one that contradicts the concept of *dishonor* with which *illegal* motherhood has been stigmatized.

The more modern Codes confer equal rights to the father and the mother. In the United States, for example, the concept of the family in the Roman sense does not exist. The father's power, the foundation of the family in the ancient regime, is almost nil. A father's rights have been transformed into the duty to care for his children. Just as in our Code, he also has the obligation of feeding his children, keeping them with him, raising them according to his means and representing them in all actions that might benefit them. But in North America children do not need permission or advice to marry, and the mother's authority is identical to the father's. The tendency is to make marriage easy and unions out of wedlock nearly impossible; for this reason, North Americans dispense with solemn formulas and formalities that hinder a couple's marrying, they facilitate divorce and, in the first place, they strengthen the rights of the children and the equality of the spouses.

Marriages entered into in good faith have civil effects for the innocent spouse and the children, even if they are annulled, or even if they are entered into in bad faith, because the legal rights of the

---

277   Author's note: Article 46 of the Civil Code.

children must be independent of those of the parents – a principle that, unfortunately, is not always respected. Above all, the rights of illegitimate children must be the same as those of legitimate offspring. The distinction should disappear and birth certificates should only include the names of the parents without indicating whether they are married or not, since regardless of this their legal rights must be the same. In the case of divorce or annulment children younger than three years of age remain with the mother. When they are older they are placed in the care of the innocent spouse, and if both are guilty of bad faith the Courts determine with whom the children will reside. In the case of an annulment, with both spouses' good faith, the daughters stay with their mother and the sons with their father once they are older than three. This is a tacit acknowledgement of the importance that a mother's care has for the infant.

An incongruity can occur that allows the guilty spouse to regain parental authority once the innocent spouse dies if the cause for divorce was adultery, battering or serious insults. If the cause is something else a guardian for the children is named.

The mother has the obligation of recognizing the child as long as there is proof of his or her identity and birth. She can recognize a child born out of wedlock alone or jointly with the father. When she does so alone, she cannot reveal the name of the person with whom she had the child due to the prohibition on investigating paternity. When the father alone recognizes the child, he also cannot reveal the name of the mother.

One of the new cases of legal rights that the war[278] has raised is the declaration of presumed death of those who disappeared. After a man has been absent for four years, his wife remains married to him, but his mother is released from any responsibilities toward him.

One can clearly see the various ways that motherhood is considered in theory, in practice and in the Codes. In theory, everything suggests a lyrical exaltation of maternity, going so far as to turn a purely animal function —since the act of giving birth is not in itself meritorious or commendable— into something semi-divine. True motherhood, one that is worthy of all praises, is arrived at later through the work of bringing up and educating the child and the sacrifices the woman endures for the love of him or her. In this sense, we could even say that some virgins are mothers while others who have children do not deserve this name. Ambition, which Napoleon

---

278   This is a reference to World War I (1914-1918).

was unable to hide, has had a great deal to do with the exaltation of motherhood. His "Praise be to mothers!" meant: "Praise be to the makers of cannon fodder!" much like what we might say about the brooding hen that gives us more chicks.

There have been times when patriarchy shaped everything, such as during the Hellenic era. Then they sang the praises of the father. Killing a mother was not considered parricide and the laws absolved Orestes of the murder of Clytemnestra;[279] let us recall the words of the famous tragedy: "Would you deprive of light the one who has given you life? Incomprehensible crime!" says the unfortunate woman. And the hero responds: "My father alone has given me life. The gods give man alone the ability to propagate the human species. Children must love their fathers, not their mothers."

Some of this absurdity persists in the custom of calling the sons of the same father brothers and those of the same mother half-brothers, as though the male and female principles did not have the same value in the mysterious sprouting of existence. But just as absurd as this concept of the superiority of the paternal function and the excessive authority of the father is, it is also absurd to put motherhood on a pedestal above fatherhood. Any inequality in the home, whatever it may be, harms the entire family. Fortunately, there are many of us who, while defending the rights of women, can also have an excellent opinion of the men, because we were lucky to have fathers and brothers who were worthy of respect, are acquainted with honorable men who are models of fidelity, and know happy homes.

There are women who exploit motherhood and see themselves as having the right to be placed in a situation of privilege above those who have not had children. There are women who do not fulfill their maternal duties, but because they have given birth they take advantage of their maternal status. During her trip to Paris in 1896, Hilda Sahs[280] said: "Ever since I arrived in France I have been hearing women exclaim how proud they are of being mothers, and consequently bore everyone by showing off their children. I also have children and I don't praise myself. It is a natural function of which one should not be proud." The missions of father and mother are equally respectable when they are filled with tenderness, selflessness and love. But motherhood has been turned into something engrossing,

---

279   This is from Aeschylus' *Oresteia* (6th Century BCE). The second play in the trilogy, *Choephoroi* (*The Libation Bearers*), has the story of her death.

280   Sahs (1857-1935) was a Swedish novelist, journalist and feminist who campaigned for women's suffrage.

which constitutes a woman's entire horizon of expectations: an honor that proves to be another link in the chains that bind her.

Although a mother's role in reproduction and childbirth is more painful than that of the father, this is not enough to proclaim her superiority. She breastfeeds the child and cares for the infant while the father works so that she can look after him/her. The child soon reaches a phase of his/her life in which the mother and father are equally as important for his/her upbringing, since they must surround the child with both tenderness and steadfastness. The duties of each are equally admirable when they are carried out with love. Lubbock[281] has said: "Those who only cared for their children because it is a duty would be bad parents."

But at the same time that in theory motherhood is ennobled in order to encourage women, by appealing to their vanity, not to shy away from propagating the species —an act which causes them so much pain—, in practice they are chained to what can be called *obligatory motherhood*. Motherhood is invoked as one of the reasons why women must stay in the home removed from any other activity, as if women's exclusive role is to be mothers and wives. There are many women who do not marry, others who are not mothers and still others who, having fulfilled their duty towards their children, have time to devote to other things. This is borne out when we see mothers leave their children to go for a walk, shopping, dancing, to the theater, etc. If they leave them for such frivolities, why can't they leave them to attend to serious occupations? Jeanne Schmahl[282] asks: "what reason is there for wives and mothers to be less free than husbands and fathers?" It is absurd to argue that because a woman is a *mother* she cannot be something else. It is as if we could forbid a man from taking on any other role because he is a father.

To be a mother one especially needs to have great physical strength and resistance. Pregnancy, childbirth and breastfeeding are work that requires much natural self-assurance. In order to bring up her children, shape their character, and awaken their emotions a woman needs a great deal of knowledge and real aptitude. Her mission is not inferior to the work men boast about. And if she can demonstrate physical and intellectual strength, why be opposed to

---

281   Sir John Lubbock, British archeologist and member of Parliament who published *Prehistoric Times* in 1865.

282   Jeanne Elizabeth Archer (1846-1916) was born in England, but married a Frenchman. She practiced as a midwife until 1893, and co-founded the French Union for Women's Suffrage in 1909.

her contributing to all areas for which she has talent, just as she collaborates with her husband in propagating the species, raising their children, and even supporting them?

Some might say that the painful and important maternal mission leaves a woman no time for other things; but this is not true. Once the period of bed rest needed after childbirth is over, she is capable of all kinds of work. A housewife carries out rough and complicated tasks, a worker returns to a factory, they all resume their work. There is no reason to deny them the option of intervening in public affairs. Gabriela Mistral, with an excess of maternal zeal —perhaps due to the anxiety of not having had children—, and being more of a poet than a thinker, wants the whole life of a woman to be limited to the care of children. She says: "As shoemakers, we will make children's shoes; as carpenters, we will make their toys; as journalists, we will write their section in the newspaper; as interns in medical school, we will go to the Gota de leche[283] center." It is easy to see how false this notion is; it so limits and subordinates women's activities. The more educated a woman is, the better she will fulfill her maternal duties, but they are not only the roles of wet nurse and nursemaid.

The mother type is almost always falsified; even in literature the lack of this female figure was not filled until Gorky.[284] That is, a *normal* mother, great in her simplicity, without grandeur, had not appeared; rather, what we had was an absurd mother, at times pure flashiness, at others quiet and fleeting. In the theater mothers hardly appear in the work of Lope or Calderón. It is fathers who occupy their place. But it is not fair to blame these authors for doing without them; they faithfully portray how mothers lacked authority, their role was less important in both the family and society. Undoubtedly feminism strengthens maternal authority and influence.

Moreover, it is absurd to sing the praises of motherhood while humiliating mothers who have children out of wedlock. In the Russian Code a married mother and an unmarried one have the same rights with regard to their children and their fathers.[285] All children enjoy equal rights and their parents must support them

---

283   At the start of the 20th Century, these were places where women who could not breastfeed and did not have the means to hire a wet nurse could go for assistance in feeding their children. The term means "drop of milk".

284   Maxim Gorky published *Mother* in 1907. The novel deals with the lives of working class women in pre-revolutionary Russia.

285   Author's note: See the previous chapter.

until they are seventeen years old with a third of their income. In Burma, there are towns in which a law regulates the status of children of unmarried parents. Once the filiation is proven, whether or not the parents marry, the children have their rights. The man gives the woman's father a sum of money to raise them. They swear that this is a happy country where infidelity is non-existent.

We still have to consider the rights of a widowed mother. Widowhood allows a woman to recover the greatest amount of legal capacity granted to her if she is an adult. While she is a minor she is subject to guardianship and until she turns twenty-three she cannot borrow money, take on a mortgage or sell her real estate. However, once the husband dies, even if she is a minor, she has parental authority over her children and the legal capacity to represent them, according to a declaration by the Public Records Office. She can only exercise parental authority while she remains a widow; if she marries again she loses this right, but will regain it if she is widowed again. The law is based on the idea that a married mother is under the influence of her husband, and this might be harmful to the children. The same could be said of a widower who remarries, he is also under the influence of his new wife, and yet he does not lose his parental authority over the children of his first marriage. Experience shows that there are more stepmothers than stepfathers who mistreat their stepchildren. Yet it can even happen that the mother loses her parental authority and it is granted to the new husband.

All of the procedures having to do with motherhood after becoming a widow are tiresome. If the birth takes place within the three hundred days after the death of the husband, the child is considered legitimate, but if s/he is born after the three hundred days s/he is considered illegitimate; this can give rise to the absurd notion that the mother is a corrupting influence on her young children, and she will then lose her parental authority over the ones she had during her marriage, but keeps it over the newborn. This is as if the law, which watches over the morality of some children, does not care about that of the others. The Code is so malleable when it comes to morality that adultery committed by the mother is not considered to be included among the cases that, according to article 171, can deprive her of her parental authority.[286] When a widow believes that she is pregnant she must let her husband's heirs know, and they can have a judge make the necessary rulings so as to avoid all trickery or prevent

---

286   Author's note: This interpretation of the law was set down by the Supreme Court in an opinion issued on November 9, 1898.

the child that is born from passing as legitimate when s/he is not. The Code provides for the judge to decree the necessary measures so that the widows' modesty is not offended and her freedom is not limited; but she has to suffer the humiliation of the presence of the interested party's trusted representative at the birth, or if she rejects this person, the presence of a physician or a woman appointed by the judge.

If the husband recognized his wife's pregnant state in a private or public document, she does not need to notify his heirs, but she has to put up with the witnesses' investigation at childbirth. The omission of this last formality does not endanger the legitimacy of the child, since if it were challenged it could be proven by the mother or a legitimate representative of the child.

A widow who becomes pregnant, even if she is independently wealthy, must be supported by the inheritance, since part of this belongs to the posthumous child if it survives. In the case of an error with regard to the pregnancy or a miscarriage, the goods or property, which should have been under the control of an administrator, will go to their rightful owners. For the newborn to acquire and transmit rights, s/he must be born with human characteristics and live twenty-four hours entirely independent of the maternal womb.

The span of time that the law requires before a widow may remarry is too long. To establish the paternity of a child, it is not necessary for nine months from the death of the husband to elapse. A period of four moths is enough and some Codes establish this period.

Another oddity – which in no way benefits morality – is that of prohibiting the marriage between adulterers who have been found guilty in court. If, because they cannot marry, they live together out of wedlock, since this is not prohibited by law, yet it is a much greater sin. If they have a child, s/he will be born destined not to be recognized by an ensuing marriage. So, it is not the parents who are punished, but the children.

A widow does not inherit ownership of property and goods, but rather the usufruct[287] of a part of the inheritance that is equal to that of each of her children. If there are no children, she receives the usufruct of half the inheritance. In Catalonia, a widow who does not have a dowry, is poor, has lived with her husband until his death without seriously offending him, does not hide any information about the inheritance and leads an honorable life has the right to what is called *cuarta-marital*, which constitutes one fourth of the husband's

---

287   The right to use and enjoy the benefits (such as interest, rental income, etc..) of something.

property as long as there are fewer than four children; if there are four children the widow inherits a fifth; if there are five, a sixth, and so on. The *cuarta-marital* cannot exceed 25,000 pesetas. In Aragón and Navarra, the widow inherits the usufruct of all the goods and property that the husband contributed to the marriage. In Vizcaya, she enjoys the usufruct of all his goods and property for a year and a half. The surviving spouse receives her bed and the linen she uses. The widow's mourning clothes are purchased with money from the husband's inheritance.

Widowers of either gender who remarry are required to reserve ownership of all goods and property of the deceased spouse acquired through the marriage —but not the shared possessions— for his/her children and descendants by means of a will, intestate succession, donation or they may be granted for valuable consideration or by lucrative title.[288] Upon remarrying widows must take inventory of all goods and property subject to being reserved, may use the chattel[289] and must register all real estate in the Property Registry as reserved, according to Mortgage Law requirements. The obligation of reserving property applies to widows, whether they remarry or not, who have an illegitimate child who is recognized or a child who is declared legitimate, during their widowhood.

Administrative Law awards a widow half the pension left by a civil servant when he dies, the other half goes to their legitimate and illegitimate, legally recognized children. Any others only enjoy half of what is granted to the legitimate children. When she remarries, the widow loses the pension forever. Daughters lose it when they marry, but they recover it if they become widows when they are poor and if no one else lives off it. Poor, widowed daughters who have lived in the paternal residence for at least a year before the death of the father will also have a right to the pension. A man's legitimate or illegitimate mother also has a right to the pension. As one can see, Administrative Law is more favorable to women. They always maintain their pension, as long as they do not marry or become nuns, while the sons' pension ceases at the age of twenty-three.

The Statute on Pensioners passed in Barcelona in 1926 talks about female public employees. This is one of the statutes that

---

288   These last two are legal terms that have to do with the granting of a property title. The first, "for valuable consideration" implies that there is a financial exchange between two parties; the second, "lucrative title" means the title was acquired by gift, inheritance or succession.

289   Moveable property, such as furniture, bedding, etc., as opposed to real estate.

distinguishes between the rights of each gender, when the same rights should be legislated for both, without making distinctions. According to these last resolutions a woman has the same rights as a man, with the only exception that she will in no case pass on her pension to the widower and her children will not have access to the orphan's pension while their father is alive, unless he is disabled and cannot support his children, has abandoned them, or has been sentenced to jail for more than one year. In these cases, the pension ends when the disability disappears, he returns to the home, or recovers his freedom. One must claim the pension before three years have passed since the death of the mother. In this case the injustice is committed against the man. A home that was established on the basis of two incomes must suffer from the lack of one, and just as the children receive a pension when the father dies, regardless of the status of the mother, they should in this instance as well. There is also no reason why the widower should not receive a pension, just as the widow does, especially when he is ill or disabled. We need complete equality in the laws, not privileges for one gender or the other.

In the Portuguese Republic, according to the bill authored by Alejandro Braga and presented to the House of Representatives in 1912, an adult woman has the legal capacity to be a testamentary guardian, a supervisory guardian and a member of a family council.[290] She can be witness to a will or attesting witness, attorney in fact,[291] even in a trial; in the same way as she can be an executrix, she can act as a guarantor, and exercise the parental authority along with her husband. We already know that divorce is legal and that neither spouse may sell their property and goods without mutual consent. Single women are protected, and when a marriage does not take place through the fault of the groom, the bride is entitled to compensation. It is the most favorable Code for women in all the Latin countries of Europe.

The demands that the International League has formulated with regard to the Civil and Penal Codes are the following:

- ∘ "Article 44 must be amended in the following way: 'An engaged woman whose wedding does not take place through the fault of the groom, will be entitled to demand compensation from him in proportion to the harm suffered, by way of moral reparations. For the purposes of this directive only a woman who has been asked for in marriage will be considered engaged. A maiden who loses her honor, either

---

290   See chapter 7, note 215.

291   This is a person acting on behalf of another through a power of attorney.

deceived by a promise or through force or abuse of authority, will be entitled to compensation, to be financially supported in all cases, and to demand reparations or the punishment of the guilty man in the case of pregnancy or a contagious disease."

○ "It is necessary that the following sentence be stricken from Article 155 and subsequent ones: 'The father, and absent him, the mother.' It should be replaced with 'The father and the mother, and absent one of them, the other spouse.' Women reclaim for themselves their involvement in the sacred duty of watching over the upbringing of their children and satisfying all their needs, and in this matter, do not want to dispense with having equal obligations as their husbands."

○ "It is also just that in Title IX, Chapter I and the following ones, all the legal requirements which give preference to men in their appointments as guardians and the carrying out of a guardianship be modified so that women can be appointed guardians and supervisory guardians the same as men."

○ "The irritating omission of women in Article 249 that gives preference to male progenitors and descendants, and even the husbands of living sisters over a wife when it comes to establishing a family council must disappear."

○ "Title XI, that deals with emancipation and legal adulthood must be modified to establish complete equality between the father and the mother with regard to the emancipation of a minor and complete equality of benefits for all Spaniards who are of age regardless of gender."

○ "*All laws that abusively close off certain careers or trades should be repealed*; both should be accessible to women who have the same capabilities as men; women should be able to practice law, be notaries, judges, etc., and in these professions just as in those that they are already permitted to practice (telegraph, mail, teaching, etc.) they may, just like men, legally reach the highest positions, with no other limitations than the ones imposed by their aptitude. This is already recognized in Calcutta; thus, it turns out that Indian women are more emancipated than we are."

○ "*A Jury should be constituted by the same number of people of each gender with similar backgrounds*, for this is just and equitable."

○ "*Women should also be equal to men in the Penal Code.* We do not wish any privileges in favor of women, but at the same time we want adultery no longer to be considered a crime for the woman, and only a misdemeanor for the man; once it has been proven, there should not be a need for aggravating circumstances for the man's infidelity to be criminal, since these are not necessary when it comes to the woman. And may the attenuating *flagrante delicto* that Article 438 establishes disappear for the crime of the man who kills his wife, as well as for the father who surprises his daughters who are younger than twenty-three and living in the parental home and their corrupters."

○ *"The investigation of paternity must be established.* And this is one of the fairest demands, since the law authorizes the investigation of maternity, showing with this that the Codes were made by men solely for their own benefit, since it is they who are the main culprits of illegal procreation, because of our customs and the certainty of impunity. Protected by the law, as well, are the ones who skirt their responsibility of raising and educating a child who is theirs as much as of the unfortunate woman who, after being a mother without being a wife, is disqualified by society, and the great majority of the times, in terrible economic circumstances. It is a hateful privilege of men that the law protects the investigation of maternity, and at the same time prohibits that of paternity. And, since to achieve complete equality we need to either abolish the former or allow for the latter, we demand this last one, since it is more beneficial for the innocent child who begins life, and whose rights as a human being should be respected.

○ *"We demand that legitimate and illegitimate children always have the same legal rights,* that is: a) that the articles of the Code that do not recognize some children or that deny others equal rights be modified; b) that as soon as the filiation of the new being is discovered, the father and the mother – whatever their status and circumstances – have with this child all the obligations that the law establishes for those who, until now, have been considered legitimate children to the exclusion of the others; c) that, by virtue of these modifications, the classification of children as legitimate, out of wedlock and illegitimate disappear from now on."

All these are indispensable reforms for women to conquer social esteem and to put things right by attending to their needs with what we might call their *own resources*, without having to reach out with their hands and beg for what they are justly owed.

CHAPTER 10
THE LAW AND RELIGION

The Influence of Religion on the Fate of Women. –Ancient Priestesses. – Women in Christianity. –Various Sects. –The Female Messiah. –Deaconesses. –Abbesses. –Spanish Legislation on Nuns. –Canon Law and Civil Law.

The conception of theogony[292] held by a people greatly influences the fate of women. In Asia the essential principle of Nature, which was worshiped religiously, was feminine: the worship of the Moon and the Goddesses whose supremacy ennobles women. The enthronement of the male divinity of the sun brought about the decadence of female power, although not without a fight. There are some who consider the Amazons to be no more than a myth that symbolizes the battle between sun and moon worship, that is, between the feminine and the masculine principles.

The Goddesses had priestesses, and some demanded bloody sacrifices, such as Ma-Belona[293] who, like Artemis of Turide[294] or the Indian Kali,[295] demanded male blood. So it is that these priestesses and the Druidesses[296] were considered "men-killers." Women also performed the role of Great Priestess of Ishtar,[297] "the Mother Goddess." As is well known, centuries before Jesus Christ Egypt gave us an example of equality of the sexes that we have not yet achieved in Europe in the 20th Century of the Common Era. Women were prophets in all Egyptian, Chaldean, Assyrian, Hebrew, Greek and Roman towns. This gives rise to the recently renewed belief of the Greeks that the feminine temperament is more adept at perceiving

---

292   The origin and descent of the gods.
293   The Roman goddess of war.
294   In Greek mythology, she is the virgin goddess of the hunt and the moon and twin sister of Apollo.
295   Kali is the fearful and ferocious form of the mother goddess.
296   In ancient Celtic society, the Druids and Druidesses were priests and considered the elite class.
297   Ishtar, a goddess of both fertility and war, is the Akkadian name of the Sumerian goddess Inanna and the Semitic goddess Astarte, the three names referring to the same deity in different cultural contexts. She inspired great devotion in the ancient Babylonian empire, as evidenced by the many grand temples, altars, inscriptions, and art objects devoted to her.

ultra-sensitive impressions and exerting influences on unknown forces. This belief persists even among the modern spiritists, whose best mediums are women: Eusapia Paladino,[298] Miss Florence[299] and many others.

In Greek culture, we can see the influence of the Goddesses; almost all the statues found in the excavations of Cypress and Crete are of Hera,[300] Demeter[301] and A[riadn]e[302] and of priestesses praying or dancing behind a procession or around divinities. There is not a single priest. The battle between the two principles must have persisted there still, since when Athena and Poseidon competed for hegemony, she triumphed, thanks to the female vote. Among the Romans the role of sibyls did not have a priestly nature, but the vestal virgins possessed priestly privileges at the same time as they symbolized the worship of the home.

Christianity, if we heed Jesus' doctrine, is favorable to women. He does not want serfs or slaves, he does not allow for inequality. The Divine Principle, although Jesus names it in the masculine "My Father," is conceived as immaterial, and therefore, genderless. Christ emancipates women socially, as he does all oppressed people. His doctrine is potentially feminist, but it turns out that Christian Theology is impregnated with a Germanic despotism that the northern hordes brought with them when they broke up and overwhelmed the ancient world and, in their savagery, they enslaved women. Additionally, Christian Theology, as we have already seen, includes the traditions of the Hebrew people, on which it bases itself and becomes frankly unfavorable to women.

The tribes of Israel never had marriage and, given the tradition of the origin of man and the sin of the first parents — of which Eve is considered worthy of blame — the responsibility for the perdition of the entire human race is heaped on women. Solomon said, "There is no woman who is not thoughtless and treacherous, a wicked slave of her passions and subject to her whims." Without a doubt, the women who looked upon the physical squalor, the corruption and the vices

---

298 Italian psychic of the late Nineteenth and early Twentieth Centuries whose skills were said to include levitation, elongation, spirit materialization and channeling.

299 Miss Florence Cook, one of the most famous British mediums who was supposed to produce an actual materialization of the spirit.

300 Queen of marriage, women, childbirth, heirs, kings and empires.

301 Goddess of agriculture, horticulture, grain and harvest.

302 A Cretan princess who became the immortal wife of Dionysus.

of the wise king would not have a better opinion of him; but it is his judgment that prevails and in Jewish society women continue to be enslaved: they do not share in the teachings of the doctors, nor can any religious ceremony be held solely for them. Although the temple may be filled with women one cannot officiate unless there are ten men. Women are unfit even to work on priestly ornaments.

It is inconceivable that Christians, who maintain that Christ —incarnated through a woman— came to redeem slaves and to right wrongs, would leave women unredeemed, without falsifying the doctrines that they support and were preached by him. Even assuming Eve's guilt, among other absurdities, one must confess that Christ came to redeem both sexes and that the drama of the Calvary with its supreme pain was embodied in Mary. The Mother at the foot of the Cross would suffice to redeem all women. There is perhaps an excess of zeal, of religious fervor in the Patristic writers that makes them look at women with apprehension because they see in them an obstacle to the supreme purity and chastity to which they aspire. It is because of this that they fight against women with a brutality so unlike Christian piety that it seems unfathomable, and they dedicate to them a bouquet of mystical flowers such as these:

San Juan de Damas says, "Woman is an evil donkey, a disgusting tapeworm that burrows into the heart of man."

San Juan Crisóstomo adds "Woman is the fountain of evil, the author of sin, the headstone of a tomb, the gates to hell, the fatality of our misfortunes."

Saint Jerome carries the persecution to a climax and calls her "Road to iniquity, spear, scorpion and dangerous species." He repeats, echoing Ecclesiastes, that she is "more bitter than death," and that "a *blameless* woman is rarer than a Phoenix." Without a doubt, he did not think to look for a blameless man who could, accordingly, throw the first stone.

San Gregorio Magno assures us that "woman has no sense of right."

Saint Thomas writes in his *Summa* that "she is an accidental and incomplete being, inferior to man in virtue and dignity, since she was not created by God without mediation."

Tertulian says, "Woman, you are the gates to hell. You are who persuaded the one whom the devil did not dare attack face to face. It is your fault that the son of God had to die. You should always be dressed in mourning."

This lovely litany is repeated throughout time. Lamennais writes, "Woman is a smiling machine, a living statue of stupidity.

Speak to her reason and her gaze floats aimlessly. Insist and she will yawn behind her fan. The truth is a closed door to her. The creator, who made her from a bit of sludge, forgot her intelligence; a shadow occupies the place of her soul in her brain." One can see the disrespect they show when they proclaim that God could be forgetful and imperfect and make a poor, incomplete work with that bit of mire that was a piece of a man.

The son of Saint Monica said, "Woman is an animal whose only pleasure is adorning herself."

There has even been a debate about whether a woman is a *human being*, and in the Council of Macon[303] there was a serious discussion about whether *she has a soul or not*.

All of this neglects Jesus' words and spirit entirely: "a man leaves his father and mother and is united to his wife, and they become one flesh" (Genesis 2:24). Can there be a greater declaration of the most absolute equality?

Many have not dared fight against the opinions of the Holy Fathers, believing that this was unorthodox, but we have to take into account that the Church only grants them infallibility when they speak ex cathedra[304] and are all *in agreement* with the opinion. Fortunately, when it comes to these interpretations of women, they were not enlightened by the Holy Spirit... Saint Paul explains women's subordination by saying: "Man is head of the family because he is not of woman, but woman of man. Neither was man created for woman; but woman for man" (1 Corinthians 11: 3, 8, 9). It is true that later, in the Epistle that he dedicates to the Galatians he contradicts himself and exclaims: "There is neither Jew nor Gentile, neither slave nor free, nor is there male and female, for you are all *one* in Christ Jesus" (Galatians 3: 28).

Women's dispositions are such that — despite the ungratefulness with which they were treated — they heroically adhered to Christian

---

303   See chapter 4, note 66.

304   The First Vatican Council, Sess. IV, Const. de Ecclesiâ Christi, c. iv: "We teach and define that it is a dogma Divinely revealed that the Roman pontiff when he speaks **ex cathedra**, that is when in discharge of the office of pastor and doctor of all Christians, by virtue of his supreme Apostolic authority, he defines a doctrine regarding faith or morals to be held by the universal Church, by the Divine assistance promised to him in Blessed Peter, is possessed of that infallibility with which the Divine Redeemer willed that his Church should be endowed in defining doctrine regarding faith or morals, and that therefore such definitions of the Roman pontiff are of themselves and not from the consent of the Church irreformable"(1909).

doctrine, burning with love and faith. They influenced husbands and fathers. They did not hesitate to renounce comforts and luxury; they sacrificed themselves and their children. Christian martyrs are legion. In spite of all this, they were unable to shake off the dreadful influence of theogony. To show how true this is, all we need to do is compare it with Indian beliefs. Women there are not cursed. The nature of the fall of the human race is identical, but it is the man, Adisna, who disobeys the Creator's commands and who entices the woman. When it is time for punishment, the woman pleads not only for her own pardon, but also for that of the man who led her to sin. God, moved to pity, responds that Redemption will come through a woman, and Vishnu[305] is incarnated as Krishna[306] in the bosom of a virgin. And this difference, the guilt being the man's, is the reason women are listened to and respected. Let us look at a few opinions from the Rig-Veda[307] in order to compare them with the ones we have merited from the Patristic writers:

> "A woman's tears cause lightning to strike those who make her cry."
> "He who curses a woman is accursed by God."
> "There is no crime more hateful than to stalk a woman."
> "Women's songs are sweet to the Lord's ears. Men who wish to be heard should sing with them."
> "Unfortunate is he who laughs at a woman's suffering. God will laugh at his prayers."
> "If a woman is not happy she will not fill her husband's heart with joy."

Manu has said: "Do not hit a woman even with a flower, even if she is full of faults; where women are revered, the deities are pleased and where they are not honored, all pious acts are worthless." It is true that socially he subordinates women to men, as do the Brahmans, the Semites, the ancient Greeks, and the Romans. Each has added a link to women's chains.

The *Koran* sees Eve's daughter as a superior being, but it enslaves her and denies her the right to educate herself. In this Mohammed is the most ungrateful, since he owed all his success

---

305 A major god in Hinduism and Indian mythology; he is the preserver of the universe.
306 The embodiment of god and divine joy.
307 A collection of over 1000 hymns from 1200 to 900 BCE that contain the mythology of the Hindu gods.

to the devotion of his wives, Kadija and Aicha. The influence of the former on the Prophet of Allah was so beneficial that the verb *Kadijear* was created to refer to the positive effects of a wife's encouragement of a husband. But in all religions, we see the same phenomenon of male selfishness towards women.

The Christian sects that split off from Catholicism have treated women in diverse ways. The schismatic Greeks do not give women a role in the priesthood. The Protestants give them the right to preach and in the United States there are women who are ministers. The Reverend Anna Shaw[308] is one of most renowned pastors of American Protestantism. A woman, Mary Baker,[309] is the founder of the Christian Scientist Church that desires to reconcile science and the mystery of the Eucharist. In Norway, Mrs. Martha [Steinsvik] was the first woman to preach and officiate at an afternoon service in the church of Greenland, in Oslo. Among the Adventists, the Anabaptists and a multitude of religious sects there are women who embrace their beliefs with genuine enthusiasm; although in all of these sects they are overlooked.

The Gnostic sect — in which principles from all religions and philosophies are blended together — returned woman to, as Renan said, "her place near the throne of God." They devised a cosmological and theological novel in which *Sophia*, a woman, plays the central role. Bythos, God, creates the universe because of his love for her, and upon seeing its imperfections, she cries at his feet until she moves him to send Christ to redeem it. A woman is part of the Trinity. "God," they say, "does not distinguish between men and women, nor the wise and the ignorant, the rich or the poor. The sun shines for everyone. Everything for everyone and everyone for everything." So, women have a role in their churches; they officiate, they preach, they baptize exactly the same as men.

In the sect of the Waldenses, the *Poor of Lyon*, —whose apostle, Pierre Valdo[310] renounced all worldly goods to found his Church— women were preachers.

---

308 Anna Shaw (1847-1919) was a prominent suffragist; among her many positions, she was honorary President of the National American Woman's Suffrage Association and Chairman of the Woman's Committee of the Council of National Defense. She was the first woman ordained by the Methodist Protestant Church.

309 Mary Baker Eddy. (1821-1910). In 1879, she founded the Church of Christ; later named the Christian Science Church.

310 Pierre Valdo (1140-1217) did not manage to get permission from the Pope for lay people to preach. The Waldenses were excommunicated at the council of Verona (1184).

The most anti-feminist of all the sects is the Albigensian.[311] It could be said that they believe the story that a woman contains all evils, like Pandora's box, or the legend that the devil is not an angel, but rather a rebellious woman, Lilith, Adam's first wife, who was turned into a demon because she did not respect him; then God created Eve as a companion for the first widower. This sect believes that it is a great evil to perpetuate the human race, a Satanic creation, and its ideal is celibacy, so that the species should die out and our spirits be liberated. *The Perfect Ones*[312] renounced all commerce with the world, while the masses abandoned themselves to all manner of vices and excesses. Not only did they not allow women a role in the priesthood, but they decreed that "they would never enter into Paradise." However, it was the women who most valorously continued to defend Simon de Montfort's[313] theories, when all of his followers died in the Inquisition or sought refuge in the harsh Alps, just as the Waldenses did.

After these sects died out, in the 13th Century Guglielma of Bohemia[314] appeared in Milan stating that she was the Holy Spirit incarnate in the womb of the queen of Bohemia. She was, therefore, the third person of the "Holy Trinity, fully divine and fully human." She explained her second incarnation by pointing to the necessity of redeeming women. Guglielma was beautiful and eloquent. She did not lack supporters and soon she had disciples. Imitating Jesus, she named the young Maifreda[315] her vicar on earth, who would replace the successor of Saint Peter. The Redemption begun by a God-Man would be completed by a God-Woman, since the first time God was incarnate in the male form due to modesty, and thus chose the lesser of the two sexes. Guglielma's church, known as that of the *Blessed*, gained a large number of followers. Guglielma went to England and France preaching her Gospel and was always triumphant. After her death in Colmar (France), her disciples waited for her resurrection and attested to having seen her rise to the sky, glowing, wearing a purple dalmatic[316] and golden sandals. The Inquisition finally got involved

---

311   Also known as the Cathars; they existed from the 11th to the 13th Centuries.

312   Those of the Albigensians who were recognized as *parfaits* made up the elite, and relatively small leadership of the sect, that practiced extreme asceticism and did not marry.

313   The implication that Simon de Montfort's thought was behind the Albigensian beliefs is incorrect. In fact, he led the Crusades against them from 1209 to 1218.

314   Actually, she was Princess Blazena Vilemina, the daughter of the king of Bohemia.

315   Maifreda de Pirovano, who died at the stake for heresy in 1296.

316   A wide-sleeved tunic-like vestment open at the sides, worn by deacons and bishops.

in the matter and the new sect was soon extinguished when Maifreda and another apostle were burned at the stake in the public square.

Later Saint-Simon[317] appears and his philosophy tends to be, as an illustrious thinker has said, "the rehabilitation of the flesh." He says: "God is one and he appears at the same time as spirit and matter, as knowledge and beauty." So, for the Saint-Simonians, the flesh is as noble as the spirit, and life, in its totality, does not have anything that should be beyond the pale. Intelligence and strength are manifestations of the whole. His disciple Enfantin abused Saint-Simonian philosophy —much in the same way as Rasputin has done recently—, he used his prestige with the women followers of Saint Simon, who allowed them great influence. Enfantin deluded them into thinking that they must go to the East and look for the *Mother of the Apostles* who would give them the new doctrine; they found a mysterious Mother Joan, said to be the female Messiah, with whom the sovereignty of women would begin. Enfantin had his followers call him "King and Pontiff of the New Jerusalem." This all turned Saint Simon's philosophy into a ridiculous sect.

With respect to the Catholic Church, it hasn't changed its opinion from Saint Paul to our days regarding the subordination of women, although many pontiffs have protected them from abuses, owing to the support women have always given the church. Let us remember the names of countess Matilda of Tuscany[318] and queen Christina of Sweden,[319] who converted to Catholicism and placed all her energy and fortune at the disposal of the Popes who fought to maintain worldly power.

In the early Church, there were deaconesses who performed great service and were necessary for maintaining morality, especially during baptisms by immersion. They were chosen among the virgins and the widows devoted to God. At first, they were required to be sixty years old, but later forty year olds were admitted. Saint Paul, in his "Epistle to the Romans," already speaks of Cenchreae,[320] the deaconess of Corinth. The deaconesses were very helpful in instructing women in doctrine, caring for the sick, distributing food

---

317 Claude-Henri de Rouvroy, Comte (count) de Saint-Simon (1760- 1825), French social theorist and one of the chief founders of Christian Socialism.

318 Also known as the "Great Countess" (1046-1115), she was a strong supporter of Pope Gregory VII in his conflicts with the holy roman emperors.

319 1626-1689.

320 This is a mistake. The church was at Cenchreae, but the deaconess was Saint Phoebe (Romans 16: 1-2)

and clothing, in that communism of the early Church. A bishop ordained them, and he was the only one to have that capacity, which made some believe that they had a role in the priesthood, but it was made clear that they did not receive ordination within the ecclesiastical hierarchy, but rather a respectable ministry divested of priestly character. Justinian, in his *Novels*, spoke of the deaconesses when he dealt with the personnel that the Church of Constantinople should support, and as we can see they also shared in the wealth of the Church, since they had salaries. The same emperor established capital punishment for deaconesses who married.

Two flaws were pointed out in the deaconess institution. The first was that they cut their hair and entered the church passing as men, and causing serious scandals (this gave rise to the stories of the existence of "Pope Joan"). The second was that many of them left their possessions to the Church and the clergy, causing their families harm. To avoid this, emperor Theodosius ordered deaconesses to be older than sixty and prohibited their leaving their possessions to the Church. The first part was carried out, but the second was revoked by the emperor at the pleading of Saint Ambrose and the Holy Fathers. The Council of Epaone in 517 attempted to abolish deaconesses, who continued existing for a long time in the East, but in the West, they disappeared after the 6th Century.

However, thanks to some special privileges there remain vestiges of this early institution. Shortly before the revolution in France, the Carthusian nuns of La Salette, in the Dauphiné,[321] performed the functions of deacons and sub-deacons, and touched the sacred goblets. The abbess of Saint Pierre, in Lyon, maintained her position as deacon and performed her role as such, as well as that of sub-deacon. She chanted the Epistle and wore a maniple,[322] though not on the arm as does a priest, but on her hand.

Nuns do not have a priestly character either. The first one that we know of, the Roman Marcella, performed the duties of a deaconess. In Spain, there is evidence of virgins and widows who dedicated their life to God from the times of persecution and struggle, but they did not live in communities. In the seventh-century religious communities under the direction of monks appeared. The morality of some of these communities was so questionable that in the Second Council of Seville, Saint Isidore[323] fought against the dual sex monasteries

---

321 An archaic name for a province in the south-eastern corner of France.

322 An ornamental band formerly worn on the left arm by the celebrant at the Eucharist

323 See chapter 5, note 121.

and prohibited any contact between monks and nuns very strictly. At this time, his sister Florentina was a model nun.

Later, with the splendor of the monastic Orders abbesses appeared. The legislation that deals with them is contained in the Council of Trent, in the decrees of Pope Gregory XV and in title VII of the 1st Partida of Alphonse the Wise.[324] The most usual practice was that abbesses were elected by the community in a public voice vote; but later, Sixtus V gave the nuns of Santa Clara the privilege of a secret ballot, and all the other Orders followed them. To be abbess, one was required to have professed vows for a certain number of years, and to have reached the age of forty in some instances and sixty in others; the bishop ratified the election and the post was held for life. These practices were not always followed, since in the majority of the monasteries the monarchs appointed the abbesses and frequently they selected their illegitimate daughters at the time they professed. There have been lay abbesses, even very young girls, and, nonetheless, they collected the tithes. The Gothic, Asturian and Leonese monarchy also had the custom that the kings' widows, as well as their lovers and any divorced princesses would seek refuge in the convents. Out of respect, deference and appreciation for the donations they gave they were elected abbesses. Convents were a refuge for all these ladies as well as for the second born daughters of noble families. There are even examples of peace treaties among nations in which the appointment of abbesses has been stipulated. In Spain married abbesses were not allowed, but in other places they existed, such as: the countess Apays, wife of Began, in Saint Pierre de Reims; Berta, mother in law of Oton II, in Merestein; Ogina, mother of Louis VI, in Saint Marie de Laon, and many others. The flourishing of Abbeys in the Middle Ages is well-known. Since women's monasteries were not called Abbeys, although they had abbesses, suffice it to quote the names of men's, the famous ones of: Poblet, in Spain; Alcobaça, in Portugal; Cluny, in France; Windsor, in England; and Monte Casino, in Italy.

Abbesses are the precursors of Spanish feminism because they were the first to aspire to equal rights with the abbots. In some monasteries they surpassed them, like the abbesses of Santa Cruz de la Serós versus the abbots of San Juan de la Peña. The abbesses of Santa Cruz had their own seal, they had vassals, collected tithes and received donations, and were honored to have housed Doña Urraca,[325] daughter of the King and sister of the bishop of Jaca, in

---

324 See chapter 3, note 57.
325 See chapter 6, note 165.

their monastery. Many abbesses had countless privileges and were given the titles of *Bishopess, Deaconess, Canoness*, and even *Popess*, although these were not official, but born from habit.

The most famous of the abbesses was that of Las Huelgas, the renowned monastery founded by Alphonse VIII in the 12th Century near Burgos, in a place of leisure, to which it owes its name. People used to say that the abbess of Las Huelgas had more privileges than all the others put together and that if "the Pope had to marry he would not find a woman with a standing closer to his than the abbess of Las Huelgas." She was a *mitered abbess*, that is to say that she had the right to wear a miter and other insignias of a bishop. She also had lordship of fifty villages and jurisdiction not only over her monastery, but over the nearby hospital, served by nuns who wear the Cross of Calatrava[326] on their chest, and another fourteen convents, among which are those of Palencia and Valladolid. Among her privileges was that of appointing the mayor, sheriffs and scribes in her jurisdiction. A judge administered justice in her name and the Magistrates of Burgos had to lay down their staff of office while on her grounds. The abbesses also provided for the prelacies and curates in their dominions, and awarded commendations and chaplainries; they even went as far as to grant dimissory permits[327] and confer orders and licenses to preach and hear confession. Some said that they even heard the confessions of their nuns and chanted the Gospel.

Others believe that this is a slur engendered by the habit of *declaring their sins* that exists in some convents; but the fact is that the abuse by the abbesses and abbots was so great that the ecclesiastical and civil powers abolished their privileges. The Spanish Parliament had to put an end to the abuses, especially by the abbots, counts and commanders of religious-military orders. Today, the abbey of Monserrat is the only one left in Spain. Once Pius IX eliminated their exemptions, today's abbesses are not more than veritable prioresses, heads of a Community, who rule and govern according to Canon Law and the Legal Codes of the various countries.

The laws of the Partidas, although they were not a Code until they were considered one later, have served as a basis for our legislation and still influence it today. We have already had the opportunity to see the laws' injustice towards women, since they

---

326   One of the most important and powerful Spanish military and religious orders; founded in the 12th Century.

327   The permission a bishop gives his subjects to be ordained or to leave for another parish.

were inspired by Roman law. They contain defamatory concepts, improper of a legislator's fairness of judgment and say that "a woman is not of as good a nature and state as a man." Informed by this idea, the laws order that "women must not approach the altar or be around it while the cleric says mass nor may they help him nor answer him." They also say that "in churches women must be separate from men" and that "they cannot live with clergymen unless they are their mothers, grandmothers, sisters, aunts, nieces or relatives once removed." Titles VII and VIII of the First Partida are dedicated to the religious profession of faith and the vows of humility, chastity and obedience that women declare. Not only virgins could embark on a religious life, but also widows and married women with the permission of their husbands. Men also needed the consent of their wives, who could force them to leave a religious order if they had joined it without fulfilling this requirement. But with regard to the other vows the husband *has an advantage over* the wife and can do as he pleases without her getting in the way. There are, however, important exceptions. The husband "cannot vow to fast nor avoid eating meat nor abstain from anything that could harm the wife, because she could become ill or weak and due to this he would not have offspring from her." The ninth law establishes that the husband cannot vow to go on a pilgrimage without the approval of the wife, except to Jerusalem, but in this case the wife has the right to accompany him.

Until that time, the Fuero Viejo and the Fuero Real forbid monasteries to inherit from a monk or a nun who died intestate, and asserted explicitly their right to make a will within the first year after professing, with the understanding that if s/he did not do it, his/her children or close relatives would inherit his/her possessions. But Law 17 in Title I of the 6th Partida forbids those who profess to make a will after their profession and stipulates that all their possessions belong to the monastery, except when there are children or obligatory heirs. The essential requirements for religious profession were specified in session XXV of the Council of Trent, the stipulations of which are law in Spain, according to the Phillip II's Royal Order in 1564.

The vows can be simple or solemn, and there are four requirements for them to be valid: first, the novice must be fully sixteen years of *age* for the simple vows and nineteen for the solemn ones, although they can enter the monastery at twelve; second, a *novitiate* of one year from the moment of taking of the habit; third, *free consent*, and fourth, the *dowry* that each order determines. Any person, regardless of his/her class and status, who forces a woman to enter a monastery against her will, to take the habit or to profess, will be excommunicated. The vows are permanent and their dispensation can only be granted by the Pontiff, for whom this privilege is reserved, as is that of dispensing someone from the vows of pilgrimage to Jerusalem, Santiago de Compostela and Saint Peter and Saint Paul, Rome.

Pius X wanted to make all religious vows temporary, and some renewable for a number of years. The newest Canon Law by decree of the "Holy Congregation of Bishops and Regulars" of 1902 establishes that the nuns who have professed their simple vows maintain full ownership of the estate they possessed upon entering the convent and of any property they might acquire before they profess the solemn vows, and they can dispose of these definitively up to two months before said profession. They are prohibited, however, from administering their property; hence before they take the simple vows, they must freely relinquish the administration, usufruct[328] and use to anyone whom they please. The Law also prohibits a nun from engaging in any kind of commerce. With just cause, the Holy See can expel nuns. Whenever they leave the convent, be it through expulsion or dispensation of vows, they are handed back their full dowry, but only the principal, without any interest.

Our Civil Code requires a woman to be of age to join a convent without the permission of her parents or her guardian. She needs counsel, just as she would to marry. In terms of her legal capacity, our laws try to erode it as much as possible, since they are dealing with a woman. At times, it has been recognized on an individual basis, but denied to the Community as a whole, as one can see in the Law of July 29, 1837. Yet at other times the opposite has happened, as the Royal Decree of July 25, 1868 shows. In our day, that is since the enactment of the second edition of the Civil Code, on May 27, 1889, religious Communities and their individual members have been granted the right to own and acquire property, repealing the provisions of the first edition, which prohibited it. In 1896 the Office of Records determined that, according to the law, the *Sisters of the Poor* had the legal capacity to enter into *contracts individually, even when they were professed nuns*. The lack of a necessary ecclesiastical license does not prevent the state from registering the documents signed by a nun. The heads of the dioceses can canonically correct the infraction of a Community or an individual member who did

---

328   The right to use and derive profit from a piece of property belonging to another, provided the property itself remains undiminished and uninjured in any way

not seek such a license, but once the act or contract has been entered into, it is valid in the civil realm, unless it is explicitly prohibited by law. The Code denies the right of professed nuns to marry unless they have received dispensation from their vows.

But it happens that for the Code to be in agreement with the requirements of the Council of Trent, following Phillip the II's Royal decree, it contradicts itself. The Code upholds the theory that the religious profession of a person does not modify her legal capacity and that a professed nun retains all the rights that the laws give to single women who are of age, or widows, depending on their civil status. This is why civil laws frequently protect the secularization of nuns who seek aid to leave the Order to which they belong; and it makes no sense that they be denied the right to marry if they change their mind about vows that should only bind them with their own conscience and not as citizens.

A nun is considered to be like the mother who remarries in terms of exercising paternal authority toward children she had before professing, and the children preserve all their rights of succession. The Partidas consider children born after the profession of vows to be the result of *sacrilege,* and the Laws of Montalvo, promulgated by the Catholic Kings in 1484 forbid their inheriting anything. The Laws of Toro allowed them to receive a fifth of their mother's estate while she was alive or upon her death, which was the amount she had at her disposal for her *funeral expenses.* In the spirit of the Code, nuns should be able to recognize these children, since those whose parents could marry with special permission are considered to be "natural," and this is the case of the nuns. They are also denied the right to adopt, something inexplicable since it is clerics who are prohibited from adopting and nuns are not in that category. The law does not uphold cloistered nuns' rules, since their order does not allow them to uncover their face in front of a man, and they are required to lift their veil before a notary.[329] The Code of Commerce forbids nuns to practice a mercantile profession in that it states that those to whom it is forbidden by law or other special circumstances may not practice it, since, as we know, Canon Law bans them from trade. The fulfillment of this provision is important in order to avoid disastrous competition with capitalists and workers, but it is not always carried out.

Many convents used to dedicate themselves to teaching

---

329   Author's note: Royal Order of 1867.

without their nuns having teaching degrees or inspections by the State, something remedied by the wise laws drafted by the count of Romanones. Today nuns need a professional degree and the State has the right to inspect their facilities.

Administrative Law established that the pensions enjoyed by widows and single daughters of those who have served the State would stop when they married or professed in a religious Order; but the Royal Order of November 21st, 1890 gave professed nuns the rights to receive said pensions. The recognized right of professed nuns to acquire and own property stood in favor of this provision, but the likening of the profession to marriage stood against it. The situation has been resolved in the recent Statute on Pensioners of the State, ratified in Barcelona on October 22, 1926. Pensions will cease upon marriage or profession, but if one professes or marries before the age of forty she will receive twelve monthly payments of the pension or part of the pension as a dowry, but in no case may the total sum be more than 1,500 pesetas. The pension they enjoy will not increase that of the other co-participants until the amount granted the nun is paid off.

In Conscription Law nuns are not granted any rights as mothers or sisters of the recruits since it is the Community, and not the soldiers, who supports them.

With regard to *Penal Law*, the 7th Partida established that a man who did not respect a nun's modesty and who committed the crime using force be sentenced to death and his estate be confiscated to benefit the monastery. If he committed it through deception or flattery, the punishment was only the confiscation of his property for the King's Chamber, in the case of an honest man, and lashes and exile to an island for five years if he was immoral. The current Penal Law does not take into account the religious profession of the victim. Attacks on modesty are punished with the sentences established for attacks on maidens. There is, however, the aggravating factor stipulated in article 10, number 20 of the Penal Code: "An act committed with disregard for or affront to the respect the injured party merits due to her position is an aggravating circumstance." Regarding the crimes that a professed nun commits, she is subject to ordinary law; her religious status has no influence on the punishment she receives. When it comes to Penal Law the justice system is much more generous in granting equality!

There are countries where nuns have even achieved political

rights. In Hungary Margarita Slachta,[330] of the Order of "Sisters of Social Service," was elected to Parliament as a member of the Christian Social party, which she represented before Congress in Washington. It is the first case of a Parliamentarian nun or a nun Parliamentarian.

---

330 Slachta (1884-1974) was a founding member of the order and is also remembered for resisting against the Nazis and trying to save Jewish lives during World War II.

CHAPTER 11
MILITARY RIGHTS

Historical precedents. –The ancient world. –The country of women. –Amazons. –Warriors of the Middle Ages. –In the Crusades. –The Lady of the Golden Legs. –Spanish women warriors. –The "she-male" of Castille. –The lieutenant nun. –Heroines. –The Code of the Partidas. –Twentieth-century women warriors.

Women have recently shown their extraordinary ease at adapting. During the Great War women took over all agricultural jobs, factories, workshops, department stores, and offices in the belligerent nations. We have seen them perform in all trades without exception, confirming the truth in that famous statement by Voltaire: "woman is capable of everything that man is capable of." Lloyd George[331] has confessed that: "without women's hard work the allies would not have won." Wilson said that: "the voluntary mobilization of women allowed the allied nations to employ all their strength in the world-wide conflict."

Women's performance in trades, professions and jobs has demonstrated that they are as physically able as men in all endeavors. In the same sense, when we study the organization of the family in antiquity, we see that in all primitive cultures women accompanied men to war, just as they still do now in some Asian and African tribes, and they also participate in their council's deliberations. It has been shown that initially men and women were considered suitable for the same work, and the more we have diverged from the laws of nature, the more marked the difference between the genders has become. In remote antiquity, Egypt showed us the example of women who were fit for warlike arts. Queen Hatason (c. 1500 BCE) was a Napoleon of her time. Before the Greeks sought the *golden fleece*, she fit galleys that sailed seas which were unexplored until then, and they returned loaded with treasure, scents and exotic plants, which she later grew in her gardens. A woman, Amten,[332] was *general and commander of the*

---

331   David Lloyd George (1863-1945) was a British liberal politician and Prime Minister of the U.K. from 1916-1922.

332   It appears that Antem, also known as the "Great Huntsman" and the "Primate of the Western Gate," was actually a man. However, in 1898, the ethnographer Jean Cidbat published a volume titled *Le Tombeau de la dame Antem*, 'The Tomb of Lady Antem.'

Gateway to the West, and defended it against the bandits of the desert. The Hittite people – whose women were warlike and dominating – were ensconced between Mesopotamia and Egypt.

Some historians place the people of Su-fa-la-min-Ko-chu-lo (country of eastern women) in the middle of the mountains of Western China. Only the women ruled and governed there, using the men to defend the borders. The head of this State, which consisted of nineteen cities, was a queen, whose nine-story palace built at the top of a bluff merited brilliant descriptions. She is pictured with a helmet covering her beautiful, black mane, a long-trained dress, and large earrings. Her title means: "She who goes first." During the 7th Century, the empress of China Wou-Heo[u] named Lio[u]-P[i], queen of Su-fa-la-nin-Ko-chu-lo, general of fort Ya-Khian-We[i]. [333] China is a country that has always had Amazons. History records their battles against the ferocious Huns. Among them Thingtoc stands out for her courage, she took sixty villages in the name of the emperor, half a century before Jesus Christ. The Amazons are always depicted with soldiers' armors.

The legend of the Amazons is so universal, that without a doubt it represents a historical fact, although people have fantasized about it a good deal, and some have tried to find symbolic explanations for it. In all proto-history there are vestiges of the Amazons, but the state where the most well-known legend hails from was located at the foot of the Caucasus, in Sarmatia, where it is said that Pompeius[334] found Amazons. The origins of these Amazons lie in a Scythian[335] town whose women rose up when their men were killed by an enemy people. The women were accustomed to military exercises so they quickly became ferocious warriors who not only avenged their dead, but also formed an independent state and vowed to eternally hate the other gender, to such a degree that they became known as Men Killers – a name which has led some to believe that Amazons are only a myth and represent the feminine principle and its battle with the masculine principle in ancient theogonies, in which the Sun and the Moon fought for dominance. Others consider them to have been priestesses and construe the nickname as referring to sacrifices of male blood that they offered their Goddesses. According to legend,

---

333 Burgos' source for this information is Léon Abensour's *Histoire générale du féminisme des origines à nos jours* (Paris: Delagrave, 1921) 38.

334 Gnaeus Pompeius Magnus (106-48 BCE).

335 A nomadic people originally of Iranian stock who migrated from Central Asia to southern Russia in the 8th and 7th Centuries BCE.

their fame as strong women aroused Greece's envy. Hercules[336] reached the city of Themiscyra[337] and fought the women warriors who wore outfits made from animal skins: pants, tall boots with curved toes, pointed hats. And they were armed with double axes, arrows and spears and carried a shield in the form of a quarter moon. They had cut off their left breast in order to better handle the bow. As humanly courageous as they were, they were unable to defeat those who were protected by Jupiter. Antiope, the queen, was taken prisoner and the beautiful Hyppolite was led to Greece. There she forgot her sisters, for the love of Theseus, to the point that she fought against them when they, wishing to avenge their defeat, crossed over the ice of the Bosphorus [Istanbul Strait] and laid siege to Athens for four months, a blockade that ended with a treaty of alliance.

Penthesilea's combat is a poetic episode. The most beautiful Amazon appeared before Troy with twelve courageous comrades; stunning, with her helmet and golden arms, she fought Achilles, who plunged the magic sword that Vulcan had forged into her throat. It is true that the Greek hero cried over his deed when he saw Penthesilea's sculptural beauty, as great as that of Minerva and Aphrodite.

The Amazons scattered throughout Assyria, India and Africa; only after many centuries did those who had established a colony on the shore of lake Tritonis[338] return to Asia, where their queen Thalestris, fascinated by Alexander's courage, paid homage to him. Despite the legend of the Amazons' beauty and the pretty statues with which artists have portrayed them, the portrait of an authentic Amazon, found in the ruins of Boghazkoi[339] casts doubt on this idealized representation. It is the image of a shrew, scraggly haired, big bellied, ghastly, but on the other hand it testifies to the existence of those masculine women who, like all Scythian women and those living in the settlements near the Caucasus, the Danube and the steppes of the Taur[us] Mountains rode horses and shared the perils of war with their men.

There also exists a tradition of Amazons in Bohemia; during the time of Charles Martel (c. 688—741) they left their country, founded the city of Drevvin (city of Virgins) on a high bluff, and banned men from entering it. Wlasta, their queen, was known for the beauty of her

---

336 This is a reference to the legendary ninth labor of Hercules, the "Girdle of the Amazon."
337 In Greek mythology, the capital of the Amazons.
338 A mythological lake in northern Libya.
339 An ancient Hittite city in Turkey that archaeologists began to excavate in the early 20th Century, and which yielded some 10,000 clay tablets.

magnificent red tresses and for keeping her breast bare. Bohemian warriors founded the city of [V]isegrad in front of Drevvin, but they were unable to defeat the Amazons in battle. The combat lasted until they tricked them into celebrating a banquet to mark the occasion of a truce, and at dessert each man seized the woman he had next to him and carried her away to his city.

The Romans remember Clelia, an Amazon who broke through Etruscan troops and crossed the Tiber on horseback. Zanobia, queen of Palmyra,[340] can be considered an Amazon, so can the courageous Kahina, who led the Berbers and died fighting the Arab general Hassan. No one should believe that the Amazons existed only in antiquity. We find them transformed in the Middle Ages. During their husbands' long absences, the ladies of the castle did more than watch over their interests, they armed their serfs against invaders and sometimes they themselves took part in the lucrative pillaging of their neighbors' lands. Feudal legislation recognized women's military abilities. So, we see many ride horses and do battle like men.

During the Crusades, the women —both of humble origins and grand ladies—who fought to rescue the Holy Sepulcher from the hands of the infidels are legion. One of the first who died fighting against the Turks was Florina, the daughter of the duke of Bourgogne, who accompanied her fiancé, the prince of Denmark, and died with him in the deserts of Anatolia. Eleanor of Aquitaine and Margaret of Provence both accompanied their husbands. A great lady fit out a ship and steered it herself. Of the humble women who fought like soldiers the most famous are the ones who climbed the city walls of Antioch during the siege [in 1098] and threw stones and burning oil on the Saracens. Three hundred women warriors led by the renowned *Lady of the golden legs* were imprisoned by the Turks, who only realized what gender they were when they took off their helmets and saw their tresses unfurl.

There are plenty of heroines all over Europe. In France, a Spaniard, lady Blanca of Castille, personally besieged the city of Bailén while her son, San Luis, was still a minor, and Blanche of Champagne battled against the enemy of Thibault, her son, whom she challenged to a duel. Joanna de Montfort fought for twenty years to gain possession of her duchy of Brittany and forced Charles de Blois to end the siege of Anneban. There are innumerable examples of women warriors that culminate in the well-known example of

---

340   An ancient city in central Syria.

Joan of Arc: Queen Emma, who protected Verdun; the wives of Saint Riquier, la Rochela and Péronne defending their cities, with all the courage of the princess of Epinay, whose statue stands in Tournai.[341]

At the beginning of the 17th Century, when Cardinal Mazzarino[342] took the prince of Condé prisoner, the princess went personally to incite Bordeaux to revolt and spoke with such eloquence that she achieved her aim. Among the ladies who went with her was Mlle. Gerbier, a pretty, young 18-year-old, and Mmes. Fierque and Fontenac. Mlle. Montpensier stood in for her sick father and went to the aid of Orléans, which she entered through a breach in the wall.

Without a doubt, the French Revolution succeeded due to the support of women. Thereoigne de Mericourt appears with her squadron of Amazons declaring the famous phrase: "Can men really believe that they are the only ones who deserve glory?" In almost all provinces legions of Amazons were formed. Lodoiska Carneska[343] dressed in military clothing with Turkish bloomers and a red velvet Hungarian cavalry jacket and hung two guns from her belt. The renowned Mother Duchène, a decrepit little old lady, was the first one to expound the entire Bolshevik[344] theory to the revolutionaries, with its process of socialization, the dictatorship of the proletariat, and the terror. Pauline Leon presented the Legislative Assembly with a petition for military rights from 800 women.

Many women have died in the streets of Paris with a rifle in their hands in various occasions. One of them defended the Montparnasse station against the supporters of Versailles. The Fernig sisters reached the rank of officers, and General Dumouriez mentioned them in a military communiqué. Rosa Doullon accompanied her husband to Alsace and fought boldly at his side. Mme. Marthes conquered an Austrian flag, and General Anselme's sister completed an entire campaign and entered Nice at the head of 500 warriors.

---

341   While her husband was away, Christine de Lalaing defended Tournai from the duke of Parma in 1581. The city withstood two months of siege before it fell.

342   Mazzarino was a French-Italian cardinal, diplomat, and politician, who served as the chief minister of France from 1642 until his death.

343   Wife of Jean Baptiste Louvet de Couvray (1760-1798)? French writer and politician, whose novel *Les Amours du chevalier de Faublas* is the basis for Cherubini's opera Lodoiska.

344   Mother Duchene was a popular fictional character who appeared in a series of propagandistic publications during the French Revolution. Of course, Burgos is being anachronistic by talking about Bolsheviks in the late 18th Century when they only existed in the 20th, but, as she has before, she is pointing out the similarities in thinking between revolutionary communists of her time and earlier revolutionaries or activists.

The example of Louise Michel clearly shows that in each woman there is a spirit that is capable of sacrificing for the motherland and being a brave soldier when it is needed. This saintly woman, unjustly slandered by her enemies, burned with human love for all beings, like Saint Francis of Assisi, and, despite this, she did not hesitate to organize female battalions against the invaders[345] in 1870, and wore a national guard's uniform. Louise Michel, who was called the Red Virgin because of her red hair, is one of the most beautiful examples of peace and love. Her delightful spirit made her an optimist, she thought life was beautiful and humanity good, it was only our being temporarily off course that produced the turmoil, and she waited for the day in which everyone would live happily, without killing or enslaving each other. In the meantime, she aided all who approached her without asking them who they were or what they thought. She housed the first stranger who asked her to, she had the compassion to pick up those who had fallen, the selflessness to care for the sick, the love to console the abandoned. She practiced true communism, distributing whatever she had among the vagabonds who had no bread or work; she never closed the door to her home. Her protection went so far as to rescue our brother cats and dogs who were cruelly abandoned by humans. She even begged for alms so that she could hand them out. Her sweet words preached the forgetting of grudges: "Forget it all," she said, "forgive it all, give whatever you have if you wish never to lack anything." And this woman put on a warrior's uniform to defend her fatherland and she led the hungry hordes and gave them bread from the bakery. She is proof of the courage and goodness that can appear together when justice demands it.

In Italy, one can recall the names of heroines like: Bianca Visconti, the wife of Francesco Sforza, who defended Cremona against the Venetians and repulsed their ships; Catalina Sforza defended Forle; Countess Malespina, aided by other courageous ladies, defended Pavia against Francis I[346] and Lady Constanza D'Avalos remained on the island of Ischia fighting in the name of Charles V.[347]

In Spain, there have always been Amazons. Cantabrian women

---

345   During the Franco-Prussian war, Paris was under siege. Michel helped to defend the city.

346   Feb. 24, 1525, during the war between Spain and France.

347   Constanza D'Avalos took up arms and defended Ischia for four months against 40 French galleys in 1502, two years after Charles V's birth, so it would have been in the name of the Catholic Kings that she defended Ischia.

worked the fields in peacetime and took part in war just like their men. In the 8th Century the women of Jaca went out armed with spears, knives and stones in defense of the men who were fighting against the Moors; they made such a show of strength and such noise that they frightened the enemy and determined the victorious outcome.[348] Even now every year they celebrate a pilgrimage to the Virgen de las Victorias, which all the women attend wearing the gold cross of Sobrarbe and a red banner on which one can see the decapitated heads of the four Moorish kings whom they defeated in the memorable battle. During the reign of Ramón Berenguer IV [1131-1162], the women of Tortosa defended the city so valiantly that the king allowed them to wear a double axe embroidered in red or scarlet on their dresses as a memento of their courage.

Epic poems tell us of heroines like Tarquira, in *La Bética Conquistada*,[349] who fought wearing men's clothes and who are surely not the figment of a poetic imagination since, unfortunately, our epic poetry suffers from a lack of inventiveness and the artists curbed their imaginations to stick to reality, creating something closer to a rhymed history than a real poem.

But returning to the realm of history, somewhat mixed with legend, we can see the great figure of the Barona of Castille, Doña María Pérez appear. Of noble Gothic lineage, brought up in the castle of Villanañe along with her brothers engaged in masculine pursuits, she did not want to be away from them and accompanied them to war, dressed as a man. Many were the heroic feats that María Pérez carried out: she took Mayor and Torquemada, and the castle, which was named *las Dueñas* because it was conquered by women. But her most significant and legendary victory was her defeat of King Alphonse I of Aragón, the Warrior, when the heroic maiden came upon him on the plains of Atienza. The king fought her, thinking her a man, and, defeated, he begged her to tell him her name to make sure he was surrendering to a nobleman before he gave her his sword. Imagine his surprise and confusion when he realized he had been defeated by a woman. He kept the deed so much in mind, that once peace was restored with his stepson, Alphonse of Castille, he gave him a ring to give to Doña María that bore the Aragonese coat of arms as a sign of his having been vanquished. The Castilian monarch then bestowed on her the title of Baron of Castille, which

---

348 This is one of the legendary deeds surrounding the battle between the Moors and Conde Aznar Galíndez in 758.

349 By Juan de la Cueva, 1603.

people turned into "Barona"[350] of Castille. When Doña María became widowed from don Vela, son of the king of Navarre, she ended her days in a convent to do penance for the years she had spent killing, and according to Monje,[351] in the Cloister of San Salvador de Oña one could read this epitaph until recently: "Here rests in peace the very illustrious and courageous Captain María Pérez, conqueror of Kingdoms and provinces. The wars with a sword earned her the name Varón, which turned into the feminine "Varona." Vivit caelo illa quae tal in muros et judeos in Hispania occidit."[352]

In the 16th Century, the heroic Galician María Pita appears to defend La Coruña, besieged by the British. She wielded a dead soldier's sword and buckler and shouted at the men who were disheartened and ready to surrender: "Let he who has honor follow me." She attacked so valiantly that she revived everyone's courage, so much so that the besiegers had to retreat. Phillip II gave this admirable woman the rank and pay of a lieutenant, which he sustained into perpetuity for her descendants. Her house is preserved in La Coruña, and recently a commemorative stone plaque has been placed there.

Another Spanish heroine who could have come out of a novel is the renowned *Lieutenant Nun* Doña Catalina de Erauso, born in San Sebastián. At an early age, she showed masculine tendencies and when she was very young she ran away from the convent of Dominican nuns of San Sebastián the Older. The vicissitudes of the first part of her life emulate those of *Guzmán de Alfarache* or *Gil Blas de Santillana*.[353] She finally appeared in Veracruz (Mexico), where she earned a living by hauling goods as the owner of a train of mules. Later, *Mule Driver Nun* became a soldier in Peru and Chile. Her determination to hide her gender is admirable; she even went as far as to live next to her brother, Don Miguel de Erauso, as a comrade without revealing her secret. It was only when she was seriously wounded and in danger of dying that she made her confession to the

---

350   This is a play on words between "Barón" and "varón" (male, man) which in Spanish are pronounced the same way, and "Barona" and "varona", the first meaning a female baron (but not exactly baroness, with its feminine connotations) and a masculine woman, or "she male."

351   Rafael Monje published "La varona castellana" in the *Semanario Pintoresco Español* in 1848.

352   May she who killed so many Moors and Jews in Spain live in heaven.

353   These are both picaresque novels in which the heroes –of lower class extraction and poor moral character– undergo a series of adventures with their masters that usually turn out poorly for them.

Bishop of Guanaza. Love did not intercede, as some of the literary works inspired by her have fantasized, such as Castillo Solórzano's novel *El Bachiller Trapaza* or Montalván and Coello's comedies.

Catalina de Erauso's birth certificate is kept in the parochial records of San Vicente, in San Sebastián, and is dated February 10, 1592. The Basque heroine stood out in the war using the name Alonso Díaz Ramírez de Guzmán and her feats are confirmed by irrefutable testimony. Don Luis de Céspedes Xeria issued the following document: "I certify and attest to Your Honor, that I have known Doña Catalina de Erauso for more than eighteen years, and that she started to serve as a soldier dressed as a man." Don Guillén de Casanova, governor of the Castle of Arauco chose her from the rest of her company, "for being courageous and a good soldier," to go out onto the battlefield against the enemy, those ferocious Indians, whose valor Ercilla noted in *La araucana*. Captain Don Franciso Pérez de Navarrete also praises her bravery and Captain Don Gonzalo Rodríguez says that in the battle of Purén "she distinguished herself for her valor and resolve and she was wounded many times." One of her biographers who met her in Rome says that her face and her body looked like a man's, and that she told him when she was very young she had had an operation to avoid the development of her breasts. Don Diego Ignacio Góngora met her in Seville, in 1626, upon his return from Rome, where he had gone to beg the Pontiff's pardon for her escape from the monastery.

It is frequent to see the combination of religious and bellicose feelings in knights and warriors of this time. They went easily from the convent to the battlefield or vice versa. When war was waged among peoples of different religions, and killing men did not rule out canonization, it had something of the holiness that it maintains for the Arabs.

Spain still had Amazons in the 19th Century. In the first place, one should mention Doña María Consolación Azloz, countess of Bureta, who earned the name of *Heroine of Aragon*. Although she was a widow, young, beautiful, the mother of young children whom she worshipped, she did not hesitate to give up everything and go offer General Palafox her fortune and her person to fight as a soldier in the defense of Zaragoza, against Napoleon's armies. One could see the countess fighting in the most dangerous places, with a cartridge belt around her waist and a rifle in her hand. On August 4, 1808, at the Arch of Cineja she had two cannons dragged in front of her own house, and with a skillful tactic she caught the enemy between two lines of fire and forced them to retreat, chased by the courageous

Calvo de Rojaza. Palafox ordered steel sheets engraved in which the countess appeared with a rifle in hand, rallying the troops.

Agustina Zaragoza Domenech immortalized her name in this same siege of Zaragoza. She began by accompanying her boyfriend, an artillery sergeant, and giving out water, food and ammunition among the fighters. "Take heart, artillerymen," she would say. "When you can no longer fight, there are women here." Her words were not bravado. At the most dangerous time, when her boyfriend was dead and the artillerymen were destroyed, the enemy was going to come in through a breach in the wall, she walked over the dead bodies and fired the 42-caliber cannon, an extraordinary feat at that time. The example enlivened the men and they returned the fire. Agustina Zaragoza continued fighting in the most dangerous positions until the end of the siege. Despite her being sick with the plague in the hospital, the French made her prisoner, but she managed to escape while she was being transferred across the countryside, carrying her son —who died soon after arriving into safety— in her arms. General Palafox decorated her himself after the first battle and pinned the ribbon of honor on her chest on December 31, when she defended the Puerta del Carmen. In his portrayal of her Palafox says: "She is twenty to twenty-two years old, tall, shapely, brunette, and charming." She passed away when she was second lieutenant of Infantry in the Ceuta regiment.

There were many heroic women in Zaragoza. Palafox declared that "they asked to be placed in the most dangerous positions and some were carried out suffering from horrendous wounds." He added that they were "the envy of everyone and an example of valor." We must also mention: Casta Álvarez, wounded in the neck and Manuela Sancho, wounded in the stomach, both of whom returned to fight as soon as they were treated.

Benita Portales was the first person who went into the middle of the Plaza de la Magdalena encouraging everyone, including her own husband. When she was imprisoned and condemned to death, General Suchet, admiring her courage, pardoned her. Catalan women were no less heroic at the siege of Gerona. One hundred and twenty women appeared before Don Mariano Álvarez asking to take part in the battle as soldiers. The general formed four female companies, under the leadership of *Commander* Doña Cándida Moles and *Captains* Doña Luisa Fonama, Doña Ángeles Pinerua, Doña Ramira Nouvilas and Doña Carmen Custs. Once the siege of Gerona was over, these Amazons fought in Tortosa and Tarragona. Worthy of mention is Doña Francisca Artigas, who saw her father die at the hands of the invaders and to avenge him fought boldly in all of the cities mentioned above, distinguishing herself through her fierceness and the number of casualties she caused the enemy. This heroic woman also deserves a place among the martyrs, because once they took her prisoner, already badly wounded, the French treated her with iniquitous cruelty. They tied her to the mouth of a cannon and whipped her and committed all kinds of atrocities.

Women of all the regions behaved with the same bravery. Let it suffice to remember in Castile, the women of Madrid on the Second of May and in Andalucía, the women of Cádiz, last bastion of liberty, and the famous ditty:

> With the bullets
> That the braggarts fire
> The Cádiz ladies
> make ringlets [in their hair]

In the present day, women's bravery has not waned. There are some very recent examples. When Viviani[354] called all men to defend France in 1914, even though they had no training, women valiantly threw themselves into the work in military offices, factories, and workshops to such a degree that everyone has confessed that a large part of the victory is due to the *municionettes* [women munitions workers]. President Wilson called on women during the mobilization the same as men. Mrs. Violette and Markham[355] occupied high posts in the National Service Department of the United States, and Mrs. Tenant was Assistant Secretary of State.

Wanting to participate in all the battles and dangers, German women demanded the creation of the National Women's Army, and also served as courageous examples by carrying out work in the fields and the mines.

In England women took on the coarsest jobs, they carried out all the public works, labored in the explosives factories and as cooks, telephone operators and military cyclists, they even served as policewomen.

In Russia, from ancient times on, women have served as examples of bravery. During the time of the czars they were the first to protest against the tyranny. The jails were full of admirable women: well educated mothers and wives, of high standing, abandoned it

---

354 See chapter 8, note 237.

355 This is actually one person: Violet Markham, (1872–1959) a British writer, social reformer and public servant. In 1917, she became deputy director of women's section of The Office of National Service, which was a British agency as well.

all to defend the holy cause of the oppressed people. There were those who were as beautiful as Maria Kulinoskaia, whom even the jailers called Kupidanskaia, who sacrificed herself as did Sigida Novakarski, Vera Zassouliny, Maria Woronzof, Sophia Boyomdetz, Essia Hoffmann and Elisabeth Olaveriskof: some died in jail; others went mad with pain; the rest were murdered.

During the Great War, the Russians not only went to work, but they formed battalions of women soldiers. The revolution has not been able to be ungrateful towards them as was the French Revolution, not because their men are more just or more consistent, but because the most experienced women *demanded* instead of *begging*. A demonstration of 45,000 women preceded by a squadron of Amazons placed themselves in front of Tauride Palace [Saint Petersburg] and the presidents of the Soviets and the Duma,[356] Techeidze and Rodzianko had to break their silence and recognize their civil and political rights.

It is true that when they reached the most radical period, Russian women repeated the terrible scenes of the Terror in France, demonstrating that in cruelty just as in heroism they can be equal to men. One half of humanity has the same vices and virtues as the other half. The bravery of the Russian women was admirable when on November 3rd, 1917 they created the *Battalion of Death*. They were the first victims to fall before the Winter Palace, fighting against the coup and defending order and the republic. Russian women hurled a manifesto into the world against Bolshevik tyranny and the dissolution of the Parliament.

If we think about these examples of wars, we will see that women can be suitable for military service. It is true that, as a legislator a woman would always try to avoid war, but once it was accepted, its inevitability would overcome any false sentimentalism, but this does not imply a lack of tenderness, as it does not for men either. It is precisely because of love that women have always leaped into battle, to defend their own. They always see the son, the eternal child in a man, and wish to protect him in the battlefields just as they do at home. The selflessness, with which women accompany Armies —be it with the esteemed Red Cross, or as water carriers—, is proof of their courage. It is unfair that they should be kept from participating in battle and carrying arms when they are allowed to

---

356 Soviets were elected governmental councils, and the Duma was a representative body, mostly during the Tsarist era, since during the revolution it elected members of a provisional committee and was dissolved.

put their life at risk by accompanying armies. If they can go to work as water carriers, they can equally go as officers or commanders. Women can carry out a very important mission in ambulances, in the General Staff, in offices, in the administration and in many positions that men monopolize both in the Navy and in the land Army. During the Great War, there were already women performing as officers in the North American Navy.

Hence, we must demand the right of women to form part of the Army, receive military training like men and be prepared like them, lest we again require that prodigious effort that they put forth in the warring countries in 1914. Women's services were only organized in the last two years of the war, to avoid a greater waste of energy, and to allow women to do their work under better conditions. After the example women have given, no one doubts the advantages of female mobilization in times of war, but it should not be organized precipitately, improvising everything.

Today, it is in Poland where the idea of making military service extend to women is progressing most quickly. The top military authorities, presided by Marshall Pilsudski, are trying to declare the military preparation of young women obligatory; in case of conflict, they would make up an Auxiliary Military Service Corps.

The Spanish Constitution does not deny women the right to defend the fatherland, since it does not distinguish between the genders when it talks about citizens. This right is virtually recognized in that Queens and female members of the royal family are granted army ranks, and they have the same rights of citizenship before the law as other women. There also exist the precedents of women who held ranks, such as María Pita, Agustina Zaragoza and a few others. In our early legislation, a woman was not excluded from military service either, since the law of the Partidas states that: "she will be compelled to go to war in the case of a rebellion against the King." Reading closely, we can see that women are allowed to be imperiled, but they are not given a position in which they will have subordinates. With regard to ability one must remember Tacitus' renowned statement: "when in danger, a woman's spirit can outdo in bravery and suffering that of great and illustrious men." But since all ideas of superiority in a gendered sense are absurd, we must agree that both sexes can be exactly the same.

CHAPTER 12
EMANCIPATION THROUGH FASHION

The law and fashion. —Reasons for the existence of fashion. —Its influence on the lives of women. —The influence that literature has. —Emancipation of women through fashion. —Modern customs. —Clubs and sports. —The uniformity of beauty.

Fashion is as old as human beings. From the earliest of times, by consensus we have been inclined to adopt specific forms in customs: eating, dressing, speaking and behaving. This is what constitutes fashion, although generally the meaning is restricted to dress, or at most, social practices.

Fashion is, by its very nature, variable. The very fact of living brings with it a wearing out which ends in the negation that we call death, which occupies our thoughts for barely a moment, if at all, when we open our window each day for the new sunlight to enter. Fashion trends die out when they are worn out and are reborn, each one of its phases replaced with new and different ones, which at bottom are always the same. But fashion is not erratic and arbitrary as Simmel[357] believes when he states: "We can almost never discover a material, esthetic or other kind of reason that will explain the variations of fashion." Older writers, such as Feijóo[358], held this opinion; he tells the anecdote of a fool who walked around naked, carrying a bolt of fabric on his shoulder, not daring to make himself a suit for fear of the variations of fashion.[359]

Dr. Marañón[360] admirably synthesizes the reasons behind those variations, saying, "Fashion always obeys perfectly recognizable and fixed causes, which have to do with: *usefulness, economics* and *sexuality*. Consider all trends in clothing and body shape and you will see that these three causes, combined in different proportions, can always be uncovered." My experience, after having studied the matter for many

---

357   See chapter 1, note 24.

358   Benito Jerónimo Feijóo (1676-1764) was a Benedictine monk who taught theology and philosophy at the University of Oviedo. He was a major figure of the Spanish Enlightenment who combatted superstitions and injustices.

359   Author's note: *Teatro Crítico.*

360   See chapter 2, note 26.

years in order to deal with it in newspapers and books, compels me to be in complete agreement with this theory. How usefulness and necessity have influenced fashion can be proven. In fashion trends, there is always something very important, very hidden, capable of revealing on its own the essence of an age and the spirit of a people.

If we limit ourselves to dealing only with sartorial fashion, we can observe that it is always influenced by usefulness, even if ornamentation is mixed into it, which expresses the tendency towards art that exists in the human spirit. Dress comes into being due to need, but soon an artistic instinct, a sense of beauty embellishes it. It is an attempt to beautify clothing. At the beginning men and women's clothing differed little, and only a few centuries ago men exceeded women in the lavishness of their dress, made with embroideries that contained pearls and precious stones, prized lace and sumptuous fabrics. Conflicts and battles created the armors of the warriors, and work and men's occupations forced them to leave their robes and their ancient clothes and adopt trousers. Taine says that the sign of the evolution of the world is this change in male clothing: the conquest of trousers. Men came to make pants into a sign of virility. When they want to assert their dominance, it is common to hear: "In my home no one wears the pants but me."

We can study the customs of an age in women's clothing. We need only see the luxurious and heavy dresses of the castle dwellers in the Middle Ages to think how they harmonized with the coffered ceilings and tall mantelpieces of their dining rooms, or with the hunting excursion on horseback, falcon in hand. The age in which a woman was no more than a charming toy brings us the enormous hair styles that required a wire scaffolding to hold them up, and shoes that were so fragile that when, at the time of Louis XV, one lady complained to her shoemaker, he replied with surprise: "What, lady, you need shoes to walk!" Those hair styles, those shoes, those fragile and lavish outfits are appropriate for the ladies that inherited the privileges of Courtly Love[361] and the chivalrous age, occupying themselves only with gallantries in their salons and carried about on a litter.

The ringlets, crinolines, and bustles worn less than a century ago could not be worn by a woman who gets on a tram, in a car or on an airplane. It happened that in the theaters where, at that time,

---

361   In the middle ages, this was a mostly literary relationship based on a set of strict rules whereby the woman is placed in the position of authority, she is the lady, and the man is her servant.

women were forbidden to be among men,[362] there were *squeezers* in the *cazuela* – which was the name of the place reserved for women – who would crush their dresses to fit them in, since each one took up the room of half a dozen. All that expensive, heavy, cumbersome, hard to wear clothing would be impossible today for women who participate in active life, in work and in sports – some driven by economic need, others by habit.

Dress reveals the customs of a people, as we can see in Indian women, obliged to wear a *purdah*, that prevents them from showing themselves in public; Arabic women hide their face with a veil, a custom that has left traces in the Algarve, where women cover their faces with their long shawls, and in towns of Andalusia, where it is customary for village women not to show themselves without a scarf on their head. Until recently, women in Constantinople, Angora and Smyrna, have been subject to hiding in their loose dress, the caftan and their veil. Now that they have gained their freedom in such large part, they are forbidden in Trabzon to wear those garments on the street, under penalty of jail.

With respect to fashion, women have shown their spirit of independence since antiquity. In Rome, when the Oppian Law[363] forbade women to wear different color dresses, they all rose up against Cato. Women invaded all the streets leading to the Forum, carrying the citizens in their wake, and they whistled at the wise man when they went by. He then delivered his most violent speech against women. He said, "Restrain the tyrannical nature of that untamed animal. Our forefathers wanted women to be under the guardianship of their fathers and brothers or husbands. Remember that all laws have chained women, have locked them up under the power of men and, despite their being serfs, you can hardly contain them. Do not allow them to snatch away your rights one by one and become your equals, because soon enough they will be your superiors." Lucius Valerius and Fundan[i]us, who defended the women's cause and managed to repeal the Oppian Law, can be considered among the first feminists.

The promulgation of sumptuary laws[364] has been attempted many times with only temporary success. There was a desire to establish a separation of castes through clothing, forbidding peasants to wear what ladies were allowed. The laws of the Partidas prohibited

---

362 Author's note: *Novísima Recopilación*
363 The law forbade women to wear dresses with purple trim. It also prohibited women from riding in carriages, and limited the amount of gold women could possess.
364 These are laws made to restrain extravagant expenditures.

honest women from wearing jerkins[365] and farthingales.[366] They established that a woman who was "virtuous or honest and wears the clothing of disreputable women, cannot sue someone who shows her a lack of respect or offends her."

For a long time, women have not had an area other than fashion in which to use their imagination, hence the passion with which they have devoted themselves to creating and reproducing new styles of dress, hairdos and accessories. All women's art is in the history of clothing. Their paintings, their sculptures, their literature had to be condensed into their sartorial creations. Undoubtedly, the industry —jewelry, textiles, dry cleaning, embroidery, etc.—, was developed by them. At times, their talent took motifs from nature, imitating shades and forms; at others, it reflected things they admired, like the corset influenced by Northern warriors, whose bodies, in their armors, resembled those of wasps. Fashion was a type of freemasonry among women in every country. The renowned dolls of Saint Honoré Street,[367] which travelled to show their French genius' new creations, were a precursor to sewing patterns, which universalized outfits, replacing the labor of individual women who created and imposed their tastes, with a model created by seamstresses and professional designers, who sometimes look for inspiration to artists and painters.

Literature influenced fashion. *Paul and Virginia* by Bernadin de Saint-Pierre inspired the fashion of romantic muslin, light and thin, just as the fashion immortalized by Watteau is due to *Repose in the village* by Rousseau.[368] Fondness for fashion has been considered a feminine frivolity. A writer says, "When it is a matter of buttoning a dress, a woman's instructions to the maid, her looks in the mirror, her turns, her steps forward and back, the movements of her arms, her bending of the waist will exasperate the most patient husband watching those interminable preparations that never end. They cannot get dressed without help; they even need someone to button their gloves." For this author, making a man wait is a crime and he chronicles the fact that queens Cristina and Victoria of Spain made Alphonse XII wait a few minutes on the day of their marriage. As proof of female inferiority, he says that "a woman could spend an hour gazing at a hat."

---

365   Short tight-fitting jackets, usually sleeveless.

366   Hoopskirts.

367   In the 18th Century, these were also called Pandoras, and were small dolls about 12" tall that were used to show new outfits, much like mannequins. They often travelled throughout Europe.

368   See chapter 4, note 80.

And, yet, men fear that women will lose their flirtatiousness. This is precisely one of the arguments used against feminism. Mme. Paquin has said that "the feminist movement means the end of women's beauty and for this reason feminism will never prevail in France." But it is precisely the opposite. Feminism has come to save fashion because it has emancipated women. In the past, there were only restrictions for women. Make-up was considered especially sinful, and whether it was allowable or not was debated. Let us remember the Archpriest of Hita's books,[369] in which he peers into women's chests and criticizes their cosmetics, and the viciousness with which the Archpriest of Talavera speaks about their attire in the *Corbacho*, where he clings to the habit of speaking poorly of women, which he resurrected from Simonides, Aristophanes and Plato; motivated by a wish for revenge, Boccaccio wrote against a woman, while he also desired to entertain Fiammetta, that is the princess Maria, sister of Joanna I of Naples, and to enjoy the laughter of both when he read to them in the famous Neapolitan Egg castle.[370] Since it was inspired by Eastern texts, our early literature presents women as treacherous, while the books of chivalry convert them into sleeping beauties of the woods, who can only allow themselves to be adored.

Mr. Well,[371] a Jesuit, defended the right of women to adorn themselves, with decency, to please their husbands. This already points to the *sexual* motivation that Marañón[372] speaks about when he says, "It has been said many times that there is no stronger enemy of love than habit, and with good reason. A man and a woman who love each other need to renew the external cause of their attraction constantly so that it will last: new outfits, the celebration of certain anniversaries, absences, fights and subsequent reconciliations are only different ways of renewing the power of attraction, and fighting against the monotony of habit and routine." In fact, a woman is never more brilliant and visible than when fashion trends vary greatly. Her variations bring about a constant renewal of her figure, it is as if she placed herself in front of a beam of light that illuminated her and she showed off now an arm, now a hand, now a neckline or her hair, and this creates an exaltation of passion, although, as even Marañón

---

369   This is the semi-autobiographical *Book of Good Love*, written in the 14th Century, which includes a variety of women with whom the protagonist has relationships.

370   Giovanni Boccaccio wrote *The Elegy of Lady Fiammetta* between 1343 and 1345. In it Fiammetta recounts the vicissitudes of her extramarital love affair with Panfilo.

371   This is likely Herber Manning Wells, governor of Utah from 1896 to 1905, and he was a Mormon, not a Jesuit.

372   See chapter 2, note 26.

recognizes, there are times when the emotional and psychic life of a couple is rich enough to find in itself causes for renewed curiosity.

Once their primitive desire for luxury was simplified, men looked for comfort rather than beauty in clothing. As Marañón explains it, this is because a man loves a woman *generically*, and she has to make an effort to stand out, individualize herself, attract him and retain him. A woman, on the other hand, loves the *individual* in a man. He assures us that during a few years, a man desires a woman in a specific way. Eventually the attraction weakens and he desires to change. For this reason, a fashion trend is not limited only to the dress itself, but rather it determines a preference for white over brown, blonde or brunette hair, blue, green or dark eyes. What is rare is the unanimity of tastes in these cases. At times an hourglass shape is preferred, at others a more matronly body and sometimes, like now, says Marañón, "We are going through a time of a slim sexual archetype. Almost without exception women of our time are obsessed with what is called the *figure*, incorrectly, since the wide and curvy figure, which is now out of style, is also a figure that will some time regain its prestige over the straight shape that now dominates."

Maybe here we find the motive of *usefulness* because in this dizzying time of work and sports, women need to be agile and light. Perhaps a new type of feminine beauty will be created that will change the way we conceive of it. Through sports a woman becomes strong, her arms develop biceps, the muscles in her neck become more pronounced, her feet enlarge and lose that delightful curvature and the ankles and wrists lose their delicate slimness and hands and skin are rougher. But this does not mean she loses beauty. It is a new form of beauty.

The *economic* motive has much to do with modern fashion. Complicated dresses made of lace and many yards of cloth, which required great designers, have been replaced by smooth, simple dresses that are easy to wear. The new fashion styles, with short skirts and low necklines, have also shown up the conventionality of the laws of modesty, in that there is nothing fundamental about them. The antithesis of this fashion are the "Meninas" painted by Velázquez during a time when women seemed to hide the fact that they had a body, and this gave them a strange and conventional look so that we cannot guess their shape. The Yankee shoe, the military heel, the masculine hat and British style suit are indispensable garments that correspond to the necessities of modern women. At the same time, along with their new style women have freed their movements.

Simmel[373] says that "Through his gestures a man takes spiritual possession of a portion of space and the individual gestures of women externally reveal the particularities of the feminine spirit." In fact, gestures are not simply bodily movements, but the expressions of a spirit. Just as dress reveals a different mood, gestures change and one could say paradoxically that it is as if the dress created the gesture.

The expressions and movements of a woman who once lived relegated to the domestic sphere must have been very different from that of our women today. An active woman's liveliness is very different from those quiet and contained ladies depicted in old portraits holding a handkerchief, wearing dresses whose creases look as though they had been hanging in a closet for a long time. Still, a woman does not lose her poise with her new look. There is something fundamental in her that avoids angular movements, a harsh voice and unseemly gestures. With fashion women have achieved it all. One of their greatest conquests has been the right to *walk*, to leave the house… and to leave by themselves, breaking the ancestral dictum that women should be at home spinning wool. N[ovikov], in his beautiful book *The [Emancipation] of Women*, argued that the most important cause of women's slavery was the lack of the right to go out alone. Additionally, women were separated from men when they went for walks, were in the theater, in school, and even in church. But this did not mean that women were more respected, on the contrary. Women now go out alone dressed in the flashiest of clothes and no one bothers them, as men did they did to the *tapadas*,[374] obliging good gentlemen like Francisco de Quevedo to take out their swords in their defense.

When men and women are more used to dealing with each other, they lose the preconceived notions about the other gender that really harm true morality. Women become sincerer, they do not hide their desires or their character; they are not like that falsely demure type who could not speak in front of people, who had to keep her eyes lowered, cowering and looking like a doll moved by strings. Or that type of mischievous, *nitwit* or *phantom lady* from the theater of Lope and Calderón.[375] Mischievous, hypocritically naïve, respectable and,

---

373   See chapter 1, note 24.

374   See chapter 9, note 271.

375   Félix Lope de Vega (1562-1635) was the most popular playwright in Golden Age Spain, and is believed to have written as many as 1800 plays. Pedro Calderón de la Barca (1600-1681) was an important baroque playwright whose most famous play is *Life is a dream*. He also wrote *The Phantom Lady* in 1629.

at bottom, strong women, are oppressed to the degree that under the forced layer of exaggerated innocence they hide a devilish cunning, it is these whom Lope de Vega defended in *The Reward for Speaking Well*, when he said:

> To respect women is
> a thing to which all good men
> are born obliged
> for they owe them
> their first lodging of nine months
> and it is fair they pay them.

But it was not until Moratín[376] in *The Maiden's Consent*, that anyone dared to proclaim a woman's independence and freedom. The literary types that had the most influence on 19th-century women were Goethe's, derived therefore, from Locke's theories, which do not allow for any other source of knowledge than the senses, as well as from Condillac who, in his regression to Decartes, reaches an ideal sensationalism. Margaret[377] and Charlotte[378] are unstable and sick women who harm the reader's spirit. The first embodies the doubts of her time; she represents a hint of a daydream, fog and fantastic clouds and wind that rattles the windows of ruined feudal castles. Charlotte with her flirtatiousness, hidden behind the shield of innocence and goodness has, within her apparent simplicity, a complicated and dangerous spirit.

Other female types are Jean-Jacques Rousseau's, spiritual relatives of Schilling's system, which tends towards Pantheism; they extol motherly love and the return to the countryside. Other literary types that also had great influence are Richardson's Pamela and Clarissa Harlowe,[379] who can be affiliated spiritually with Kant, who causes Fichte to establish human responsibility, independent of God and without falling victim to fatalism. They are daughters of the most severe Calvinism, with full Christian austerity, "super-rigorous," a veritable excess of perfection, which creates rigid, cold

---

376　See chapter 6, note 163.

377　She is the main female character in *Faust*, for whose love the protagonist sells his soul to the devil.

378　She is a main character in *Werther*, with whom the protagonist falls in love and because she is married, he eventually commits suicide.

379　Samuel Richardson (1689-1761) wrote the novels *Pamela or Virtue Rewarded* –the letters of a servant to her father asking advice when her master makes advances –and *Clarissa or The History of a Young Lady* –the story of a girl who flees with her lover and is later abandoned.

women who control their passion and are shaped in that fanaticism that made Bernard Shaw[380] exclaim: "God save us from a world where everyone wants to act righteously, most inconsiderately."

Victor Margueritte's[381] *The Boyish Girl* portrays today's woman well. One cannot understand the scandal it caused. *Monique* is a noble type. Injured by the unfaithfulness of a man, mad with pain because he took advantage of her innocence, in a moment of fever and derangement she goes astray and hits that moral rock bottom that society always has prepared for women, because there is always a man next to them ready to make them fall. But *Monique* redeems herself through work and recovers her full dignity along with her independence, and she is able to love again, to be loved, to be an exemplary wife, a loving mother and head of a happy household. Readers who are used to novels in which a woman who has strayed morally dies in a hospital or becomes a nun have been alarmed by such a beautiful and human redemption, achieved through her own efforts alone.

I have said that feminism has proclaimed a woman's right to care for her beauty. The ability to openly dress and make herself up as she likes, is one of her great victories; having lost the freedom with which Egyptian, Greek and Roman women used to do it, fighting against the prejudices that imposed a style of dress and forbade her to use perfumes and products that would increase her beauty, when a woman would hear moralists advise, "be good in order to be loved," her instinct would reply, "be beautiful also." Artists and aristocratic ladies were the first to break with these prejudices and excessive strictness, which went so far as to consider the cleanliness of their bodies as improper for respectable women. Perhaps because it was associated with the Gentile idea of Roman baths and Arab ablutions. Maybe women went too far propelled by the impulse of that first push, but there was the advantage of courageously breaking the molds, of getting used to the cohabitation of the two genders and equality during celebrations and public acts. In this sense, worldly feminism has aided a great deal in resolving serious and significant problems related to the slavery of the female gender.

Victories over prejudices have been difficult. The struggle over short hair is still not completely resolved; the bob has been considered a lewd style, improper for serious and respectable ladies, as if these

---

380   See chapter 5, note 160.
381   Margueritte (1866-1942) lost his Legion of Honor decoration due to the scandals provoked by this novel.

qualities were fused together with long hair in the same way as was Sampson's strength. Hair has had exceptional importance especially in Spain. J. Lavalle, on a trip through the peninsula, speaks of *long-haired maidens,* that is girls who wore their braids down as a sign that they had not yet reached the age for marriage. When they reached it, they put their hair up and donned long dresses, in other words, dresses with trains, since girls used to wear longer skirts than today's matrons. This debut was a huge party to celebrate the opening of the doors to the world that had been closed to the girl. In the villages, after marriage women no longer bared their heads.

Even today certain churches ban the entrance of women wearing low necklines, short skirts and short hair. The female employees of certain centers are abusively forced to disregard their taste in dress and are forbidden to follow the fashion trends. There is an attempt to impose by force that which can only be achieved through education and conviction. Only an esthetic education will strengthen a woman's good sense to reject ridiculous styles. It is odd that a strong personality is most needed when it comes to not allowing oneself to be swept away by the general current of fashion. In Spain, there has been such an attachment to national styles that to replace the mantilla with a hat is considered to be *frenchified;* men's *handlebar mustache* was like a national emblem, and the famous mutiny against Esquilache in defense of the hat, the cape and cloak is well known.[382] One can gauge the strength of women's perseverance needed to break through the crust of preconceptions in such a country.

There are now trends and customs that allow a woman to go out on foot or driving her own car without having to take the indispensable chaperone with her or obliging her mother to accompany her. She can dress as she likes, go to parties, go into a café or the theater, play a game of polo with her friends and dance in a tea house. Women take part in all sports regardless of how violent they might be. They swim like sirens next to their male friends and win swimming prizes in difficult contests, they row, sail, are cyclists, Amazons and aviatrixes; they practice all sports: tennis, ball, even boxing.

The development has been so fast that it seems many centuries separate women from 1899 to today. These latter are slim, have short hair, wear short skirts, have wide necklines and plucked eyebrows, they go around smoking their cigarettes, painting their lips, cheeks

---

382   This is a well-known riot that occurred in Madrid in 1766 when the Marquis of Esquilache, a Neapolitan, attempted to legislate the use of short capes and three-cornered hats.

and eyelashes publicly. They have their own clubs like men, which some believe is a sign of feminism, when anything that does not entail work to attain the rights owed to every human being falls outside the field of action of feminism, even if it is carried out by women.

Men were the first to complete that labor of distancing themselves from the companionship of women by creating clubs in which the latter were not permitted entrance except when there was a party, so that the men could have more fun. Men's clubs and life in the cafés that separate men from the intimacy of their home are not prudent activities. As a general rule, women's clubs are more austere than men's. They do not usually have that fishbowl or large window open onto the street that allows snooping or the start of a fling. They are not places in which to receive a letter that should not go home or to make a date with someone who cannot be received at home. Most especially, in women's clubs there is no gambling. But the problem with women's clubs is the same as with men's: the separation of the sexes.

W. Fernández Flores[383] used to say these words that are full of wisdom, with his charming, humorous tone: "Women should tell men: I have shown that I can do the same as you; that I can be a good doctor, a good lawyer, a good accountant, a good town councilor, a good writer…; I have even been a soldier, not during the mythological time of the Amazons, but in Bolshevik Russia. Why do you think the entrance to the casinos should still be closed to me? Don't you understand that when I cross the threshold, out of the highest window would go the boredom, which is the oldest and most persistent member of your men only lairs. Come on! Hand over my armchair next to the window where the old people cackle! And tell them to put an ashtray on top of the little table where I can flick the ashes of my Virginia cigarette with my crystalline nails." It is truly the essence of what women should demand. No privileges for one or the other gender, no antagonisms, no isolation. We must live together in society and at home, with the same dignity and the same rights. In particular, no separation.

Fashion tends to equalize everything. The difference that existed among the appearances of the great lady, the bourgeois and the woman of questionable behavior has disappeared. They all dress alike. We cannot distinguish among an average woman, a princess or a queen. Everything is allowed. Even the garments that working-

---

383 Wenceslao Fernández Flores (1889-1964) was a popular Spanish writer and journalist.

class women never wore are now within their sphere. Regional dress is only worn in some distant places, as in Lagartera[384] in Spain, or traditionally they are worn on holidays and Carnivals.

But what is really odd is that the clothing of both genders is becoming more alike. Sometimes it is difficult at first glance to distinguish a woman with her hair done up in a boyish style, wearing a shirtwaist blouse, a British cut frock coat or smoking jacket, a masculine hat and a tight skirt, from a light bearded man, in large sports collar and wide trousers. Gómez de la Serna[385] has portrayed the androgynous woman, who welcomes that subterfuge to counteract her masculine influence in *A Woman Dressed as a Man*. We can tell a boy from a girl only when she is wearing earrings.

Trousers have been the only success women have not achieved in fashion. The attempt at a split skirt was noisily rejected by men. Women have only satisfied their desire to wear that garment with pajamas, just as men wear a skirt when they have on balloon trousers, which are a veritable pants-skirt.

Uniformity of beauty does not benefit women. An illustrious artist explained that the success of a black dancer in Paris was due to her being the only one to stand out from the monotony of women, all sporting the same silhouette and the same mask.

---

384 Lagartera is a tiny municipality located in the province of Toledo, Castile-La Mancha, Spain. The village is renowned for its ancient tradition of embroidery, needlework and lace-making

385 Ramón Gómez de la Serna (1888-1963) was an important Avant guard writer with whom Burgos had a relationship until 1929.

CHAPTER 13
POLITICAL RIGHTS

Political rights. –The importance of women's suffrage. –Its true meaning. – Suffrage in Spain. –Campaigns and distinguished opinions. –The injustice of statements against women's suffrage. –The Work of the International League of Iberian and Hispanic American Women and the Crusade of Spanish Women. –Manifesto submitted to Parliament. –The granting of a limited vote. –Current state of affairs.

Women's suffrage does not yet form part of all feminist programs. There are associations that refrain from demanding it either because they wrongly believe it to be of secondary importance, or because they are afraid to oppose the supporters of a *sensible feminism* that only demands protection for women. It is a new ruse to keep women passive that has come to replace the medieval songs of gallantry. They invoke femininity, which in this case is no more than submission to instincts. There are those who applaud a *sensible feminism* that asks for equality in civil rights, without realizing that aligning themselves with the conservative perspective is more detrimental to the organization of the family than equality of political rights.

But the educated women of all countries have understood that the ballot is a weapon and that if they do not have the right to suffrage they will not easily obtain the reforms they request from Parliaments. Women who are interested in issues of morality, hygiene, education and pacifism know well that they need to demand suffrage, not because of vain pride, but to have the means of working to improve the future. There is nothing better than the words of Mme. d'Abbadie d'Arrast in the beautiful book in which she studies women's situations in various countries: "Once they possess the political vote, form part of the electorate and can run for office, women will defend their own interests and collaborate with the legislators on their work, and watch over it so that the laws are made in their favor and not against them.

"Who denies," she adds, "that women's activism is above all an altruistic act? This activism is inspired by higher goals, related to the family, work, safety, the protection of children; most of all women want to instill a moral and physical hygiene in the bosom of the society that they want to regenerate, purify, cleanse for the safety and education of its children. The eyes of a mother can judge the state of the environment. She soars towards the ideal that a woman must achieve as long as she is really a woman; she wants the vote because of love, unselfishly. Her actions will be a woman's actions, not a poor copy of a man's actions. She sees evil because her eyes know how to look; she turns against vice because her children and she herself are victims of the evils of our time." How different this ideal is from the one which people who do not think or who have ill will suspect feminists of having!

Spain has been the nation that has remained disengaged from the issue of politics for the longest time because even men themselves have not understood its importance and that politics —that is to say everything that shapes the national environment— is at the same time a right and a duty for all citizens and the vote is an unavoidable obligation for both genders, since sovereignty is not essentially male. And it is not that Spanish tradition is backward, as has been shown in almost all the prior chapters. The prevalence of women in ancient times in the entire Peninsula is well known. In the Balearic Islands, there is a funerary inscription that praises a woman who held all the public offices in her town. In Spain we have had, on the one hand, the unconscious indifference of some, the fears of the liberals, and the paralysis of the conservatives. Women, for their part, have taken a long time to begin to realize their situation and their interests. It is a traditional country that fears progressive ideas as though they were revolutionary and polarizing, upper class women entrench themselves in their privileged status and consider middle class feminists who work to be eccentric or hotheaded. Working class women, lacking an education, do not realize their poverty or the social injustice they live in. Aristocrats, revered and oblivious, only think about parties and philanthropic work. To be a feminist has not been considered fashionable.

I must, necessarily, speak of my work when dealing with the history of suffrage in Spain, since I had to be a precursor of this movement. In 1907, I carried out an opinion poll in the *Heraldo de Madrid* to learn what people thought. I have to confess that the result was not very encouraging. Most of the prominent men and a majority of ladies avoided committing themselves to a view. There were, however, some important politicians who did not hesitate to express their opinion. The Count of Romanones[386] answered frankly by saying: "You raise one of the most discussed and most debatable

---

386 Don Álvaro Figueroa y Torres (1863-1950) belonged to the Liberal Party and was president of the Senate 17 times, and of the Council of Ministers 3 times.

issues of political rights: active and passive suffrage for women. As a politician and leader, my opinion is quite explicit: I consider that, for now at least, women cannot be part of the electorate or eligible to run for office. The reasons on which I base my opinion are not appropriate for a letter, but there is nothing in these reasons that presupposes the inferiority of the most beautiful half of the human race. If among us [men] electoral practice can lead to so much corruption, what would happen if a feminine influence intervened? And this is certainly not because of a greater lack of moral sense, but rather due to the weaker resistance to passions that the exercise of suffrage provokes."

This fear of increasing the immorality that they recognize in men has been one of the most cited arguments. Charles Turgeon[387] said: "I, for my part, would dislike it if our mothers, our daughters, our sisters, went into the wild animal's cage that is a Legislative Assembly, or descended into the bear's den that is a municipal council."

The great thinker, Max Nordau[388] told me: "Women who are of age should have political suffrage just as men, since they have the same interests to defend and no less intelligence. I would want to grant eligibility for office only to married women and widowed mothers. But my logic requires that men also be eligible only if they are fathers. The community should require that the legislator have a lively interest in the future of the State and of the nation and only persons who think about the future of their descendants can feel that interest in a concrete way. For celibate people or those without children the future is an abstraction, something that belongs to others, and it is well known that even the most conscientious people will work on others' matters with less zeal than they would on their own."

The illustrious journalist Luis Morote[389] said: "Since suffrage is a political right, the entire discussion surrounding women's votes should be about whether they are fit to influence public life and participate in sovereignty."

"In Spain, more than in any other country of the world, the actual facts are in their favor, since we have been *governed by women* in the highest position of the State, there is no logical or juridical reason that they should be excluded from the polls if we have a modicum of equity."

---

387   A well-known professor of law and political economy, author of a two-volume work titled *French Feminism* (1902) which is opposed to the feminist movement.

388   See chapter 4, note 115.

389   Morote (1862-1913) was also elected to the Spanish Parliament in 1905 and 1907 as a member of the Republican Party.

"During the 19th Century and even at the beginning of the 20th, we had two Queen Regents and one actual Queen: the governing Queen, from 1833 to 1840, Queen Isabella, from 1843 to 1868, and Regent Doña Cristina, from 1885-1902; in total, fifty-two years of reign or rule by women. Would it not be an iniquitous, monstrous, irritating inequity to grant the fair sex the total and supreme power of the Nation and deny it a small bit of sovereignty, the one contained in a ballot?"

"Now I will let the reader decide, not the absolutely unquestionable problem of law which is favorable to women, but that of experience and life, thinking back throughout History to see how Spain did during such a long, turbulent and catastrophic period, *Glissez, n'appuyez pas...*"[390]

Women themselves were against the vote. The elderly writer Doña Patrocinio de Biedma[391] stated that: "for Spanish women the vote would be something like a joke, which the father, friend or husband would decide on a whim, and not women themselves with their own judgment." The illustrious doctor Aleixandre told me that "before thinking about the vote, women should ask men to refrain from drinking, fighting and even committing crimes on election days."

As almost always happens, the humorists took it as a joke. Mariano de Cavia[392] told me: "Allow me to get out of the awkward situation with a Kantian response. With the Critique of Pure Reason, I will say yes. With the Critique of Practical Reason, I will say no." The Quintero brothers answered: "A woman talking like someone from the majority would be a reason for leaving the country or shooting oneself under the beard."

Some said that neither women nor men should vote. They took advantage of the opportunity to attack universal suffrage. There was no lack of supporters of the vote, in principle, but it was a limited vote. Others said that the day a woman were elected town councilor or mayor would be the last day that there would be beautiful and attractive women, as if we would grow a beard and a mustache because of voting. Some said that they accepted women everywhere, even in the

---

390   This is a quote from Pierre Charles Roy, a French satirist and dramatic poet, meaning "Thus lightly touch and quickly go," and implying this verse: "Where mischief lurks in gay disguise"

391   Biedma (1858-1927) published widely in women's magazines, under the pen name of Ticiano Imab. While she published more than 20 books, she is now largely forgotten.

392   Cavia (1855-1920) was an important journalist of the time who wrote political commentary.

Royal Academy of the Spanish Language,[393] but not in the government of the State, because they had "a more sacred mission to fulfill at home." Many declared that women "were only meant to please."

As one can see, except for a very few, the opinions were inconsequential, routine, and ordinary. The foreign Press, which followed the plebiscite with interest, did not declare the signers of the letters to be great thinkers. We were defeated: 30,640 votes against suffrage and 20,025 in favor. Of these 9,500 were against eligibility to run for office. The fruit was still green, but at least the *Heraldo* managed to stir up a debate around this forgotten issue. That same year, Mr. Buen, Mr. Palomo and Mr. Salvatella presented various amendments in Parliament when electoral reform bills were debated, and among these was the granting of the vote in municipal elections to women; but it was thrown out. Without losing heart I continued to be interested in achieving political rights. The examples of countries that had suffrage, which I saw during my long and frequent travels, strengthened my opinion, and I noted with sadness that only Spanish women did not worry about vindicating their rights. In newspapers, in books, even in novels and lectures I continued to work for women and especially for suffrage.

In 1908, on the occasion of a project by the local administration, Mr. Pi Aruaga requested that women be allowed to vote in municipal elections. The conservative Parliamentary Commission rejected the proposal due to "bad timing and lack of education on the part of the Spanish public." The government allowed for a free vote, but the measure failed since many Liberals, Democrats and Republicans voted against it.

In 1920, I again carried out another opinion poll using the podium of the *Heraldo de Madrid*, which was inspired by the noble spirit of Don Miguel Moya, and I was happily able to ascertain that the feminist cause was gaining ground, and that many people had changed their mind. The Count of Romanones himself thought like Condorcet,[394] when he said: "Men have violated the principle of equality of rights, calmly depriving half the human race of contributing to the creation of laws." The Count wrote: "We Liberals were so pleased with ourselves a few years ago when we

---

393 This is a body that decides grammar rules, issues a dictionary, as well as edits other works. Its members are important writers. Women were not eligible to enter the Academia until 1978.

394 Marie Jean Antoine Nicolas Caritat, Marquis de Condorcet (1743 1794), was a French aristocrat, a mathematician, and an official of the Academy of Sciences.

proclaimed universal suffrage. Universal, even though we had excluded something more than half the human race! Women should be voters and eligible for public office, there can be no doubt about this; the doubt creeps in when we consider if women's inclusion on the electoral rolls will not currently harm liberal principles, since in the Spain of today women are not very independent politically, although I acknowledge that one might say men are not either."

Alejandro Lerroux[395] declared: "One thing is that women should be and another is that they could be voters. I believe they should be, but I also believe that they cannot be without evident risks. However, fears of danger to freedom cannot justify the relinquishing of freedom; if women, who should have voting rights, cannot have them it is because society has legislated in such a way that they have been consigned to impotence, but since no intellectual, moral, social or ethical reasons can be opposed to a human being's intervention in the guidance and administration of public policy, whatever her/his gender, what matters now is that we prepare –as quickly as is possible without impairing perfection – to modify the state of affairs that causes that impotence.

"This does not mean that I would refuse it my vote if the issue were posed seriously, because today's circumstances are such that it is necessary to take advantage of the tremendous unrest that seizes society to gain positions from which we can defend ourselves and can defend the progress civilization has made, and this means, in the final analysis, that if, reversing the order of events, we now made women voters and eligible for public office in Spain, the commotions and disturbances that this could produce would cause a healthy reaction, it would force everyone to improve the political environment, legislation and customs so that women-citizens were and could be the same as men-citizens."

The illustrious writer, Don Baldomero Argente,[396]stated: "It is difficult to answer soberly so that both the nuances and the scope of my thinking are clearly delineated. Nevertheless, considering the reasons in favor and against, I will only say: Yes, I believe that Spanish women should vote and be eligible for public office under the same conditions as men. Taking into account the reality of the situation

---

395   Lerroux (1864-1949) founded the Radical Republican Party in 1911 and later shifted to the right during the Second Republic in 1931, he was minister of foreign affairs. From 1933 to 1935 he headed a number of rightist governments.

396   Argente (1877-1965) was a liberal politician, sociologist and publicist who was elected numerous times to Parliament.

and not including exceptional cases, however, this does not prevent me from believing that women should not vote or be eligible for office, even if the law should not impose artificial restrictions. To influence politics women do not need to vote; they have perhaps too much influence already. Within the current social organization, their participation in Assemblies would have such deplorable circumstances, in my view, that they would greatly surpass the presumed advantages of contributing a superior sensitivity to the deliberation of public affairs. Women were not born to fight in the public sphere, and they stop being women when in practice they become equal to men; they were born to be men's helpers, to keep that fire that symbolizes the life of the species lit, and for many other things sung in lyrical poems, many of which are true."

"If today, in part, women need to go outside of that sphere, it is because the social organization is corrupt, wrong, lost and what matters is that we modify this social organization, returning it to its foundation in justice, which will permit the spirits of both genders to flower naturally; this is not to say that in the civil realm women do not need an opening of doors that today are legally closed to them."

On the conservative side, witty Azorín[397] responded: "One more time I will say that for me women should be totally, absolutely equal to men. Equal in law, in politics, in the social economy, in work, in pay..."

Don Antonio Maura[398] was inclined to the active participation of women in public life, as he had already demonstrated in one of his brilliant lectures in the Spanish Academy.

Don Juan de la Cierva said: "Of course, I am pleased to declare my opinion is frankly favorable to the granting of said rights, under the same conditions as they were granted to men, with the certainty that doing this would render a great service to the cause of progress."

The illustrious don Antonio Goicoechea, told me: "The crusade in favor of women's emancipation would be more smoke and mirrors than real if it did not have the three goals of achieving civil, economic and political liberty for women, all at the same time, with the elimination of the inequalities that place them at an inferior level than men in these three fundamental aspects of life. Doña Concepción Arenal used to say, quite correctly, that in the current legislation, 'there is no logic, because there is no justice. Replacing it or correcting it, if at

---

397 See chapter 8, note 261.
398 Maura (1853-1925) was head of the Conservative Party and Prime Minister on five separate occasions.

all possible, will be a generous act in which the effort expended should be accompanied by the affection and support of all men of good will.'"

Such a competent person as Don Ángel Ossorio[399] said, "I am an unwavering supporter of women's vote and eligibility for public office; they should absolutely enjoy the same political rights as men. But instituting the complete reform in one fell swoop seems reckless to me and runs the risk of failure. Women's lack of political education, the inevitable and authoritarian interference of men and the lack of an atmosphere of true civil and political freedom would be more than ample reasons why we would not achieve a greater degree of citizenship, but rather a sterile upheaval. Because of this I believe that at this time active and passive voting rights should only be granted to women who enjoy full legal freedom, that is, single or widowed women who are not dependent on any male relative."

Don Manuel Burgos y Mazo,[400] to whom Spanish women owe such special gratitude for being the first Minister to propose the granting of political rights to women, wrote: "I have already given my answer beforehand, when I presented the first bill in our nation that would grant wide ranging votes to women twenty-one and older in a Congress meeting on electoral matters. That is where I put down my thoughts on the matter, written in accordance with my true and sincere convictions, as I always try to do."

As this brief review shows, the objections against women's suffrage add up to very little. They all recognize a woman's right to vote: but even so they want to deprive her of exercising it due to selfishness and fear that greater harm to the community might emerge. They oppose freedom in the name of freedom itself, as if veritable rights could be counterbalanced with usefulness. The objections are:

> That women's votes would hand power over to reactionary parties.
> That women would be susceptible to their husbands' or fathers' influence.
> That women would lose their charm and cease caring for their home and children.
> That women do not have the same intellectual and moral attributes as men.

---

399 See chapter 7, note 188.
400 Burgos y Mazo (1862-1946), sociologist and politician, belonged to the Conservative Party and was Minister of Justice (1915-1917) and later of the Interior (1919).

That they are not prepared for public life.

That they do not serve in the military and are always pacifists.

The most common argument in Spain is the first one, but when he presented the bill for women's votes in his country, Dr. Brun, President of the Republic of Uruguay, and one of the staunchest feminists, said: "Does a reason exist perhaps to believe that a woman will abandon the parties that defend high social principles and that fight to achieve the general wellbeing? Could she desire the victory of a party, like the Catholic party, which will not have to defend any fundamental issue related to its beliefs in Parliament, and that does not have a defined program meant to further the nation's progress and the greater happiness of its inhabitants? It is more logical to suppose that family or emotional interests and motivations will prevail above the influence of the priests, and that the political attitude of a woman will be determined in each case by the opinion she herself has formed of the interests and needs of the country." The British example supports these statements. The first woman Member of Parliament, Lady Astor, was a conservative, but soon women affiliated with the Labor Party —among whom there are factory workers and women like Miss Jessie Stephens,[401] who worked as a domestic servant— have achieved predominance.

Regarding the second part of the objection, Dr. Bard, defender of women's rights in the Parliament of Argentina, responds: "The adversaries of feminism hold that even if the influence of the Church did not constitute a decisive factor in a woman's decision to vote a particular way, the husband, or the father, etc. would be. Those who put forward this argument assert that a woman will issue her vote freely in very few cases. The truth is that there is no one, man or woman, who is not subject to the legitimate influence of the people with whom s/he lives. This natural result of living with relationships affects men and women, yet it has not been a sufficient motive to deny men the right to suffrage. When men vote, they do not proceed with absolute freedom of action. They often subordinate their preferences to other considerations. The lists of candidates contain names that could be replaced advantageously by others. However, in the name

---

401   Born in Glasgow (1894? -1977?), Stephens was forced to leave school and work as a domestic due to her family's finances. She became a member of the Independent Labour Party and the Women's Social and Political Union in 1910. She later went to London and worked with Sylvia Pankhurst. In 1922 she ran for Parliament, but was not elected, instead she became borough councilor for Bermondsey.

of solidarity and partisan interests, they accept them as they are and not as they wished they were."

In addition, the same could be objected with regard to the influence of women on men, and, according to this argument, it would be worse, since they believe male inspiration to be more reasoned and just. Aristotle said: "It's all the same if women govern personally or if they control the leaders. The result is always the same." And Cato said: "We govern men and we are governed by our women." And what is worse about that government, which has all the evils of hidden power, is that women exercise it without the responsibility that elevates the level of morality and the motivation for the acts.

Voting will not cause women to stop looking after their home when the inclination or need induces them to do so, but not all of them care for their homes when their economic position allows them to entrust that task to a housekeeper or governess. Citizens do not stop dedicating themselves to their work because of voting. The exercise of political rights will not wrench women from their houses, just as it does not tear farmers from their fields or workers from the factories. But those who say that a woman will allow her husband to influence her vote, also say the exact opposite, when they assure us that the difference in political opinions between husband and wife will destroy the peace of the home. With regard to this, Jules Simon[402] has said: "A family has one vote; if it had two it would be divided and would die." But these are only empty words. If there is a disparity of opinions in the family, voting is not necessary for the introduction of discord. Surely one would not go so far as to get a divorce for voting incompatibility. There are more serious things than electing a councilman or a member of parliament. In one of my trips to Norway, the Spanish Consul in Bergen was town councilman and his wife was as well. I asked them if there were ever arguments between them because of their political views. "Absolutely not," they replied. "When there are differences in these it is because they already exist in other areas as well." In fact, one can keep women from voting, but one cannot keep them from thinking and therefore if there is not full harmony in the home, if the spirits of the couple haven't married, if there is not a union of interests and views, discord takes over the home with or without the vote.

They say that emancipated women will lose their charm and

---

402   The French philosopher, writer, and statesman Jules François Simon (1814-1896) was a leader of the moderate republican faction in the early years of the Third Republic.

there will be fewer marriages. Although it is important, the ballot is not an extraordinary amulet that will change female nature. The same passions and marriages will always exist. Equality, freedom are the most beloved dream of human beings. A woman will not abandon her home due to voting and being eligible for office more than she does now for frivolous pursuits. A woman who does not like to flirt, who does not have responsibilities at home, can perform social service in the arts, the trades, industry and politics. Mme. Edmond Adam[403] asserts that when the age of passion has passed there is a metamorphosis in which once the instinct decreases reason prevails in men as well as in women and they are more alike.

Women are considered suitable for molding their children's character and raising entire generations, because generally women are the ones in charge of infants; and we deny them the paramount right to instill civic responsibility. We should allow that positive influence we recognize women have in the home to radiate from them, as John Ruskin[404] puts it, and let their great gifts of strength, sensibility and economy exercise a beneficial influence in public life.

The argument of mental and moral inferiority has already been discarded. If in universal history great and talented women are not plentiful, it is because of the difference in upbringing and the state in which they have been kept, but in proportion to the number of women who practice professions and dedicate themselves to the arts and sciences, we can assert that they are not fewer than great men. Brilliant women have stood out in the arts and letters, and we have already mentioned glorious names in the sciences. The supposed superiority of men's spirit is, in general, a consequence of their upbringing. But if this were a reason for denying women their rights, they could only be granted to brilliant men. Condorcet has said: "Among the human spirit's most important signs of progress toward the general happiness, we must count the full destruction of the prejudices that establish a dreadful inequality of rights between the two genders. Vain is the search for reasons to justify it through the differences in psychic organization, in which some would like to find the strength of one's intelligence and moral sense. This is no

---

403 Juliette Adam (1836-1936) was a French writer and feminist, author of numerous novels and founder of the *Nouvelle Revue* that published works of important writers. She also wrote *Anti-proudhomian ideas on love, women and marriage*, a defense of George Sand and Daniel Stern (another woman writer who used a male pseudonym).

404 British Socialist, Ruskin (1819-1900) was also considered to be the most important writer on art and culture of his time.

more than the abuse of force which they ineffectively try to excuse with sophisms."

A consequence of this objection made against women is that they are not prepared for public life. Here we could say, as does the Count of Romanones: "Are men prepared perhaps?" One cannot think that free beings can be brought up within a reactionary environment. That women are not prepared is a ruse to deviously gain time. Necessity is the best teacher; driven by necessity, women's intelligence will reach its full development. If education were not free and spontaneous, born from the desire to know the truth that exists in human beings, how could women have managed to escape the tyranny of prejudices and learn the ideas that they now hold. They would not have been taught them on purpose, because the instructors were interested in keeping them ignorant so they would remain submissive. Women have lacked the stimulation to develop their mental acuity. Ramiro de Maeztu[405] said in one of his chronicles from England: "So women are not educated in politics? Neither were the working masses when they were granted suffrage. So they are not soldiers or marines? But soldiers and marines are the only adult British citizens, aside from madmen, criminals and the indigent, who do not have the right to vote." In effect, the law treats women like it does the disabled, excluding them from the rights of citizenship and of expressing their opinion. However, dim-witted, illiterate men have the right to vote and determine the path of their country. Women are likened to madmen, the mentally challenged and criminals only because of their gender.

Alexander Dumas[406] wrote his dialogue *Women Who Kill and Women Who Vote* about this:

> "'Why shouldn't Mme. de Sevigné vote when her gardener can?'
> 'Because Mme. de Sevigné is an exception and the customs, ideas and laws of a country should not be changed for one exception.'
> 'And her grandmother, Mme. de Chantal, and Mesdames de Lafayette, de Maintenon, Dacier, Guyon, de Longueville,

---

405　Maeztu (1875-1936) was a Spanish journalist and sociopolitical theorist. Between 1905 and 1919 he was the London correspondent for several Spanish newspapers.

406　This would be French dramatist, Dumas the younger (1824-1895). In this book, he argues that women should vote but not hold office.

du Chatelet, du Deffand, de Staël,[407] Rolland, Sand and...'
'All exceptions.'
'A sex that has such exceptions has won the right to give its opinion in the appointments of mayors, municipal councilmen and members of Parliament. But the exceptions do not end here. What about Clotilde, who converted the Franks, and therefore us, to Catholicism. Do you think she has had an influence in our country? What about Anne de Beaujeu? And the good Queen Anne and Blanca de Castilla and Elizabeth of Hungary? And Queen Elizabeth of England and Catherine the Great and Marie-Thérèse?'
'They were Queens.'
'That does not change their sex, and if they have reigned, as they have, it proves that they could reign with intelligence and strength as well as men. No one will ever convince me that women, who can be Queens like them, in spite of their sex, cannot vote because of their sex.'
'But in the end, there are only those women and the majority of women have no idea of any sense about politics and government.'
'A sense that is easy to acquire if we go by the men who pretend to have it.'"

But the theory that women are beings with duties and without rights is maintained. They shamelessly dub it *universal suffrage*, the one in which women do not participate. Women cannot issue an opinion when it is a matter of deciding on peace or war, which can result in the happiness or ruin of home and country. However, a woman who is not wealthy or does not have a man who will support her, works and bears all the burdens just like a man, and she pays exactly the same taxes. When Napoleon said: "I do not want women to concern themselves with politics." Condorcet's widow replied: "You are right, sire, but in a country where their heads are cut off, it is natural that they have the right to know why."

Women pay taxes and duties, just like men, like them they give their children to the motherland, but they cannot express their opinion. There are cases of servants voting and their female employers cannot, or of an illiterate man voting, but not a woman teacher. Taine[408]

---

407 See chapter 4, note 75.
408 Hyppolite Taine (1828-1893) was a French philosopher, historian and critic. He is best known for his *History of English Literature* (1863) which develops his determinist views.

said, in favor of universal suffrage: "Whether I wear a blouse or a tailcoat, whether I am a capitalist or a worker, no one has the right to manage my life and my money without my consent. For five hundred people united as one to send me to the border and decide my fate, it is necessary that I tacitly and spontaneously authorize them and the way to authorize is to elect. It is, then, reasonable for a villager, a worker, to vote just like a bourgeois or a nobleman and for a woman to vote as well as a man. They all should exercise their right."

Paul Bourget[409] has written: "I don't understand why women should not vote in the countries that practice universal suffrage. From the moment that an illiterate man votes just like a literate man, a servant like his employer, a villager like a city dweller, because the differences in education, fitness, or in general are not taken into account, why does the wife of the villager, the servant or the city dweller not have a voice by the same token as their husbands? Their votes would not be more incompetent, or more imprudent. Maybe the love they have for their children and their economic sense would make them wiser in certain matters, such as education, protection and tax laws."

The argument that women do not pay a "blood tax" is absurd. In times of war, as we have already shown, women contribute their work, endure dangers and injuries just like men and, as Michelet has said: "Mothers are the ones who pay a blood tax." Relegated to having no mission other than motherhood, they have put all their effort into it. Their love for their children, who constitute their only hope, is more passionate. They have been allowed nothing other than that son, and he is taken from their arms. This is why women suffer more than men who, while loving their children, have many other things that demand their attention and distract them. In the renowned Greek tragedy Lisistrata[410] exclaimed early on: "Oh men! Do we not carry half of the burden of war? We, who painfully give birth to our children and see them leave bearing arms."

The admirable Severine,[411] defender of all just causes, says: "We are creatures of intimacy. We do not want to conceive children, carry them for nine months in our wombs – because we are the live

---

409 French novelist and critic, Bourget (1852-1935), held conservative social views and wrote psychological novels.

410 A play by Aristophanes of the same name that takes place during the Peloponnesian War and in which she tells the women of Greece to withhold sex from their husbands until a peace treaty has been signed.

411 Caroline Rémy de Guebhard (18551929) was a French socialist, journalist, and feminist.

cradles of humanity – nourish them with our milk, raise them to be men, so that they will be taken away and sent to battlefields where mutilated and bleeding they still scream our names with their last breath in their last convulsions." It is thought that Jesus himself took pity on mothers' pain caused by the cruelty of wars that sprouted throughout humanity, when he uttered the famous words: "Daughters of Jerusalem, do not weep for me; weep for yourselves and for your children. For the time will come when you will say, 'Blessed are the childless women, the wombs that never bore and the breasts that never nursed.'"[412]

It is true that women are pacifists because their feelings and reason demand it. They believe in reducing to the utmost the enormous expenses of war and that replacing acts that cause death with life affirming acts must be humanity's mission. German women, so courageous during the war, are now planting a Peace tree in front of the Cathedral of Reims. Women's feelings are more virginal because they have not committed violence against their humanitarian instincts and they reject all negatives: ugliness, evil, death. They love all positive ideas, all affirmatives: beauty, goodness, life. The more aware women are, the more against war they are. But this is not only a feminine condition. Many men are also pacifists. We need only remember the admirable examples of the Doukhobors,[413] Tolstoy, Roman Rolland[414] and all the men of good conscience who have preferred to die rather than live with their hands stained with blood. But the pacifist struggle undertaken by women is not weakness. Once the moment of inevitable war has arrived, women have borne its burden with the same courage and resignation as men; among the horrors of combat they have spread the balm of their mercy, consoling the combatants without regard to their own lives. Spanish women are pacifists, but not "defectors." They try to avoid war, but once the struggle has started they do not place obstacles in the way; there are examples that show that in these cases women have known how to help achieve victory and have even been heroic.

In 1921, the "Crusade of Spanish Women" and the "International League of Iberian and Hispanic American Women,"

---

412   Author's note: Luke 23: [28-29].

413   A Russian peasant group which sought a simpler more spiritual version of Christianity and were persecuted by the Orthodox Church. In the last part of the 19th Century they became pacifists.

414   Rolland (1866 –1944) was a French dramatist, novelist, essayist, art historian and mystic who was awarded the Nobel Prize for Literature in 1915.

convinced of the justice of the feminist cause and that there was nothing in the Spanish Constitution that opposed women's voting, went to Parliament to present their demands and their program for the vindication of all civil and political rights. Groups of women from all social classes handed out the manifesto in the streets and presented it in the Congress and the Senate, thus carrying out the first public act of the Spanish suffragists. The well thought out preamble stated:

"In the name of a well-educated minority of women in this country, and interpreting feelings which have not been entirely expressed by that majority that still lives in ignorance of their rights and duties in the lethargy of their inactivity, The International League of Iberian and Hispanic American Women and the Crusade of Spanish Women have resolved to go to the highest representatives of public Power to express our demands, the satisfaction of which we deem urgently necessary for individual progress and our social renewal."

"While in the more enlightened countries the issue of the legal dignity of women has ceased to be a matter of academic controversy to become a strong and urgent legislative necessity, in large part already satisfied by wise and just laws, in Spain, the traditional resistance to any progressive reform, and the privileged men's fearful interest in opposing egalitarian innovations, place women in such an awkward situation —so inadequate for intelligent and free beings—, in the eyes of the law and customs, that, considering the limitations placed on women, one can declare that human slavery has not been erased entirely from History; since the regulations legally survive to humiliate, oppress and tie the hands of the physically weaker half of Humanity, as if freedom in women's hands were a terrible weapon that could be wielded against the other half."

"But this is not the most appropriate time to set out theories that today enjoy almost universal approval, or to consider problems that have already been satisfactorily resolved, the beneficial solutions of which are a strong example of convenience and justice that will force us to imitate them sooner or later. We demand equality of treatment that will place us in the same and just level as other civilized women; and what interests us most is what also interests all of Spanish society during moments of danger in which it is necessary for all to join forces to defend civilization and social organization, which are being rudely threatened. Our words will be simple, just, concrete; each one of them will summarize a goal that is the liberation from prejudices that represent centuries of servitude, humiliation and suffering for half of Humanity."

"For Spanish women to occupy the place that they deserve in modern society, it is necessary that the incontrovertible strength of wise and just laws help them, and their creation does not pose any problem, since in no brain are there vestiges of those absurd theories of inferiority or superiority of one of the two halves of the human race."

"So, leaving out thoughts that are surely on everyone's mind, we will present our just demands, which are the following: Complete equality of political rights, and therefore, to be voters and eligible for public office under the same conditions that men are, without any other restriction than the legal capacity that is required of men."

After expounding on the example of countries in which women's suffrage exists, the manifesto reads: "On this point our demands do not request any privilege for women, but rather complete equality, cohabitation with men in a citizen's life, as we have it with our parents, our brothers and our husbands at the hearth of every home. With this we desire to eradicate from our sons the belief that we are inferior beings. And we desire not to be deprived of fulfilling the duty of voting, for the benefit of our country, without the reprehensible indifference we are forced into and of which men themselves partake."

"On the other hand, in Spain the spirit of the law has never been to eliminate our political rights. Aside from the fact that women can be queens proves this, there is no article in the Constitution or the Electoral law that strictly forbids us from exercising that right. Title I of the Constitution, 'On Spaniards and their Rights,' states: 'The following are Spaniards: 1) People born in Spanish territory; 2) Children of a Spanish father or mother, even if they were born outside of Spain...' etc. Afterwards all rights common to Spaniards are enumerated, without distinguishing between genders. In title III, 'On the Senate,' there is an article 26 that says: 'To be seated in the Senate it is necessary to be Spanish, be at least thirty-five years old, not have a criminal record, or be disqualified from exercising political rights, and not have property that was confiscated.' In title IV, 'About the Congress,' article 29 says: 'To be elected member of Parliament it is necessary to be Spanish, a layperson, of legal age and enjoy all civil rights.' In neither article does a prohibition regarding women appear, but for greater certainty, we will examine the Civil Code, and its Book I, title I, article 17, which repeats article 1 of the current Constitution in the same way that we have just quoted, and that contains an article 22 which adds: 'A married woman has the same status and nationality as her husband.' So, then, a woman who marries a Spaniard is also a Spaniard. In the strict sense of our language, it should be understood that the legislator did not speak only of men, but also of women. When one says that Spain has x million inhabitants, it is understood that this number refers to both sexes; otherwise one would say, for example, x million women and z million men, which would be ridiculous and inappropriate."

"It is clear, then, that when the Constitution refers to the civic rights of Spaniards, it is not a matter only of men, but also of women. If the legislator had wanted to exclude women from the voting rosters, he could have and should have said so, thus closing the doors that, conversely, he generously and justly left open."

These petitions that the Crusade of Spanish Women presented to Parliament are contained in the eleven articles of the *Woman's Letter*, sanctioned by the VIII International Women's Congress of Geneva,[415] with the only differences being that these demands are justified by and molded to our special circumstances.

"Women cannot continue to be an inert mass excluded from men's social activity, rather they aspire to share obligations at the same time as rights with men.; in a word, they want to become conscious and worthy beings who can be called on to collaborate and shape a happy future."

Thousands of women of all social classes signed the manifesto: aristocratic ladies, workers' associations from many provinces and a great majority of intellectual women, teachers, students and artists. The press, which unanimously praised the act without reservations, said: "It is the dawn of a serious feminist movement and this first act of the Spanish suffragists surprised the members of Parliament, who politely and kindly offered their support even when they belonged to different parties like Don Francisco Bergamín,[416] Conservative, the Count of Romanones, Liberal and Lerroux, Republican. The president of Parliament, Mr. Allendesalazar,[417] spoke pleasantly with a group of suffragists and had his picture taken among them."[418] Another

---

415   This would be the 8th International Woman Suffrage Alliance Congress held June 6-12 of 1920.

416   As a career politician, Bergamín (1855-1937) occupied a variety of posts: Member of Parliament, Minister of Education, Minister of the Economy, Vice-President of the Congress, etc. In 1914, he was named Senator for life.

417   Conservative politician, Manuel Allendesalazar (1856-1923) served twice as Prime Minister and also occupied other political posts such as Minister of the Interior and Mayor of Madrid among many others.

418   Author's note: *Heraldo de Madrid*.

newspaper added: "All people sympathized with the feminist cause, without regard to gender."

There was a contrast between the treatment of the Spanish suffragists and the difficulties that the British women encountered, which proves that the environment had been prepared. In addition, the situation of Spanish women is favorable to this concession. There is a balance between the sexes. There are only half a million more women than men; there is a greater number of widows than widowers and a majority of women know how to read and write, as we have already seen. The new electoral law says,[419]

> "Article 83. The post of councilman is obligatory, unrenounceable and not for sale.
> Article 84. To be councilman one must:
> Appear on the Voting Rosters of the respective municipality.
> Know how to read and write, except in Municipalities with fewer than 1,000 inhabitants.
> Be twenty-five years old.
> Women heads of households are eligible, as long as this status does not change, if they meet the requirements listed in the prior paragraph."
> ....
> "Spaniards older than twenty-one may vote in each Municipality, and those older than twenty-five and that appear in the Voting Rosters compiled by the corresponding Center of the State are eligible. Women heads of households will have the same right to vote; their names will be added to the Voting Roster of each Municipality as an appendix. The names of Spanish women older than twenty-three who are not subject to parental authority, marital authority or guardianship, are inhabitants of the Municipality and head a household within it will appear in this appendix."

Recently the vote has been extended to other elections, but only the vote, limiting the right to single women, widows and those legally divorced. This concession has not completely satisfied women. To be placed on an appendix, as an afterthought like always, their rights separate from the rights of the general population due to their gender, they are belittled by the lack of voting rights of married

---

419   Author's note: chapter III, that deals with the requirements for the post of councilman.

women, of only being eligible to hold for municipal positions and by the inability of single women and widows to be so if they are not heads of household with full authority over their home. In this way, voting rights are reduced to a very small number of women, with limitations that are not placed on men.

But the majority of the Spanish population has such a poor idea of the importance of political rights —perhaps because among us we do not have an idea of what politics is, discredited as it is by its confusion with the Government—, that the matter did not receive much attention. So when the first female councilmen and mayors were appointed, people only concerned themselves with whether they should be called "consejal" or "consejala", an issue that has already been resolved in our language, which uses "Regent" for the woman who exercises the "Regency" and "Regentess" for the wife of the [male] "Regent," and which determines nouns that can grammatically be used in either the masculine or the feminine, a function which is decided by the masculine or feminine article, depending on whether one is dealing with a man or a women: "el consejal" [councilman] "la consejal" [councilwoman] in the same way as "el testigo" [male witness] and "la testigo" [female witness].

Perhaps the lack of interest in Spanish women stems from the fact that the right to vote has been conceded at a time when there is no real suffrage even for men. Women who serve in Spanish Municipal positions have yet to obtain them through elections.

CHAPTER 14
WOMEN'S SUFFRAGE

Brief summary of the development of women's suffrage. –Homage to British suffragists. –Women's suffrage in European countries. –Suffrage in the United States. –In Latin America. –In the countries of Asia, Africa and Oceania. –Evidence of the advantages of women's suffrage. –The supreme reason.

In speaking about women's suffrage, it would be unfair not to start with England, whose women have been veritable heroines in favor of the rights of their gender. The struggle began with Mary Wollstonecraft's book, *A Vindication of the Rights of Women*, in 1790. This beautiful writer —who according to one of her biographies had the demeanor of a goddess, huge eyes and a magnificent head of hair, like one of Titian's women— sowed the seed that John Stuart Mill[420] later sprouted with his book, *The Subjection of Women*, sixty-seven years later, in 1869. Stuart Mill was not just a theoretical champion of feminism. He was president of the first association for women's suffrage and presented their petitions to Parliament. In spite of losing by a large margin of votes, from that moment on the demands of the suffragists did not cease to be presented every year.

Mary Wollstonecraft had a painful upbringing: daughter of a drunkard father who mistreated her mother, and sister of a wretched young woman whose husband beat her, she left home to earn her daily bread by working. She fought valiantly against Rousseau's[421] theories on the education of women. She was a precursor of modern educational ideas and demanded: that both genders be educated together from infancy, and that women be educated just like men and be able to work in all trades and professions. The economic facet of feminism that Mary Wollstonecraft established was an innovation, and she demanded the election of women to Parliament and the right to vote for their representatives as a means of achieving her theories.

---

420 See chapter 6, note 167.
421 See chapter 4.

Stuart Mill worked alongside Mrs. Fawcett,[422] an admirable woman who, at seventy-two years of age, was full of vivacity and charm, and was never discouraged from supporting the cause that she had defended for forty years. That married lady, of high standing, related to the most aristocratic families, was the champion who won over a great number of supporters of feminism. John Bright[423] continued that work and in 1869 passed a law that granted equal rights to both genders in municipal voting. Later, in 1883, Gladstone[424] promoted the cause, pointing out that one seventh of property owners were women, 20,000 were tenants, and three million single women and one hundred thousand married women worked to support themselves. Although conservative England denied Gladstone a victory, the feminist unrest grew; both conservative and liberal associations were established with the same goal, such as the "Primrose league"[425] and the "Women's Liberal Federation,"[426] that managed to nominate candidates in the elections of 1884. At the International Feminist Congress, held in London in 1898, the women obtained favorable promises from the leaders of the Liberal Party that they would include women's suffrage in their platforms.

During the struggle women had achieved a few partial victories, like that of being able to vote and run for school boards and parochial councils. They already had the precedent that some independent women property owners had had the right to vote, such as Dorothea Packington[427] who elected two members of Parliament with her vote alone during the time of Queen Elizabeth I, in 1572. Finally, in 1907 the campaign intensified and a new bill was presented to Parliament and again defeated, but now there was a division between the political parties, and even within the Government itself.

---

422   Millicent Garrett Fawcett (1847-1929) was a leader of the women's suffrage movement for 50 years. She was against the violent methods used by the Pankhursts, and believed in a more constitutional approach. She was for a time the leader of the National Union of Women's Suffrage Societies. She was, of course, not 72 when she worked with Mill, but rather when Burgos saw her work.

423   See chapter 7, note 212.

424   William Ewart Gladstone (1809-1897) served as British Prime Minister four times, was a member of the liberal party, a scholar, financier, theologian, orator and humanitarian,

425   A conservative organization founded in 1883 that combined political and social activities. By 1891 it had over a million members, half of them women.

426   This was formed between 1886 and 1887 under the presidency of Gladstone's daughter, Catherine and by the turn of the century, it had approximately 60,000 members and almost 500 local branches.

427   Dame Packington appointed two Members of Parliament to represent her interests in the 1590s.

A majority of Cabinet Ministers voted in favor. The majority of Labor Party members also voted in favor as did the Liberals and the Irish. Among the Conservatives, a majority voted against, most notably Lord Morpath, the son of the Countess of Carlyle, one of the most ardent suffragettes, and he did so in spite of the presence of his mother, who was among the women in the gallery.

The fighters felt their drive renewed by this. Among them Christabel and Sylvia Pankhurst and their friend Annie Kenney stood out when in 1905, at a public meeting, they violently interrupted the speaker and took over the leadership of the movement.[428] The Pankhurst sisters had been nursed on feminist ideas, their mother was the founder of the "Women's Franchise League," and had inculcated in them the principles of freedom. Abensour[429] describes Sylvia as tall, strong, with noble features and large, dark rimmed eyes, and Christabel as having a tortured body; Annie, a factory worker, was charming and concealed her energy under a childish appearance. The three of them, visionaries, devoted themselves to fulfilling their mission. That is the only way to succeed, the only way enthusiasm and faith are communicated. I remember seeing their struggles on my trips to London. Those marches in which they brandished the green and purple flag, and the thousands of women who followed. Among them I could clearly make out Miss Drummond,[430] very elderly and stout, riding her horse, like a general who was leading them to victory. You could see posters, signs, placards all with the war cry: *Votes for Women*. Women from all social classes, all ages, turned into "Women Sandwiches," with their signs in front and back. They never ceased their campaign; there was no approach they would not try. "It is necessary," they would say, "to act like cooks when they make a steak, and not stop turning it until it is cooked."

Finally, they turned to terrorism, bombs, violence, sabotage, convinced that the Government would sneer at their goals "if they did not resort to the means by which men had achieved their rights." They were made to suffer all sorts of humiliations. The opposition resorted to caricaturing the suffragettes; they wielded the weapon of

---

428   This was a Liberal Party meeting that Christabel and Annie disrupted to gain publicity for their cause; they deliberately were arrested and went to prison when they refused to pay the fine.

429   Leon Abensour wrote *Histoire générale du féminisme des origines à nos jours* (Paris: Delagrave, 1921).

430   Flora Drummond (1878-1949) was a Scottish suffragette, nicknamed the "General," and a member of the Women's Social and Political Union.

ridicule. One of their meetings broke up because someone let loose a hundred rats in the room; but they always continued working with an admirable perseverance. One day they blockaded a minister's house and did not end the siege until he listened to them. Another, they fought to get close to the Royal carriage and Miss Davidson, a voluntary martyr allowed herself to be trampled by the king's horse, in Epsom.[431] They demonstrated at the theaters, unfurled banners, flung manifestoes, appealed to the Royal Place and the Parliament. They even swept the streets to collect funds.

They were truly admirable, never retreating in the face of scandal and punishment just as they did not retreat in the face of ridicule. They went to prison and on hunger strikes, with such determination that Sylvia had to be artificially fed.[432] The imprisonment of the daughter of the renowned British economist Richard Cobden[433] produced a large protest. Posters appeared everywhere with this question: "Who jailed the daughter of Richard Cobden?" When they tried to free her, she refused to leave her comrades. They would all leave jail unrepentant, ready to continue their work; some looked like skeletons surrounded by flowers in the cars that drove them around. War interrupted the struggle, allowing patriotism to rise above other interests.

But England was not ungrateful for the efforts of its women. Chamberlain hired Mistress Tenant and Mistress Violet Markham as undersecretaries;[434] many women wore the khaki uniform and carried out men's work, and finally, in 1918, when Mistress Fawcett was ready to lead her army anew in battle and face the enemy, among whom there were women like Humphry Ward,[435] the bill presented to Parliament the year before, which gave women aged thirty and older the right to vote and be elected, succeeded. In this way six million British women have the vote and assert their strength and their rights.

---

431   Miss Emily Wilding Davidson entered the race track in 1913 while a race was going on and intentionally stepped in front of the King's horse to bring attention to the suffragettes' cause.

432   This is force feeding which was extremely painful, dangerous and severely damaged many suffragettes.

433   Cobden (1804-1865) was best known for his defense of free trade among nations. He was a member of the Radical Liberal Party.

434   Neville Chamberlain was Director General of the Department of National Service from 1916 to 1917, when Violet Markham was appointed Deputy Director of its women's section. We can find no information on Mrs. Tenant, but in chapter 12 Burgos identifies her as Assistant Secretary of State of the US.

435   Mary Augusta Ward (1851-1920), a British novelist who wrote under her husband's name and was the first president of the Anti-Suffrage League.

The ignorant multitudes that yesterday whistled at the suffragettes now enthusiastically applaud the women who take their seats in Parliament. The Pankhurst sisters have not been elected; the first who crossed the threshold was Countess Markievicz,[436] leader of the Sinn Fein Party. Later Lady Astor, an elegant woman and mother of several children, was elected in Plymouth by the supporters of her husband and she was the first woman *Peer*[437] in Parliament. The Conservatives, then, the ones who most fought against women's suffrage were the first ones to take advantage of it. But soon other parties had women representatives, like Miss Wintringham,[438] a Liberal, Miss Jessie Stephen[s][439] who had been a domestic servant, and Mabel Russell,[440] the well-known actress, who earned such acclaim with the first performance of *The Merry Widow*; of the eight women elected lately, three belong to the Labor Party, which shows that it is not true that women predominantly vote for reactionary parties.[441]

Once they have achieved victory, and had their impact confirmed, suffragist associations evolve; the International Woman Suffrage Alliance, for example, which fought for the vote for 20 years and is presided by such an active and intelligent lady as Miss Carrie Chapman Catt,[442] dedicates itself to civil, economic and moral rights within a coherent program, and it has changed its title to the International Alliance of Women. Women's competence and their healthy influence on public life shows itself more and more. In April

---

436   Countess Constance Markievicz was the first woman elected to the House of Commons in 1918. However, she did not take her seat, in protest against Britain's policies in Ireland.

437   A member of any of the five degrees of the nobility in Great Britain and Ireland (duke, marquis, earl, viscount, and baron).

438   Margaret Longbottom Wintringham (1879-1955) succeeded her husband in a seat in Parliament in 1920. She had long been a supporter of women's suffrage and was a member of the National Union of Women's Suffrage Societies.

439   See chapter 13, note 401.

440   Also known by her married name as Mabel Phipson (1887-1951), she was elected in 1923 and was a member of the Conservative Party.

441   By 1927, ten women had been elected to the House of Commons, 4 of them Conservatives, 2 Liberals and 4 Labor.

442   Born Carrie Clinton Lane (1859-1947) in Wisconsin, she trained as a teacher, and was appointed a high school principal a year after graduation from Iowa State College. Her effective organizing work brought her quickly into the inner circles of the suffrage movement. She became head of field organizing for the National American Woman Suffrage Association in 1895 and in 1900, having earned the trust of the leaders of that organization, including Susan B. Anthony, was elected to succeed Anthony as President. She was key to the passage of the 19th Amendment.

of 1927 the Prime Minister declared that he plans to present a bill that grants the vote to women twenty-one years of age and older. With this, one can say that the future of England will be in the hands of women because there are several million more women than men. It is believed that the victory will be for the progressive parties, since the majority of women, as we have said, are not conservative. Some newspapers evince the fear that women will only vote for women and that there will be a Parliament in which men will have little representation.

In Ireland, several women have been elected to its new Parliament. Six belong to Sinn Fein, from the states in the south and two to the Unionist Party, from those in the north. In the British colonies in East Africa women have had political rights since 1913.

In France, the right to vote existed in ancient days. Although Saint Paul excluded women from public matters and they could not speak in the assemblies thanks to the famous argument that Eve had corrupted Adam, Innocent IV[443] ordered that: "All men and single, married or widowed women over the age of fourteen must be called on to speak in any plenary lay assembly." So, in the French villages, women formed part of the assemblies that elected the magistrates. Noblewomen sent representatives, and in Tours, in 1308 the election of ministers took place. In the age of Philippe the Fair [1285-1314] women took part in the general elections and noble ladies had the same rights as their men. The Countess of Flanders was a Peer of the Kingdom. There were also votes for representation for communities of women. The husbands of women who had property, who paid more than 50 pounds in taxes, had the right to vote and were eligible to run for office.

Even after losing their rights, women still maintained their interest in politics. Mazzarino[444] complained that they did not think about fashion or love affairs, they were not flirts, they only wanted to "see all and know all, which is how they foul up everything," he said. In fact, at that time, during the reign of Louis XIV every great lady had her politics, and fights or intrigues dominated Versailles. But the influence belonged only to beautiful, noble and wealthy ladies. It did not reach the common people. Taking into account the way that women joined the revolutionary cause, it seemed that the revolution would make Condorcet's[445] proposal come true and concede the rights

---

443 Sinibaldo de' Fieschi (? - 1254).

444 See chapter 11, note 342.

445 Chapter 13, note 438.

of citizenship to women. Mme. Moitte, a delegate for women artists, took her jewelry to the Constituent Assembly to offer "all the last bits of her vanity to the altar of the fatherland." But the revolution was ungrateful to women. Olympe de Gouges,[446] daughter of the poet Lefran de Pompignan, a beautiful artist, embraced the women's cause with enthusiasm. "A woman," she said, "has the right to climb up to the gallows, so she should have the right to climb up to the speaker's podium." Sadly, she only reached the first. Although generous and noble, she was slandered, and in spite of being a passionate Republican, she tried to defend Louis XVI and Robespierre[447] sent her to the guillotine. Goncourt[448] compares her with Malesherbes.[449] The revolution only made men and women equal in the executioner's basket. It is true that it was punished for its ingratitude, since women stopped being interested in and collaborating with the revolution and this was one of the main causes of the Thermidorian Reaction[450] on which Mme. Tallien[451] and the "Marvelous Women"[452] had enormous influence.

In the last years of the Convention and the Directory [1792-1799] women again had political influence; but Napoleon repressed any women's movement, and his despotic Code placed them in an inferior position. He put an end to their independence. With the Restoration, the women's clubs were reborn. The revolutionary

---

446 In 1791, she wrote the "Declaration of the Rights of Woman and of the Citizen" modeled after the "Declaration of the Rights of Man and of the Citizen" adopted by the National Assembly in 1789.

447 Maximilien Robespierre (1758 -1794) was the leader of the twelve man Committee of Public Safety elected by the National Convention, and which effectively governed France at the height of the radical phase of the revolution known as the "Terror" due to the large number of beheadings.

448 See chapter 7, note 232.

449 Chrétien Guillaume de Lamoignon de Malesherbes (1721-1794) was a royal administrator throughout the century. During the French Revolution, he helped conduct the defense of Louis XVI; he was arrested in 1793, tried for treason and guillotined.

450 On July 27, 1794 (9 Thermidor, Year II, in the revolutionary calendar), Robespierre and his close followers were arrested on the convention floor. During the next two days, Robespierre and 82 of his associates were guillotined.

451 Teresa Cabarrus (1773-1835) was the lover and later wife of revolutionary Jean Lambert Tallien. She was nicknamed Notre Dame de Thermidor as an allusion to the influence she had over her husband's part in the coup that overthrew Robespierre.

452 During the period immediately following the French Revolution, fashionable Parisians wore wildly exaggerated Greek-inspired tunics that were often very revealing. The women who dressed this way were known as "les Merveilleuses" 'the marvelous ones.'

women, Claire Lacambre, Efta d'Ollders and Olympe de Gouges had their successors, working class women who came to take part in the struggle added to their contingent, moved by the desire to improve their working conditions and their miserable pay. There were women's clubs whose members shared everything with each other, and Eugenia Niboyet,[453] Jeanne Deroin[454] and all the "Vesuvians"[455] who had a volcano in their hearts, held meetings in public squares preaching the most advanced and radical theories. There were also many women's newspapers. *The Voice of Women* told the provisional government: "Since we have all taken part in the revolution, we should all partake of its benefits. If the people are sovereign as was said, the people are constituted by both men and women. You must establish the people-Queen alongside the people-King and not allow men to say: 'We are the only humanity.' Women pay taxes and obey the laws of the State, let them participate in the benefits and privileges that the State gives its citizens. No duties without rights." It proclaimed the principle that sovereignty was not essentially male.

Finally, in 1849, Jeanne Deroin went to the city hall of the fourth district of Paris and asked to be placed among the candidates. The mayor included her on the list of candidates, but the following week, when she appeared in public to explain her program, she was detained by the same authorities. After much work and many meetings, during which her faith and her eloquence prevailed over the mockery of the crowd, she succeeded in getting the social democratic committee to register her name in the list of candidates where the name of George Sand,[456] proposed by some men, was already present. Neither received more than a handful of votes, but they familiarized the masses with the cause of women's rights.

During the second Empire, with the example of Empress Eugenia, who liked to be involved in politics, women again

---

453   Niboyet (1799-1883) was initially a moderate feminist, slowly became more radical, especially after being subject to much ridicule as president of a women's club. She founded and was president of the *Société de la Voix des Femmes 'Society for the Women's Voice'* which demanded the right to vote and be elected. She was editor and contributor to the newspaper *Voix des Femmes*.

454   Deroin (1805-1852) was an embroiderer, a schoolteacher, journalist and activist for the rights of women and workers. She collaborated in Niboyet's paper.

455   This was a group of radical feminists that formed in the mid-nineteenth Century. Their demands included women's military service, the right of women to dress the same as men, and legal and domestic equality between husband and wife. Like dress reformers, they wore bloomers.

456   See chapter 3, note 60.

participated in public life, but, distracted by an atmosphere of luxury and comfort, very few tried to demand their rights, as did Jenny D'Hericourt[457] in *The Liberated Woman*, where she showed herself to be more violent than rational. Juliette Lambert,[458] who later became Mme. Adam, and who still lives and works in her nineties, wrote a book to combat Proudhon's[459] theories in which she says, "The degree of civilization of a people is in direct proportion to the role of women. Society will not progress without the influence of women." Andrea Leo,[460] sweet and timid in appearance, but endowed with a rare energy, requested the freedom of married women and moral equality. Olympe Audouard,[461] who worked with Michelet,[462] edited a journal, but she was forbidden to run a political newspaper, and because of this demanded civil and political rights for women. After the Franco-Prussian War and the Commune [1871], women became combative. There was Lodoüka Carreska, Amazon of the revolution, mother Duchêne who preached modern Bolshevik theory, and the admirable and generous Louise Michel.[463] In 1870 Maria Deraisme[s],[464] champion of free thinking and masonry, carried out a large campaign in defense of women in her lectures and books. A great, wealthy lady who enjoyed much influence, her activity in favor of freedom was most intense. She led a very combative life, but she is beginning to be treated justly; a street in Paris already bears her name. Her sister Teresa founded the League for the "Amelioration of Woman's Condition and the Demand of her Rights," that has contributed so much to the foundation of *Human Rights*.[465] In 1844,

---

457 D'Hericourt (1809-1875) was a writer and women's rights activist who may have contributed to Niboyet's paper.

458 See chapter 13, note 447.

459 See chapter 3, note 47.

460 Pseudonym for Victoire Léodile Béra (1824-1900), a French novelist, journalist and feminist.

461 Born Felicite-Olympe de Jouval (1832-1890). She demanded complete equality for women including the right to vote and stand for election.

462 Jules Michelet (1798-1874) was a prolific historian. He was head of the National Archives and taught at the College de France until Napoleon III fired him when he refused to take an oath of allegiance to him.

463 See chapter 11.

464 Deraismes (1828-1894) founded the Association for Women's Rights in 1869 with Leon Richer. She influenced other activists in England and the U.S., particularly Elizabeth Cady Stanton who met her in 1882.

465 This is a mixed gender Masonic Order, initially founded by Maria as the Great Symbolic Scottish Mixed Lodge of France. Upon her sister's death, Teresa took it over and it

Flora Tristan,[466] mystical sister of the Russian Nihilists who showed oppressed women like herself the road to freedom, died in Bordeaux.

In 1869 Leon Richer had founded the French League for Women's Rights and a feminist newspaper in which women like Jeanne Schmahl[467] and Maria Cheliga[468] —foreigners who stand out— joined the French feminists. Madame Vincent tried to be included in the electoral rosters; Hubertine Auclerc began a suffragist campaign, and Mlle. Laoë ran in the municipal elections, but her efforts, while not sterile since she prepared the way for others, did not achieve the desired result. In 1889 the first Feminist Congress was held creating a very positive atmosphere. At the start of this century, Margueritte Durand established a feminist newspaper, printed and written entirely by women, *The Sling*, which, sadly, survived only a short time. Mme. Jeanne Misme founded *The French Woman*, where she valiantly upheld feminist theories. Today, illustrious women and men who work for the women's cause are legion, as are the number of important societies that further it. Among these are: the "National Council of Young French Women," a federation of some 150 associations that boasts 100,000 members and whose president and secretary are such prestigious ladies as Mme. Jules Siegfried and Mme. de Saint Croix; the "Fraternal Union of Women," whose president and secretary are Amelie Hammer and Juliette François de Raspail; the "League for Women's Rights," presided by Maria Verone, the great fighter for suffrage.

Women's influence has caused the issue to be taken to Parliament without cease. In 1906 Ferdinand Buisson requested that women be allowed to vote and be elected. The petition was repeated in 1910, but even in 1913, it had not yet been discussed. On February 3 of 1914 it was on the agenda, but it was not discussed then either, in spite of the 300 representatives who requested it, and it was left for the new legislature. In 1918 a commission was appointed to study the matter, but it never issued an opinion. Finally, on March 30,

---

became international, spreading throughout continental Europe and England first, then the U.S., India Latin America and Africa. We should note that Burgos was also a Mason.

466 Born in 1803, she was involved in the French workers' struggles for social justice and feminist causes. She believed that the oppression of women was directly related to the oppression of the working classes.

467 See chapter 9, note 282.

468 Also known as Szeliga (1854-1927), she was a Polish novelist, poet and social publicist. She was also a socialist, pacifist and a central figure of the international Polish women's movement.

1919, the representatives voted 344 votes for versus 99 against the bill introduced by Jean Bon and Lucien Dumont:[469] "Laws and statutory regulations on voting and eligibility to run for all elective Assemblies are applicable to all French citizens without regard to their gender." It seemed that French women had triumphed as they deserved after the noble example they gave in the Great War, but the Senate, after considering the bill, ended up by rejecting it in 1927, in spite of the many senators who were committed feminists.[470]

French women continue their struggle and, if not by law, in deed occupy many public posts. Mme. Pannevial has formed part of the National Labor Council; Mme. Paquin is in the section on sewing; Mme. Avril de Sainte Croix has worked with Beranger, Bieux, etc., on the Social Reforms Commission and she, as well as Severine and other important writers, were part of the commission to reform the marriage laws along with Poincaré, Paul and Victor Margueritte, Prèvost and Paul Adam. Currently, Mlle. Landry is the secretary for her father, the Minister of the Navy.

Portuguese women, so well educated from the fifteenth Century on that they stand out among European ladies, are accustomed to carrying out all kinds of work, and to be administrators of the house and educators of their offspring, due to the constant emigration of the men, they carry the scepter in the home and there is even the custom of the children using the mother's last name. Learned and liberal in nature, the majority of middle class women were Republicans. An English writer who visited Portugal shortly before the revolution warned Queen Amelia, "Your Majesty should be careful with the women. That is where the danger lies." In fact, women were the more active disseminators of Republican ideas and the ones who most effectively helped to proclaim that Republic which was established without spilling blood, amidst the jubilation of all the people. The Portuguese Association of Feminist Propaganda and the Republican League of Portuguese Women demanded suffrage which the wise and unforgettable Teófilo Braga,[471] president of the provisional government seemed ready to concede. But the law

---

469   Author's note: The defenders were Jules Sigfried, Bria, Viviani, Bracke, Louis Martin, Andriux, Justin Godar and Jean Bon.

470   Author's note: Merlin, Louis Martin, Henry Chèron, Paul Strauss, Cruppi, Ratiery D'Estournelles de Constant.

471   Braga (1843-1921) was a poet, playwright, and politician. He led the provisional government after the abdication of King Emmanuel II, in 1910, and was elected second of the Portuguese Republic in 1915.

proposed by Antonio José d'Almeida denied women and soldiers the vote. Then the illustrious doctor Carolina Beatriz Angelo, went to court demanding her rights, and the honorable judge don Joaô Baptista de Castro, worthy of the same renown as president Magnou[472] of France because of his intelligence and common sense, trying to make the law agree with justice, granted them to her, basing himself on the Portuguese Constitution, which, like ours, does not exclude women when it grants the vote to all citizens. The ruling, which provoked a scandalous reaction from the reactionary sides, was applauded throughout the civilized world. The Association of Feminist Propaganda published an edition of the verdict in French and the illustrious magistrate received congratulations from England, the United States, France and Spain. The incipient Republic breathed an atmosphere of friendship. But the new Constitution avenged itself for the women's victory, adding the adjective *male* to the word *citizen*. *Male citizen.*

Dona Carolina Angelo was able to exercise her right, which did not extend to the rest of the women, in spite of it being Dona Elzira Dantas, the wife of president Bernardino Machado, and Dona Ana de Castro Osório —the illustrious writer and sociologist, in whom the female intelligence of the country reaches its peak—, who brandished the feminist flag. These two ladies are presidents of the great association Crusade of Portuguese Women now united with our International League of Iberian and Spanish American Women.

In Italy, a bill was presented in 1912 allowing women to vote in elections for Administrative positions if they were older than twenty-five, and could demonstrate they were educated by practicing a profession, holding a job, authoring works or showing a certificate of studies. Representatives of Spanish feminist associations, including the International League of Iberian and Spanish American Women, attended the International Suffragist Congress recently held in Rome.[473] Of the sixty nations that constitute the civilized world, forty-four were represented in the Congress for a total of one thousand five hundred delegates. Several new Associations hailing from nations that were as yet unaffiliated, such as Egypt, Australia, British India and others, were admitted into the Alliance. The Congress, gathered

---

472 This might be Patrice de Mac-Mahon (1808-1893) who was president during the Third Republic from 1873 to 1879. Although he was a monarchist, the republican form of government was formally established by the promulgation of a constitution during his term.

473 This was the Ninth Congress of the International Woman Suffrage Alliance in 1923.

women from the five main races of the world: Caucasian, Mongolian, Malay, Polynesian and Indian – all of them motivated by one sole and common desire: to achieve the vindication of women's rights, and, by means of these, the physical and spiritual improvement of Humanity. But Italian women have not yet gained the right of suffrage. However, the admirable Gabriel D'Annunzio, when he was governor of Fiume, emancipated women and gave them the right to vote in 1921.[474]

In Belgium, after the war, women were granted the vote, and showed great enthusiasm when they participated in the first elections. Peasant women joined aristocratic ladies, all of them showing themselves worthy of exercising their rights just like men. Some wore religious habits and came out of the convent to fulfill their duty as citizens. "Please go ahead, Sister Angelica," one would say to the other, when the election supervisor said her maiden name, "Ana Vanderbane," which was almost forgotten due to her vows of renunciation. Queen Elizabeth served as an example when she appeared dressed simply, in black, at Precinct 96 to exercise a right that King Albert usually does not use. There were five voters before her, but when the supervisor recognized her and invited her to vote, she replied, "No, sir. I am here as a simple voter and will wait my turn."

In Holland women were electable before they could vote, this latter right was granted to them in 1921, and today there are women in Parliament and other deliberative bodies, a majority of them elected by men. In Germany, Theodor Hippel wrote his feminist book *On the Civic Betterment of Women* in 179[2]. Following the example of Queen Louise, ladies were interested in culture and held literary salons. But the mother of the great liberal movement was Louise Otto,[475] who formulated a feminist program for the first time. Bebel[476] and Karl Marx preached the political emancipation of women, including them in the Erfurt Program.[477] The former developed a warm defense of

---

474 The Fiume was a territory contested by Italy and Yugoslavia after World War I. In 1919, D'Annunzio and a group of men occupied it and he proclaimed himself commander of the Italian Regency of Carnaro. Under the Treaty of Rapallo, in 1920, Fiume became a free state, and D'Annunzio was forced out.

475 Louise Otto-Peters participated in the events leading up to the Revolution of 1848 with the "Speech of a German Girl" in which she described the oppression of women workers and demanded action. She later wrote novels and articles with a decidedly feminist bent. In 1865, she founded the National Organization for German Women.

476 See chapter 1, note 19.

477 In1891, the program of the Social Democratic Party of Germany (which became the

women in *Woman and Socialism* against female slavery, and proposed a universal suffrage bill in the Reichstag that was rejected. Important societies were formed, such as the Union of Socialist Women, which constituted a federation of women's unions. Elena Sauge[478] asked the Senate of Hamburg for women's rights. The wife of Kautsky, the famous socialist, collaborated with her husband. And recently, Rosa Luxemburg, that generous soul, saved the good name of German women protesting against the war, as did Baroness Bertha von S[uttner], author of the famous book *Lay Down Your Arms*, which earned her the Nobel Peace Prize. Rosa Luxemburg died a victim of her ministry during the sad days of January 1919.[479] Today there are more than 4,000 women in Municipal governments and 750 in Congress.

In Luxembourg women have had political rights since 1919. In Austria both men and women have political rights once they turn twenty-one years old and there are many women in Congress and City Councils. In Hungary, Sister Margarita Slachta[480] is, as we have already said, a Member of Parliament from the National Christian Party and is seated in Parliament wearing her nun's habit, among twenty other female Members. The Parliamentarian nun speaks so learnedly and eloquently that she has been sent to the United States to represent her party at the Interparliamentary Conference in Washington. The Hungarian ambassador to Switzerland is also a lady, Rosika.[481] In Poland, Narcyza [Zmichowska] gave her life defending her sisters, since she died a victim of her ministry, after two years of

---

Communist Party after World War I) included as its first principle: "Universal, equal, and direct suffrage, with secret ballot, for all elections, of all citizens of the realm over twenty years of age, without distinction of sex." This was written under the guidance of Eduard Bernstein, August Bebel and Karl Kautsky.

478   This might be Helene Lange (1848-1930), who was a teacher and a member of the moderate wing of the feminist movement in Germany.

479   Born in Poland in 1871, Luxemburg later became a German citizen through marriage. She was an important Communist leader in Germany, Poland and Russia, where she helped to found socialist parties and called for revolution. On January 15, 1919, she was arrested in Germany and murdered while in police custody.

480   See chapter 10, note 365.

481   Rosika Schwimmer (1877-1948) was active in her country's suffragist movement. A pacifist, Schwimmer spent the years of the First World War in the United States, and became vice president of the Women's International League for peace and freedom. After the war, she was a member of the new Hungarian government and was Minister to Switzerland until 1919.

prison in Lublin citadel.[482] In this country, as in Lithuania and Latvia equal rights now exist. In Greece, universal suffrage was instituted in 1920, and Turkish women are protesting to achieve it, but they have recently been denied this right under the pretext that they are not sufficiently prepared for it.

All the Balkan countries have taken part in this struggle. Czechoslovakia has granted political rights to women. About twelve per cent of its City Halls are occupied by women, and in 1927 a lady senator visited Spain and spoke eloquently on the benefits of women's suffrage in her country. In Yugoslavia women vote and are electable, but in Serbia only for Deliberative Councils. In Moravia and Bohemia women landowners vote for City Councils, and in Bosnia Herzegovina they also vote for Parliament. In Rumania men and women have equal rights.

The Northern countries were the first to emancipate women. Swedish women have had the right to vote in local elections since 1862, and now enjoy all kinds of freedoms; many outstanding women continue Federica Bremer and Ellen Key's work.[483] Selma Langelof[484] gave a beautiful feminist speech titled "The Home and the State" at the International Alliance. Nico Hambro[485] and Gina [Krog][486] deserve to be mentioned, among others. In Norway there is universal suffrage, and women have the same rights as men. Women also have access to all professions; there are even female judges and lawyers on the Supreme Court. In 1913, they were admitted into the King's Council, with a law that states: "The King shall choose his council among male or female Norwegian citizens who are at least 30 years of age." A lady is one of the Norwegian representatives to the League of Nations. The new Danish constitution of 1915 gave women the right to vote and be elected. Not only are there many women in its Parliament, and one is a representative to the League of Nations, but the minister of Public Education is a woman. Finland was one of the first countries to accept women's suffrage without restrictions. When the imperial proclamation gave it autonomy in 1907, nineteen women were seated

---

482   This is not entirely true: she was detained for two years in a Carmelite convent in Lublin, but was subsequently released, although she remained under police surveillance. She is considered one of the early pioneers of the Polish feminist movement (1814-1876).

483   Author's note: Died in 1927.

484   Langelof (1858-1940) was the first woman to win the Nobel Prize for literature in 1909.

485   Nicoline Christine Hambro (1861 – 1926) was a Norwegian politician and feminist activist. She was president of the Norwegian National Women's Council from 1916 to 1922.

486   Krog (1847-1916) was a Norwegian feminist, lecturer, writer and politician.

in Parliament at its first meeting, and they made themselves known by their admirable demeanor. In Iceland women also have equal rights and there is a large number of women Representatives.

In Russia women were feminists before even realizing it or setting out to be so. Although subject to their husbands, on whom their lives and freedom depended, Russian women, be they aristocratic or peasant, exercised political rights. Women landowners took part in the elections of the members of the Zemstvos[487] and the Douma.[488] When Alexander II emancipated the serfs, the role of Russian women became more central — these women, who have such a generous spirit, are so exalted, hungry for action and dreams, have sacrificed themselves in the name of their humanitarian ideals with the same fervor as the early Christian martyrs. When the Tsars disappeared, feminism became more organized in the new Russia. Kerenski offered the presidency of the temporary Parliament to Brechko Brechkovskaia,[489] *the mother of the revolution*. During the Maximalist Revolution,[490] Lenin and Trotsky relied on women. We must confess that their neophytes' zeal led many of them to commit violent acts, much like what happened in France during the Terror; but when Lenin proclaimed autocracy, women protested and issued a manifesto against those who abused Bolshevism. A woman formed part of the embassy charged by Trotsky with negotiating the Brest-Litowask peace treaty;[491] another, Mme. Spiridovna,[492] was a Maximalist candidate for the presidency of the Constituent Assembly in 1918. Not only do they vote and are electable to political offices, but they participate in diplomacy as well. Today, the ambassador of

---

487   Local assemblies.

488   The elective legislative assembly established by Tsar Nicholas II in 1905, overthrown in 1917.

489   Yekaterina Konstantinovna Breshko-Breshkovskaya (1844-1934) was actually known as the little grandmother of the revolution.

490   The Maximalists formed a Russian political party that was the principal alternative to the Russian Social-Democratic Workers' Party in the early 20th Century. It relied on terrorist tactics and carried out hundreds of political assassinations. By 1917 it was Russia's largest socialist group. The party split after the Russian Revolution of 1917, and its radical wing joined the Bolshevik government. It was suppressed by Vladimir Lenin after the Russian Civil War.

491   The treaty that brought about the end of the war between Russia and Germany in 1918.

492   Maria Spiridovna (1885-1941) was a member of the Left Socialist Revolutionary Party. She was elected to the Constituent Assembly but it was closed down by the Bolsheviks in 1918. That same year, she led an uprising protesting this action. She was arrested and spent 23 years in Siberia before she was shot.

Russia to Mexico is Aleksandra Kollontay,[493] the writer who is so well known for her revolutionary zeal and her talent.

Women in the United States of America, who today seem to enjoy the epitome of freedom, were in the beginning the most wretched. Robertson says that they were treated like beasts of burden, destined to serve men and punished as though they were domestic animals; they were not even allowed to enter the church. Roselly de Lorques[494] depicts them as dogs who had to hunt for food and row canoes while their men lay on the bottom. Lucrecia Mott, such a sweet good and charitable spirit, launched a campaign in favor of the freedom of black women in the newspapers and political meetings. Twenty years later, in 1851, this campaign produced Mrs. Harriet Beecher Stowe's wonderful book, *Uncle Tom's Cabin*, which is a model of keen observation and sensitivity, and which has so influenced public opinion in favor of the slaves. In 1840, when the World Antislavery Convention was held in London, several women, including Elizabeth Cady, Lucy Slaton and Florence Wright tried to attend as women delegates, but the doors were shut in their faces under the pretext that they were handicapped when it came to political and civil matters. In their outrage, they created the American feminist party.[495] "Men and women," they said, "have been created equal and the Creator has given them inalienable rights. Government's duty is to guarantee these rights, but men impose laws on women, when the latter do not participate in their formulation. Men monopolize all lucrative occupations and deny their companions all avenues leading to distinctions and honors. They have removed women from all church matters, and have promulgated sham feelings and false public opinions that imply there are two moral standards, one for each gender. They have also made married women into civil cadavers. And they have usurped Jehovah's privileges, which delimited the same sphere of influence for both genders." According to this, women's duty is to reject men's laws to achieve justice, and so that there may be one set of laws and one moral standard, not so that women may imitate men's immorality, but rather, so that both should exercise more restraint. Feminism spread quickly, at one with the cause of the emancipation of slaves with the slogan "neither

---

493 See chapter 8, note 244.

494 He was a French Americanist and apologist for Christopher Columbus, whose scientific objectivity is questionable.

495 In 1848, they organized the Women's Rights Convention, and in 1866 the American Equal Rights Association.

color, nor gender" as the excuse for slavery or inequality. Among the champions of reform there were also black women, such as the orator Sojourner Truth, an ex-slave. Susan B. Anthony was the Napoleon of this movement.

Women refused to pay taxes or fines if they were not granted their rights. Some allowed their property to be sold, saying: "To resist tyranny is to obey God." In 1828, Lincoln wrote: "I demand suffrage for all those who make financial contributions to the State and because of this I request it for all white people who pay taxes, without excluding women." Already in 1869, in the Western territory of Wyoming, women were allowed to vote in all elections when they turned twenty-one years old. Their rights to suffrage and to political posts are the same as the ones men are granted. What is more, married women keep their property; and they have decreed equality in education in this state. This is the Promised Land for women!

Inspired by this unqualified success, the campaign broadened. In 1893 Colorado granted women voting rights, and then Idaho and Utah did so in 1896. But the struggle continued in other states, especially in the East, where it met with the resistance of European prejudices. In the meantime, women conquered their place in society. There are two million affiliates of single women's clubs. Margaret Haley, champion of democracy, influenced the reform of education and equal wages for teachers, and due to her initiative, many cooperatives for workers were established. The International Council of Women,[496] whose objective is to establish constant communication among women of all countries, carries out wonderful work, as does the International Alliance of Women for Suffrage and Legal Citizenship.[497] The International League of Iberian and Hispanic American Women, whose presidency was generously offered to me, originated in the United States. The illustrious Elena Arizmendi, a Mexican lady of Spanish descent, founded this important federation, which today has its headquarters in Madrid and boasts important committees in Portugal and all of Latin America. This united work, which knows no frontiers, yields more fruit every day. In 1912 women in the states of Washington, California, Arizona, Kansas and Oregon were granted political rights. In 1914 Nevada, Montana and Illinois followed them. When the European War began three fourths of the

---

496 Founded in 1888, this was one of the first women's organizations and it is still in existence today as an NGO.

497 Established in 1902 and also in existence today, it changed its name to International Alliance of Women in 1946.

United States had not granted women their rights. In 1917, during the war, Indiana, Michigan and Ohio did so.

Dagget, the American writer, says in her book *Women Wanted*: "Soon we shall hear the voices of soldiers, voices of convalescents, voices of blind men and all those voices will repeat the same words: 'women have helped us, they have been admirable, it is necessary to free them.'" President Wilson called on women's groups to mobilize and enlist men. In 1916 Jeannette Rankin was elected senator[498] from Montana and so led the way for women in Congress. Finally, 36 Western and Central states granted women their rights, and on August 18, 1920 the federal law was passed allowing women to vote and run for office in the entire territory of the United States.

Equal before the law, equal in practice, North American women have access to all trades and professions, and every day they have a more important role in the direction the nation takes. Miriam Ferguson, respected mother of her children, has just been elected governor of the state of Texas. Lucille Atcherson is the first secretary of a delegation in the diplomatic annals of the country. Mabel Williebrandt is Assistant Attorney General of the nation. Hamilton Gardner, a writer by profession, is a member of the Civil Service Commission that has enormous administrative influence. Mina Van Winkle heads the Women's Bureau of the Washington Police. Kath[ryn] Sellers is a judge in the Juvenile Court system of the District of Columbia. Mary O' Toole was appointed judge in the Municipal Court system of the same district, and was the first woman to occupy such a post. Nellie Ross, elected governor of the state of Wyoming, shares the honor of being the first of her gender to occupy this office in all of North America with Mrs. Ferguson. Mary Norton was chosen by the popular vote to represent New Jersey in the House of Representatives, and, in fact, declared that she was in favor of modifying Prohibition. Clara Taylor is officially part of the Federal Rent Commission in Washington. Florence Knapp is Secretary of State – also by popular vote – of the state of New York; she won the campaign thanks to the Republican Party, even though the winning governor was a democrat. Mary Anderson has for some time occupied the important post of Head of the Women's Bureau of the Department of Labor of the United States. Bessie Brueggema[nn] works for the Employees' Compensation Commission of the US government. They

---

498   She was actually elected to the House of Representatives –not the Senate– twice, from 1917-1919 and 1941-1943. She ran as a progressive and a feminist. She was also the only member of Congress to vote against the entrance of the US into both World War I and II.

have achieved the unquestionable and definitive victory of feminism.

In South America, Uruguay stands out, where the Colorado Party was the first to propose the civil and political equality of the two genders, and in 1921 introduced a bill that stated:

The Senate and House of Representatives of the Oriental Republic of Uruguay, meeting in a General Assembly, hereby decree:

Article 1. We recognize the right of women to vote and be elected, in national as well as municipal contests.

Article 2. We recognize the same rights and responsibilities for women that the electoral laws grant men.

Article 3. Women are equal to men in the eyes of the law, whether its purpose be to regulate, punish or protect.

Doctor Baltasar Brum, president of the Republic, defended the bill with an eloquent, feminist speech that ended with these noble and moving words: "Enemies of feminism have tried to combat it with the vulgar and ignoble weapon of ridicule, publishing caricatures that deformed the beauty or elegance of women dedicated to feminist campaigning. This is an unfair attitude, because one cannot ignore the large number of beautiful, elegant and learned women who fight for suffrage, convinced that it would enhance the dignity of their gender.

But even if there were suffragists who were not beautiful or elegant, they would grow beautiful, precisely through the championing of noble ideals, and they should inspire in sincere and just men, not derision and disdain, but respect and admiration, because they are altruistic, intelligent and enthusiastic, because their rebellion is justified against a regime that keeps women in a subservient and inferior position. These women who are considered lacking in elegance or beauty have given their lives for their ideals, in the same spirit of sacrifice, and no less courage than the martyrs for universal democracy have used to defend their principles."

Because of their learning, Uruguayan women are worthy of sparking one's interest. Many women of merit stand out, as does for example Doctor Luissi, second Vice-president of the International League of Iberian and Spanish American Women, who also represented her country in the League of Nations, and has carried out superb work against white slavery.

In Argentina, women, not content with the great progress that the achievement of political rights represents, aspire to assert their influence and the National Feminist Party in Buenos Aires works boldly so that women will participate in the nation's government as voters and elected officials. In 1924, Mrs. Rosa P. M. de Vidal, president of the Radical Feminist Party and the League, presented a splendid program of vindications of the rights of women, and alongside her fought many intelligent women, as they did in other important associations. There is no lack of men who support the cause. Years ago, Senator Enrique del Valle Iberlucea and Representatives Juan Frugon[i] and Rogelio Araya raised the question of votes for women in Parliament, proposing,

> Article 1. Let Article 7 of citizenship law number 346, "On Argentine Political Rights" be modified as follows: Male Argentines who have reached the age of eighteen, and Women Argentines who have reached twenty-two years of age, enjoy all political rights granted by the Constitution and the laws of the Republic.

Doctor Bard states that he bases his project on the belief that: "The restitution of women's civil and political rights demonstrates the vast social and cultural capacity of the country that embraces in its laws these rights. I am not afraid," he adds, "of the criticism of trivial beings, which does not represent a genuine value at this time of full renewal, when, regardless of the efforts of so many reactionaries, truth marches on; when dealing with this issue, I am not interested in selfishness, or fear of what is trivial. Years ago, anyone who lightly remarked on the "eight-hour workday," defending it, or "the strike", or so many other rights that workers have achieved, was a "nut."

In Brazil, Dr. Basilio de Magalhaes presented a bill so that women could vote and be elected in the Federal Chamber, saying: "The ideal that forms the basis for the bill I am presenting for consideration in the Chamber of which I have the honor to be a part, has already triumphed in almost all the civilized world and should also be victorious here. My hope is that Brazil will not become, in this respect, a backward nation. The energy of political conquests is an amazing phenomenon due to the speed with which it is achieved in the more advanced countries. Thirty-three years ago, when the issue of women's votes was last raised in our republican assembly, the supporters of women's political emancipation had few examples of which to avail themselves in the world. We can see how quickly our planet has progressed in such a short amount of time. It would be a shame if in the midst of the civilized universe's forward march, Brazil remained stagnant, keeping politically in chains those who, overcoming men's resistance, already predominate in everything and for everything."

Women work actively for suffrage; Mrs. Souza Salles, president of Committee of the International League edits the important *Feminine Review* in the state of Sao Paolo, in which women of true merit stand out. Mrs. Bertha Lutz, fought against doctor Barcelos, an enemy of feminism, with great skill, saying: "Modern feminists take pains to assume their responsibilities and contribute to issues of a public nature, seeing the vote as a means of action. They act out of lofty ideals, not personal self-interest, wishing only to contribute with their efforts to the progress of the nation. This feminism is neither extravagant nor masculine, and has numerous supporters in Brazil."

Unfortunately, in the other countries of Latin America women's suffrage has too many enemies. Their minds are much too infected with the principles of Roman law that Spain gave them in their laws; but in all of them the feminist inclination is gaining ever more ground and Committees of the International League of Iberian and Spanish American Women, presided by eminent ladies, carry out intense campaigns.

In Oceania, a new continent, that has no prejudices, women have voted in municipal elections since 1867. Stuart Mill's[499] theories have had a great deal of influence on New Zealand's politicians; when he was minister, Joseph Ward declared: "Not to give women suffrage is to lose every day an unlimited supply of intellectual and moral strength." Women have had the vote since 1893 in both of New Zealand's islands. In Australia, they were granted the vote the same year, and became electable in 1908. In 1893 there was already a woman governor of a province.

In the East, in those ancient countries that seem, however, to be the youngest, the struggle for suffrage is already taking place. In Persia, the first bill was presented to Parliament in 1911. In Madras, the Burmese[500] city of the golden pagodas, women can vote in municipal elections. In China, that isolated country that refuses contact with foreigners even today, a violent transformation of customs is taking place. Women study, and like their male classmates, they have greater prestige than the countless illiterates. Because of this, women want to reform the institution of the family, in which the mother-in-law controls the families of all her sons, all of whom live in patriarchal homes that house more than forty people; and the daughters-in-law

---

499   See chapter 6, note 147.

500   Madras is, of course, in India. It should be noted, however, that Burma was under British colonial rule and was considered a province of India until 1937.

must serve her devoutly and humbly. Modern wives demand their own separate home, run by them, and seek the right to choose their husbands. Shandra Sere, widowed, abandoned her home in order to remarry, and Soume-Tcheng was the first to refuse mutilating her feet. The Republic was so favorable toward women that Sun-Yat-Sen[501] gave women the rights to vote and be elected, but Yuan-[S]hi-Kai's[502] dictatorship took those away. However, there is a woman at the head of the revolutionary government of Shanghai.

The facts show that in almost all the countries where women have political influence, the legal and economic situation of their gender has advanced; morality improves as does public health, thus reducing infant mortality. Women who participate in politics show an altruism that is easily perceived and that dispels the notion that the solemn duties of Parliament could be a pretext to show off. But the experience of the countries in which suffrage has been implemented proves that women, far from forgetting their roles as wives and mothers, only seek through the vote a better means to fulfill their duties.

In the United States, where divorce is so easy, the number of divorces has decreased and that of marriages has increased with the implementation of suffrage. Birth rates have not declined; on the other hand, infant mortality has dwindled. These are clear indications that a suffragist does not stop being a woman in the broadest sense of the term, and she does not neglect her home. In his book on women in Colorado, Judge Ben Lindsey states: "How could one properly assume that the mere act of voting would alter women's feminine nature? It does not take women away from their duties as mothers and homemakers for more than ten minutes when they go to the polls and deposit their vote in the ballot box, and then return to the bosom of their family. During those ten minutes, they have displayed a beneficial ability to protect their homes."

We would need a whole volume to review the significant improvements introduced in the countries where women have the vote. In England, New Zealand and the states of Wyoming, Idaho, Utah and Colorado, as well as Norway, married women dispose freely of their personal assets and the fruits of their labor. Husbands may not sell furniture or other objects without their wives' approval. In

---

501   He was a Chinese revolutionary who fought against the Qing dynasty, and then briefly became the Republic of China's first president from 1911 to 1913.

502   He was a Chinese army leader and reformist minister toward the end of the Qing dynasty and then took over the presidency of the Republic of China (1913–16).

some of these places (Colorado and Norway) they have the same rights as the husband with regard to the children. All professions are open to them and there are wise laws that regulate work, first and foremost those based on the principle of equal pay for equal work – this is the case in the aforementioned places as in Sweden and the states of Victoria and Tasmania. Professional and vocational schools have been created, as well as those for the ethical education of children. Schooling has become compulsory, circulating libraries, home economics courses and mobile kitchens have been fostered.

In Finland, the status of a "natural"[503] child is almost equal to that of the legitimate one, and there are courts for children and institutions that care for those who are abandoned and orphaned. There are also safety nets for the elderly, the widowed, the sick and the orphaned. There is aid for mothers and retirement for the aged. The sale of tobacco and alcohol to minors and those who are younger than eighteen is forbidden, and there is an active campaign against opium, cocaine and other narcotics.

In Australia and New Zealand women have carried out a hygienic campaign against the mislabeling of food and dirty streets. In Saint Louis, the "Housekeeping" Municipal Association was organized by women. They do not cut down trees or destroy clusters of flowers there. In New Jersey, thanks to the influence of women, they have built parks that are thousands of hectares in size. In Kearney women have enacted a law that protects trees. A man who has seduced and abandoned a woman cannot run for public office, and even a mere immoral proposition is punished. Miss Gertrude Buske has written that white slavery does not exist in Australia and New Zealand.

The campaign against alcoholism has resulted in Prohibition in almost all of the United States, and in a reduction of drunkenness in Europe. (In Norway and Sweden, it is now 1 in 7,000 as opposed to 1 in 400, England has gone from 7th place to 11th).

But most eloquent are the declarations hailing from those Parliaments that have had women's suffrage for a longer time, such as Wyoming's, which enjoys the glory of having been the first modern state to institute it. Wyoming's politicians state: "So far, the enjoyment and exercise of suffrage by women has not resulted in any negative effects, and has, in fact, produced great benefits in everything. Women's participation has contributed, to a large degree, to stamping out crime, poverty and vice, without recurring

---

503   See chapter 3, note 50.

to violent and oppressive laws. They have fostered peaceful and orderly elections, a good government and the state has prospered in civility and order. We note with pride that in Wyoming there is only one homeless shelter and the prisons are almost empty. We could say that crime has vanished from the state. Women have power and they know how to use it. Our schools could serve as models for other states. Women know how to get more out of a dollar and they have more restraint in spending public funds than their husbands."

The Australian senate has said: "This Senate believes that the granting of suffrage to women has had the most favorable results. It has brought about orderly elections. Women have placed more importance on legislation affecting women and children, without forsaking laws of general interest in the areas of defense and the good of the country with as much clear-sightedness as men. The reform has only had positive consequences, regardless of the dismal predictions of their opponents."

Mr. Well[s],[504] governor of Utah has said: "Legislators seem afraid of women's suffrage, due to the destructive effect that politics might have on femininity. We can declare that women have not degenerated into lowly politicians who neglect their homes and lose their noble feminine emotions. On the contrary, women continue to be as respected as before. The whole truth is that the influence of women in the politics of this state has been clearly moralizing."

James H. Brady, governor of Idaho, wrote in the *New York World*: "Once this principle of justice for women was put into practice, the best men have stepped forward as candidates, and the administration has been entrusted to honest hands."

Joseph Ward, from New Zealand, declares: "We have confirmed that writing a name on a ballot once every three years does not cause women to lose their grace, beauty or love of household duties. On the contrary, women's votes have a moralizing effect."

But the ultimate justification lies in these admirable words uttered by Lloyd George:[505] "If women, by taking part in elections, avoid the infamy of even one war, they will have justified their right to suffrage before God and men. When women have the right to vote in the entire continent, mothers will prevent the fields of Europe from being flooded with the blood of their children."

---

504   See chapter 12, note 371.
505   See chapter 11, note 331.